THE VIOLIN-MAKERS OF THE
GUARNERI FAMILY
(1626—1762)

THE VIOLIN-MAKERS OF THE
GUARNERI FAMILY
(1626–1762)

By

WILLIAM HENRY HILL, ARTHUR F. HILL
and
ALFRED EBSWORTH HILL

DOVER PUBLICATIONS, INC.
New York

This Dover edition, first published in 1989, is a republication of the work originally published by William E. Hill & Sons, London, in 1931. Some of the plates have been moved, and the list of subscribers has been deleted. The plate facing page 144 was in color in the original edition.

Manufactured in the United States of America
DOVER PUBLICATIONS, INC.
31 East 2nd Street
Mineola, N.Y. 11501

Library of Congress Cataloging-in-Publication Data

Hill, William Henry, 1857–1927.
    The violin-makers of the Guarneri family, 1626–1762 / William Henry Hill, Arthur F. Hill & Alfred Ebsworth Hill.
        p.   cm.
    Reprint. Originally published: London : W. E. Hill & Sons, 1931.
    Includes index.
    ISBN 0-486-26061-5
    1. Violin. 2. Guarneri Family. 3. Violin makers—Italy. I. Hill, Arthur F. (Arthur Frederick), 1860–1939. II. Hill, Alfred Ebsworth, 1862–1940. III. Title.
ML830.H46 1989
787.2'192'30922—dc20
                                     89-7777
                                     CIP
                                     MN

DEDICATED TO THE MEMORY OF
WILLIAM HENRY HILL
1857–1929
THIS HISTORY EMBODIES
THE KNOWLEDGE AND CONSIDERED VIEWS
OF THREE BROTHERS
WHO LIVED AND WORKED IN
A LIFE-LONG
INTIMACY

PREFACE

IN the year 1901 we published our book, *Antonio Stradivari: his Life and Work,* and its success was both immediate and lasting; more successful, in fact, than we had any right to expect.

Thirty years have since rolled by, years rich in fresh experience gained, yet, to the writers, leading daily busy lives, they seem but of yesterday.

Will the companion volume, the lives of the Guarneri, merit an equal success? We have certainly spared neither time nor effort in order to be in a position to pen a true story concerning these five Cremonese craftsmen, to convey some idea of the environment in which they passed their existence, and to present the result of their working life in all its bearings. But we are nevertheless conscious of the limitation of our subject: for the Guarneri, either singly or reviewed as a whole, have not left to posterity that rich field of material which was the case with Antonio Stradivari.

The reader will, notwithstanding, find in this book much that is new and suggestive; we have for all time established the true relationship of these master violin-makers, the correct dates of their births and deaths, and the sources whence came their knowledge and inspiration.

As regards Giuseppe del Gesù, the great genius of the family, we have revealed his true identity, and traced the growth of his fame from early days to recent years.

The numerous illustrations call for special comment. After divers experiments, we decided to reproduce various of the selected Guarneri instruments by a process of colour printing, and though the plates may seem less picturesque than those inserted in the Life of Stradivari, we feel that we have, nevertheless, gained somewhat by the more accurate representation of individual features of the work.

Other examples are due to photogravure; and we believe that the result obtained by both processes will compare favourably with all similar attempts of the past.

To Messrs. Hudson & Kearns we tender our warmest thanks for their untiring efforts to meet our oft-repeated criticisms in the preparation of the plates; and we owe a debt of gratitude to Sir Emery Walker, not only for his fine photogravure work, but for much useful advice in the preparation of the book. We succeeded in obtaining permission to make a drawing of Paganini's famed Guarneri violin, thanks to old friends, M. Camille Barrère, the ex-French Ambassador to Italy, and Signor Robert Foltzer of Genoa, both lovers of our subject; nor should we omit to thank Mr. Harry Currie for the drawings which he did at Genoa in 1925.

Lastly, we want to place on record how much this book owes in interest to our lifelong and regretted friend, the late Commendatore Giovanni Livi of Bologna. Research work is at all times both tedious and difficult; and to succeed in it calls for intuitive genius. Time and again, when we were baffled by our Guarneri researches, suggestions emanating from Signor Livi permitted of a renewal of our hopes; and we could not have attained success without the aid of his vast experience and ever ready co-operation.

To the memory of the late Miss Mary Pern, and to Miss Beatrice Harraden we offer our acknowledgement of valuable help in the final preparation of our manuscript. The book simply claims to present in clear language the story of these interesting men with whose works we have had close communion for many years.

LIST OF PLATES IN COLOUR

FOLLOWING PAGE 24

LIST OF HALFTONE PLATES

LIST OF ILLUSTRATIONS IN THE TEXT

Chap. I. ANDREA GUARNERI

Chap. II. PIETRO GUARNERI OF MANTUA

xvi   LIST OF ILLUSTRATIONS IN THE TEXT

Chap. III. GIUSEPPE GUARNERI, SON OF ANDREA

PAGE

A. (1) Baptismal certificate of Giuseppe Guarneri, 1666 (facsimile of entry in the Register of Births)   47

Fɪɢ.   I. Edge, purfling, and sound-hole of an example of the period 1710   50

A. (2) Baptismal certificate of Pietro, the son, known as Pietro Guarneri of Venice (facsimile of the entry in the Register of Births)   55

B.   Baptismal certificate of Bartolomeo Joseph, the son, 1698 (facsimile of entry in the Register of Births)   55

C.   Census Returns of the Casa Guarneri for the years 1699-1700 (facsimile reproductions)   56

D.   Census Return of the Casa Guarneri for the year 1713 (facsimile reproduction)   57

E.   Census Return of the Casa Guarneri for the year 1723 (facsimile reproduction)   57

F.   Census Return for the Casa Guarneri for the years 1738 and 1739 (facsimile reproductions)   58

G.   Death of Barbara Franchi, 1738 (facsimile of the entry in the Register of Deaths)   58

Fɪɢ. II. Edge, purfling, and sound-hole of an example of the period 1720   60

Chap. IV. GIUSEPPE GUARNERI DEL GESÙ

A.   Census Return of the Casa Guarneri, Piazza S. Domenico, for the year 1722 (facsimile reproduction)   68

B.   Death of Joseff Antonio Guarneri, (1) July 1683 (facsimile of entry in the Register of Deaths), Parish of S. Donato   69

C.   Death of Giuseppe Antonio Guarneri, (2) Oct. 1683 (facsimile of entry in the Register of Deaths), Parish of S. Donato   69

D.   Death of Joseph Antonio Guarneri, (3) Oct. 1702 (facsimile of entry in the Register of Deaths), Parish of S. Donato   69

Fɪɢ.   I. Edge, purfling, and sound-hole of an example of the period 1730-33   76

Fɪɢ. II.   „   „   „   „ a 'Stradivari' of the year 1710   77

Fɪɢ. III.   „   „   „   „ an example of the period 1734-35   79

Fɪɢ. IV.   „   „   „   „   „   „   year 1742   83

E.   Census Returns of the Casa S. Bernardo for the years 1731, 1737, and 1745 (facsimile reproductions)   86

Fɪɢ. V. Edge, purfling, and sound-hole of an example of the year 1742   91

Fɪɢ. VI.   „   „   „   „   „   period 1743-44   95

THE VIOLIN-MAKERS OF THE
GUARNERI FAMILY
(1626–1762)

THEIR LIFE AND WORK

By

WILLIAM HENRY HILL

ARTHUR F. HILL, F.S.A.

and

ALFRED EBSWORTH HILL

WITH AN INTRODUCTORY NOTE BY

EDWARD J. DENT

Professor of Music in the University of Cambridge

LONDON

WILLIAM E. HILL & SONS, *Violin-Makers*

140 NEW BOND STREET, W.

1931

Title page of the original (1931) edition

GENEALOGICAL TABLE OF THE GUARNERI VIOLIN-MAKERS

BARTOLOMEO GUARNERI
(Profession unknown)
Died prior to 1687

ANDREA GUARNERI
Born c. 1626
Died 7th Dec. 1698
Married Anna Maria Orcelli, 1652
7 Children

PIETRO GIOVANNI GUARNERI
(known as 'Peter Guarnerius of Mantua')
Born 18th Feb. 1655
Died at Mantua, 26th March 1720
Married (1) Caterina Sassagni, 1677
(2) Lucia Burani, 1694
6 Children

GIUSEPPE GIOVANNI BATTISTA GUARNERI
(known as 'Joseph Guarnerius filius Andreæ')
Born 25th Nov. 1666
Died 1739-40
Married Barbara Franchi, 1690
6 Children

PIETRO GUARNERI
(known as 'Peter Guarnerius of Venice')
Born 14th April 1695
Died 7th April 1762
Married Angiola Maria Ferrari, 5th April 1728
10 Children

BARTOLOMEO GIUSEPPE GUARNERI
(known as 'Joseph Guarnerius del Gesù')
Born 21st Aug. 1698
Died 17th Oct. 1744
Married Catterina Roda, or Rota
c. 1722-23
No Children

CONTENTS

Chapter I. ANDREA GUARNERI .   .   .   .   *page* I

Andrea Guarneri, born 1626, died 1698, founder of the family of five violin-makers, all master craftsmen. None gave proof of great productivity. The Guarneri of ancient lineage. State of violin-making previous to and at time of birth of Andrea. The Amati—their inspiration from Brescia. Comparison with Maggini. Amati decision to take pupils. Francesco Ruger. Andrea Guarneri, son of Bartolomeo, starts in workshop about 1636. His first violin dated 1638. His name figuring in census returns of N. Amati in 1641 as son of Bartolomeo Guarneri, profession unknown, wood-carver, perhaps. Andrea marries Anna Maria Orcelli in 1652. Leaves Amati household in 1654—census returns of Casa Orcelli. The master working on his own account. Criticism of Andrea as craftsman. Brescian violins, Gasparo and Maggini, Andrea Amati. Their different forms. Analysis of work of Andrea Guarneri, wood used. The varnish. Making of cheaper instruments. Viola constructed by him. His violoncellos. His assistants. Pietro of Mantua, Giuseppe Giovanni, the others. Paolo Grancino. The master's first will, 1687. Its contents. Second will of 1692. Third will of 1694. Death of Anna Maria Orcelli, his wife, in 1695. Death of the master in 1698. The succession to the workshop.

Chapter II. PIETRO GUARNERI OF MANTUA .   .   .   .   .   *page* 25

Pietro Giovanni Guarneri, commonly known as Peter Guarnerius of Mantua. Born February 1655, eldest son of Andrea Guarneri. Died March 1720. Co-operated with his father 1670–8. Married 1677. Leaves his father's home 1679. Departed for Mantua possibly prior to 1685. Was a cultivated musician playing both viol and violin. Petitioned for appointment to Mantuan Court. In due course was appointed. Reason for his settling in Mantua. Monteverdi, also Cremonese, had preceded Pietro in same capacity, Pietro occupying dual calling of maker and player. Pietro and his brother Giuseppe agree as to division of their parents' estate. Pietro the first-known violin-maker to be established at Mantua. Rarity of his production. Never made a viola or a violoncello. Originality of his work. Analysis of tonal qualities of his instruments. Comparison with that of Stainer. Earliest works dating from Mantua about 1685. Examination of his work. Ornamented certain of his instruments. After 1700 broadened his style of work. Made use of exceptionally fine material and varnish. Endowed with true sense of beauty. List of representative examples. Finding of certificate of the master's death. Extract from census return in 1694 and following years. Census return of 1718. Age of the master given. Marriage of his daughter, October 1718. Burial certificate of the master. Pietro's will. Inventory of the contents of his house, movable and immovable. Sale of piece of land to the master for 1,000 écus. Pietro enters into agreement with the monks of S. Francisco di Paola, renouncing claim to property belonging to his son. Marriage contract for master's daughter in 1718. No pupils left by the master. Names of several makers inspired by him, Pietro the one distinguished Mantuan maker.

Chapter III. GIUSEPPE GUARNERI, SON OF ANDREA .   .   .   *page* 47

Giuseppe Giovanni Battista Guarneri, known as Joseph filius Andreæ, born 1666, died 1739–40, younger brother of Pietro of Mantua, succeeded to workshop of his father Andrea, was a skilled worker. Was father of Guiseppe del Gesù. Census return of Casa Guarneri in 1692. The master's environment in 1698. The signing of his own works prior to death of Andrea. Modification of his style towards 1710. Some works inspired by those of his brother Pietro. Some after Amati. Analysis of his work. Influence of Stradivari. The master's varnish. Wood utilized. His output of instruments. His violoncellos—their proportions and construction. His private life. Departure of his son Pietro to establish himself in Venice. Departure of his son Giuseppe. Death of Barbara Franchi in 1738. Presumed death of the master. Burial certificate not found. Not buried in S. Domenico. Analysis of work of period round 1715. Actual assistants in workshop a matter for speculation. Absence of original labels. Ignorance as to authorship of certain instruments. The master's definite pupils. Suggestion as to Carlo Bergonzi. Doubts as to whether he had been a pupil of Stradivari. Points of similarity in work of Bergonzi and the master. Paucity of output from workshop between 1720–40. Latest dated example 1731. Giuseppe del Gesù, successor to workshop. Final review of the master's work. Overshadowed by Antonio Stradivari.

CONTENTS

HISTORICAL INTRODUCTION
THE MUSICAL LIFE OF CREMONA, MANTUA, AND VENICE DURING THE PERIOD OF THE GUARNERI FAMILY

THREE cities of northern Italy are associated with the work of members of the Guarneri family—Cremona, Mantua, and Venice. Each of these three represents a different and characteristic type of social life in the Italy of the seventeenth and eighteenth centuries. Venice was the prosperous capital of an important state which had been universally recognized, and still claimed to be recognized, as one of the Great Powers of Europe; Mantua was the seat of a Duke who made up for the small size of his territorial dominions by the magnificence with which he maintained his court; Cremona was a small provincial town like many others, with neither political nor social importance. After being a free independent city from 1082 to 1335, Cremona had passed into the hands of the Visconti, and thenceforward remained in possession of the Duchy of Milan. Its most interesting architectural monuments belong to the period of its independence; in the earlier years of the Renaissance it had its school of painters, who formed their style chiefly on the traditions of Venice, but from the middle of the sixteenth century onwards Cremona ceased to be of any importance in the history of painting or architecture. By the Treaty of Cateau-Cambresis (1559) the Duchy of Milan was made subject to the Crown of Spain. Holding not merely the Duchy of Milan but the Kingdom of Naples and Sardinia as well, Spain became the paramount influence in Italy, although some of the ruling dynasties in the north, such as the Gonzagas at Mantua, the Farnesi at Parma, and the house of Este at Modena, still continued to hold their territories. The Spanish domination lasted until the end of the seventeenth century; with the year 1700 began the War of the Spanish Succession which was eventually to hand over Naples, Milan, and Mantua to the Austrians.

During the hundred and forty years of Spanish rule Italy has, politically speaking, no history; her history for that period is the history of music. Spain may have dominated Italy in politics, but in music Italy dominated the world. Those years cover the age of the madrigalists, the birth of Opera and its development from the entertainment of princes into a flourishing commercial industry; they cover, too, the rise

of classical chamber music up to the days of Corelli. By the beginning of the eighteenth century, Italian music, and pre-eminently Italian Opera, had become the
supreme influence on the music of all Europe. Other countries produced isolated
great composers and to some extent developed national schools of composition; but
the universal international language of music was Italian. It was not merely the fact,
however significant it may be, that Italian words were used all over Europe for the
technical terms of music; nor was it of great moment that Italian singers, players, and
composers were given lucrative engagements in London, Madrid, Berlin, Copen-
hagen, and St. Petersburg. The actual music itself, whatever was the nationality of
the composer, was permeated by the influence of the Italian style. The northern
composers might do what they would to strike out a native line of their own; but
they could no more deny their indebtedness to Italy than the French and the
Spaniards could deny the indebtedness of their daily speech to that of Julius Caesar.

The history of Italian music in the seventeenth century is inseparably bound up
with that of the great Italian violin-makers. When Monteverdi produced his *Orfeo*
at Mantua in 1607 he collected a miscellaneous orchestra of all the instruments that
he could find; it was an isolated performance for a special occasion, and the Duke of
Mantua no doubt gave him a free hand as regards expense. But when the Venetians
began to produce operas a few years later as a commercial speculation, it was only
natural that the orchestra should be simplified and standardized with the string
quartet as its foundation. As Opera became more and more popular throughout
Italy the demand for violins must have increased. Nor was it Opera alone that
became popular. Towards the end of the century the passion for music had become
almost insane. It may have exhibited different degrees of intensity in different places;
but at Naples, Bologna, and Venice the musical activity reached a pitch that to us
of the present day may well seem almost incredible. The *Conservatori* of Naples
began their existence simply as orphanages; by the end of the seventeenth century
they had become schools of music that were famous throughout Europe. The same
may be said of the *Ospedali* of Venice. The state of musical enthusiasm in Bologna
may be judged from the futile attempts made by Popes, Cardinals, and Arch-
bishops to restrain it or even to suppress it altogether. Bologna was full of monasteries and convents, and they were fully alive to the value of Church music as an
attraction to a crowd that seems to have been generous of its alms when stirred by
the beauty of song. In May 1686 the Cardinal Legate obtained from Rome an

edict which was to put an end to the 'offences due to the immoderate application of women to the study of music'. Music, it said, was inconsistent with the modesty becoming to the female sex, distracting them from their appropriate occupations and duties, besides exposing to grave danger both themselves, those who teach them, and those who listen to them. It was therefore ordered that no woman, be she virgin, wife, or widow, of whatsoever rank or station, not even those who were living in convents or orphanages for their education or for any other reason, notably that of learning music in order to practise it in the said convents, should learn to sing or play upon any musical instrument from any man, whether layman, ecclesiastic, or member of a religious order, even if he were in any degree related to her. Severe penalties were threatened to any heads of families who dared to admit into their houses any music-masters or musicians to teach their daughters or any of their womenkind. The edict was useless. In vain the Archbishop repeated it, in vain he ordered the nuns to make no music at all, not even to sing the plain-song. He threatened excommunication, but the nuns went on singing as before, and the congregations flocked to hear them.

The general popularity of music must naturally have affected the commercial production of all kinds of musical instruments, but the supremacy of the violin was connected in a peculiarly intimate way with the artistic character of the music itself. The seventeenth century is the century of *Baroque* architecture, and the violin is a typically baroque instrument. Painting and sculpture show us that throughout the ages musical instruments exhibit the architectural lines of their ages no less than articles of domestic furniture. The shape of the violin, the curves of its outline, and the convexities of its back and table, are characteristically baroque—so much so, indeed, that the layman might well imagine that they were dictated more by artistic than by acoustic reasons.

The spirit that directed all baroque art was a spirit of passionate—of extrava-gantly passionate—energy. It is difficult for us in these days to realize that this passionate energy found expression in the music, no less than in the other arts, of the seventeenth century. It is still more difficult for us to realize that the violin was the chief instrument by which this passionate energy was expressed. The modern musician, if he has any interest in older music at all, probably regards Corelli as the typical composer of the age of the great violin-makers; but Corelli as a matter of fact stands strangely apart from the musical life of his time. He was a violinist and wrote nothing but violin music; but he was not by temperament a *virtuoso*. By the time he became an acknowledged master the violin had become the acknowledged standard instrument of music. There was no question—at any rate in Italy—of comparing its merits with those of the old viols; the viols were completely forgotten. The violin had no longer any need to assert itself and to emphasize the qualities which distinguished it from its predecessors; after another generation it was to become the regular maid-of-all-work of the Opera. We must listen to the violin in the seventeenth century with the ears of those who still remembered the sound of the viols. In England the viols seem to have survived for the greater part of the century; it was only about the time of the Restoration, according to Anthony Wood, that 'viols began to be out of fashion', and we learn from Roger North that during the greater part of Charles II's reign 'the old musick was used in the countrys, and in many meetings and societys in London'. Of the old consort of viols North says:

It is a sort of harmonious murmer, rather than musick; and in a time, when people lived in tranquillity and at ease the entertainment of it was aggreable, not unlike a confused singing of birds in a grove. It was adapted to the use of private familys, and societys.

Italian music of the seventeenth century was the exact opposite of this in every way. It was made not for private families but for the theatre; it aimed not at a harmonious murmur but at tearing a passion to tatters. It shocked the gentler minds, such as Evelyn, in England, and shocked the French, too, by its outrageous violence of expression. Even at the end of the century Dryden could paint his well-known picture of the violin:

> Sharp violins proclaim
> Their jealous pangs, and desperation,
> Fury, frantic indignation,
> Depth of pains, and height of passion,
> For the fair, disdainful dame.

The most important thing about the change which came over music after about 1600 was not the abandonment of counterpoint, nor the substitution of keys for modes; it was the change in the attitude of musicians towards rhythm. The music of the seventeenth century is based on a sense of emphatic accent and stress; it was only this vigorous periodic emphasis which made the classical key-system possible, made it indeed inevitable. It was the energy of accent that led to the new view of dissonance and to the style of counterpoint employed by Bach in which the driving force of regular rhythm carried the composer ruthlessly over every obstacle of discord.

For this new type of music the violin was the ideal instrument. It has sometimes been suggested that the Italian composers for the theatre treated the violin with timidity. This is far from the truth. They were no more timid about the violin than they were about the trumpet; but both these instruments had to be employed with care, lest they should be too overpowering. For practically the whole of the seventeenth century the accompaniment of voices, the main harmonic foundation of the music, is entrusted to the chord-playing instruments, the lute, theorbo, and harpsichord. The violins are used for colour, as we might say: they enter in the intervals when the voice is silent, unless perhaps a solo violin is used *obbligato* as a contesting force equivalent to a second human voice. Even so late as Mozart's *Requiem* (1791) we can see the survival of this tradition in Church music; the first number misses its effect completely unless accompanied by a considerable volume of organ-tone, for the fragmentary motives of the strings are intended not to provide harmonic support but to heighten dramatic and passionate expression. In the Italian theatre it was not until about 1700 that these wild horses were completely broken in and set to the humble drudgery of playing mere accompaniments. It is only after that date that the solo violin sonata and the concerto for violin solo take their rise. The great singers of the Opera had taught the violinists something new—the art of pure singing.

During the whole of the seventeenth century and for some considerable part of the eighteenth Venice might well have claimed to be the musical centre of Europe. It was the only city in which Opera was undertaken on a commercial basis. In other places Opera was dependent on the patronage of a court or the caprice of some individual nobleman; Venice opened a regular Opera House in 1637, and before the end of the century ten more theatres devoted to Opera had been established there. Naples, which in the following century became the serious rival of Venice as an operatic centre, appears never to have seen a performance of Opera until a Venetian company brought thither one of Monteverdi's in 1651; Rome, too, may be said to have been colonized by Venice when the Teatro Tordinona was opened in 1671 with a performance of Cavalli's *Giasone*. Two more Opera Houses were opened at Rome before the century ended; but Opera in Rome was hampered by Papal restrictions which were unknown in Venice. Bologna did not open its Opera House till 1690.

Venice possessed the further advantage of its geographical position. It was the natural source from which Italian music was supplied to Vienna and to the northern countries; even if the composers and singers came from Naples, they passed through Venice on their way. Venice, too, was a great centre of music-publishing; no other city in Italy could compare with it in this indispensable branch of musical industry. In addition to its eleven Opera Houses, Venice possessed four schools of music associated with its four hospitals and orphanages—the *Pietà,* the *Mendicanti,* the *Ospedaletto,* and the *Incurabili,* and although at all these institutions the pupils were restricted to the female sex, this did not prevent them from possessing complete orchestras, the performances of which drew the enthusiastic admiration of Dr. Burney and many other distinguished musicians who heard them.

The standardization of the orchestra and the multiplication of orchestras in such a city as Venice obviously brought about an increasing demand for musical instruments, more especially for violins; and it is equally obvious that there arose sooner or later a demand for violins at a cheap price within the resources of the humbler members of the musical profession, as well as for those masterpieces of craftsmanship which were no doubt required by artists of the rank of Corelli and Tartini. But that very development of instrumental music which the Italian craftsmen had made possible was to be the ruin of the Italian musical supremacy. Italy could always supply singers, but Austria, Bohemia, and Germany soon began to provide an army of instrumentalists; and with the rise of the string quartet and the orchestral symphony the centre of the musical world was transferred from Venice to Vienna.

In Mantua the conditions of musical life were very different from those of Venice. Venice was a republic and one of the world's great cities. Mantua was a ducal court, and its social and artistic existence depended entirely on the duke's pleasure.

In the early days of Opera Mantua had been the scene of Monteverdi's first triumphal experiments. His patron was Duke Vincenzo Gonzaga, who reigned from 1587 to 1612. He was succeeded by his two sons, Francesco, who survived him less than a year, and Ferdinand the Cardinal, who succeeded his brother in December 1612. Both of these princes shared their father's interest in Opera, and Ferdinand made several efforts to induce Monteverdi to return to Mantua, which he had left for good a few months before his accession. Cardinal Gonzaga was himself a composer and Monteverdi appears to have held him in some esteem as a musician. With the next Duke, Vincenzo (1626–27), the main line of the Gonzagas died out. The dukedom passed to a collateral line in the person of Charles de Nevers, who had spent all his life in France. Charles had at least time to confirm

Monteverdi in the enjoyment of his pension; but his succession involved him in war with the Emperor Ferdinand III. Mantua was sacked by the imperial troops in 1630, with the result that among other treasures the whole musical library of the Gonzagas was destroyed. This was also the year of the great plague which devastated Venice to such an extent that a third of the population perished. The plague was experienced at Bologna too, and in Cremona, which had also suffered from the invasion of the Austrian army. The Gonzaga line remained in possession of Mantua until 1703, when, as a result of the War of the Spanish Succession, it was awarded to Austria and remained Austrian until 1866.

During the greater part of the seventeenth century records of Opera at Mantua are very scanty. There seems to have been a sudden outburst of operatic activity just at the century's end. In addition to a large number of oratorios by unknown composers, Buononcini's *Il Trionfo di Camilla* was performed there in 1698, having been given at Naples two years earlier; Alessandro Scarlatti's *Il Prigioniero Fortunato,* first produced at Naples in 1698, was given at Mantua the following year. From 1696 to 1703 several of the singers who appeared in the Neapolitan Opera House were *virtuosi* or *virtuose* of His Serenest Highness the Duke of Mantua, and we find their names appearing at Bologna and Venice too. The outbreak of war and the deposition of Duke Carlo IV in 1703 did not bring Opera to an end in Mantua; an opera called *Il Gran Costanzo,* by an unknown composer, was performed there in 1706, and occasional productions seem to have taken place during the next twenty years. But the War of the Spanish Succession was followed by that of the Austrian Succession, and it was not until after the Peace of Aix-la-Chapelle in 1748 that Mantuan musical life had a chance of reviving.

During the seventeenth century and most of the eighteenth such things as public concerts were unknown in Italy; it was in England that they were first started, and there not until 1672. Private music-meetings in Italy were generally organized by the academies which sprang up in every town; these were mainly literary and philosophical societies, but their meetings often included some performance of music. Their membership was generally confined to the nobility and the clergy. It is from these institutions that the word *accademia*—more correctly, *accademia di musica*—came in the days of Dr. Burney to signify a concert. The clergy, in addition to the part which they took in the life of the Academies, were often staunch supporters of music in their churches and in their monasteries and convents, which prospered exceedingly under the Spanish dominion. The congregations were often possessed of great wealth and their members enjoyed both comfort and liberty.

Most writers on Italian literature have made fun of the academies, and, above all, of the famous Arcadian Academy at Rome; but when one studies the history of literary and musical effort in the smaller cities of Italy, one cannot help coming to the conclusion that, after the magnificent era of the Renaissance princes had closed, it was very largely the despised Academies which kept culture alive throughout the troublous times when Italian territories were being disputed by the French, the Spaniards, and the Austrians. War or pestilence might suppress for a time the actual meetings of an academy, but its memory remained alive, and as soon as peace was re-established it could collect its scattered members and start its activities afresh. The chief academy of Mantua was that of the *Invaghiti*, a society of noblemen under the direct patronage of the Gonzagas and holding its meetings in the ducal palace itself. It was at a private meeting of this body that Monteverdi's *Orfeo* was first performed on February 24th, 1607. The *Invaghiti* dated from 1564. There existed also a less socially exclusive academy, known first as the *Invitti* and later as the *Timidi*. The *Invitti* came to a temporary end at the sack of Mantua in 1630, but a few sur-vivors reconstituted the academy in 1643, and in 1645 the Duke (Charles de Nevers) took them under his protection. They had at that time thirty members. It was in 1648 that they changed their name to the *Timidi*. For sixty years they lived in prosperity; their amalgamation with the academy of the *Imperfetti* in 1689 enabled them to enlarge their theatre, in which they held their literary meetings, gave con-certs, and even performed operas of which both words and music were written by their own members. At the beginning of the eighteenth century they collapsed again, but reappeared in 1737, after the termination of the war of the Polish Succes-sion. Although originally a society of middle-class people, they were now joined by a considerable secession from the aristocratic *Invaghiti*. The survivors of the *Invaghiti* became in 1748 a 'colony' of the Arcadians, who about this time were absorbing the smaller and older academies in many parts of Italy. It was obviously an advan-tage for men of letters and musicians to be able to belong to the same corporation wherever they might happen to travel in Italy; but we may get some idea of the honour in which these older bodies had been held from the fact that the Empress Maria Theresa, in her dispatch to the *Colonia Virgiliana* (as the Mantuan branch of Arcadia was now called), which she took under her protection in 1752, recommended the new Arcadians to abide as far as possible by the constitutions of the former *Invaghiti,* though it is surprising to find the Austrian Empress taking so much interest in an institution founded by the dispossessed dynasty of the Gonzagas two centuries before. What eventually happened was that in 1767 Maria Theresa united both Academies in one, which still exists and flourishes as the *Accademia Virgiliana.* This body in 1769 absorbed an *Accademia Filarmonica* which had been started by some musical amateurs in 1761. A new theatre was built by Bibbiena and opened on December 3rd, 1769; the third meeting which took place there was the concert given by the young Mozart on the 16th of January 1770.

As regards Cremona there was no Maria Theresa to take an interest in its doings. It had for a short time belonged to the Republic of Venice, but during the seven-teenth century it formed part of the Duchy of Milan. Its society exhibited the typical stratification of nobility, clergy, and *bourgeoisie,* and under Spanish influences the clergy were in all probability the most predominant party in the life of the town. Spanish influence was strong, too, amongst the nobility, who here, as in other Italian centres, thought it their duty to maintain an exaggerated exclusiveness and pride which was really quite foreign to the normal Italian temperament.

At Cremona, even more than at Mantua, culture was dependent on the Acade-mies. The earliest and the most famous was that of the *Animosi,* founded in 1560. It was, needless to say, an aristocratic society, and from 1586 to 1606 it remained dormant owing to dissensions among the patrician families, some of whom took sides with the French, while others favoured the Spaniards. In 1606 it was revived and reconstituted with new statutes. It was now to be exclusive, but not rigidly confined to noblemen. Its first rule guards against the admission of persons of ill repute, its second lays down that the members are to be either noble by blood, even if they are not competent to take part in the activities of the society, or noble at least by *virtù,* which we may translate by 'ability'. No one was to be elected without obtaining two-thirds of the votes. Characteristic of the Spanish atmosphere is the rule that a President was to be elected every year, and that on the day of his inaugura-tion, which was to be that of some distinguished saint, a solemn mass should be sung either at his expense or at the Academy's. The saint in question was always to be the same one and to be regarded as the official patron of the Academy. The Academy held weekly meetings with discourses on literary matters or on natural and moral philosophy; but the rules inform us that both before and after the lecture there was to be a performance of music, and among the regular officers of the society there was to be one who was responsible for these and in authority over the musicians, who were presumably hired professionals. There were about sixty members, and they met regularly on Thursday evenings. The Spanish government allowed them a room on condition that two lectures a week should be given, one of which was to be on the subject of Honour. The lecturer was Ottaviano Picenardi, a member of one of the most noble families of Cremona; the Picenardi are still great land-owners in the neighbourhood and have for centuries been people of eminent distinction in the history of their city. The object of these lectures on the science of chivalry, as we learn from a fly-sheet printed at the time, was to teach people how to make up their quarrels peaceably and in accordance with Christian principles. Such an institution throws a striking light on the state of society in those days. Spanish punctilio seems to us now rather ridiculous; but it was not long since Tasso had declaimed against 'honour' as the greatest curse of contemporary life, and the only way to prevent perpetual bloodshed on trivial accounts was to reduce the whole question of personal honour to a standard code. Picenardi seems indeed to have been a man of considerable tact and in the management of the Academy he had often need of it.

The most important musical meeting of the *Animosi* in those days must have been the concert given in honour of Monteverdi on August 10th, 1607, when a selection from his *Orfeo* was performed. Another lecturer on chivalry was Alessandro Bonetti, a physician, who became president in 1619 with the usual ceremonies, trumpeters playing while he took his seat, after which there was 'a most beautiful concert of voices and instruments', followed by the customary panegyric delivered by another member of the inevitable Picenardi family. A lawyer, Giovanni Battista Ala (another famous Cremona name), is mentioned as a great musical benefactor of the Academy; he died in 1621. The Mantuan war interrupted the meetings in 1628, and the plague of 1630 kept the Academy closed until 1631. In spite of wars it managed to continue its existence, and a record of 1638 shows that the annual inaugural meeting in November was evidently the great social function of the Cremona season, attended by the Cardinal Bishop, the government authorities, the mayor, the legal and medical corporations, and all the nobility, to listen to speeches and music. But after 1646 the *Animosi* seem to have drooped. The fact was that they were too exclusive; a new spirit was making itself felt, and Spanish pride was gradually becoming rather out of date. A lawyer and man of letters, Francesco Arisi, founded a new academy in 1675, and in allusion to the quarrels that separated social strata, gave it the name of the *Disuniti*. Such societies, as we know well enough in our own days, depend mainly on the energy of one particular man for their prosperous continuance. As long as Arisi lived the *Disuniti* flourished; and fortunately for them his life was a long one. He was only eighteen when he founded the *Disuniti*, and he guided its destinies until his death in 1743, having transformed it into a colony of the Arcadians in 1719.

The *Disuniti* were under the patronage of St. Anthony of Padua, and one of their annual functions was the performance of an oratorio in his honour. The words were generally written by Arisi himself, who produced a quantity of sacred *libretti* during the last quarter of the seventeenth century, for these and other occasions, such as the reception of some young lady into a convent. Of the composers hardly any record remains. After the days of Monteverdi Cremona produced no musicians of distinction, and such musicians as happened to be born there usually sought their fortune elsewhere. One of Arisi's *libretti, Il cuore scrigno,* an oratorio for St. Anthony of Padua (1696), was set by Benedetto Vinaccesi of Brescia, who afterwards became second organist of St. Mark's at Venice and Director of the Ospedaletto there. He was in the service of the Gonzagas and some of his music was performed at Mantua too.

Besides the *Animosi* and the *Disuniti* there were various 'Philharmonic Academies'; but none of them had any long existence. They were merely groups of people who organized occasional performances, and Arisi in his monumental work, *Cremona Literata* (1702–41), expresses his scorn of them in grandiloquent Latin:

Verum hoc florente saeculo Academici nomen usurpatur a multis analphabetis, a Cantantibus scilicet, noctu diuque, modo huc, modo illuc versantibus, praeterea foeminas cantilenosas in similibus Academiis primo loco sedentes, sequuntur Histriones, aliique Comoedi Bacchanaliorum, iis fere accedunt Circumforanei, et Nugatores, pro ut in suis Theatris Citharistae, Saltatores, Ludiones, &c.

Arisi was evidently no lover of music; and we may suspect that the musical activities of Cremona had become so vigorous as to prove a dangerous counterattraction to his lectures on literature and philosophy.

Mozart passed through Cremona in 1770 and was well pleased with the orchestra which he heard there. No regular musical academy was started until the beginning of the nineteenth century.

Opera seems to have been hardly known at all in Cremona. The first theatre there was built by the Ariberti family. Marchese Giovanni Battista Ariberti, after taking part in the war against Gustavus Adolphus in Germany, retired from the profession of arms about 1646 and married Giulia Rangoni of Modena, a lady of some literary attainments. She wrote poems and dramas, including the *libretto* of an oratorio, *La Giustizia placata,* performed at Cremona in 1683. She did not present her husband with an heir until 1666; in 1687 she died. This son, Bartolomeo, inherited her interest in literature and music. His father, anxious for the succession, got him married soon after his mother's death, and in order that the young couple might enjoy the drama in their own palace built them a theatre in communication with it. The old man lived on until 1707. But he had been disappointed of his posterity. Marchese Bartolomeo had one son only and he became a priest, rising eventually to the dignity of Titular Archbishop of Palmyra. He entered the congregation of the Oratorians at Brescia, and soon after his grandfather's death persuaded his father to give him the theatre and the adjoining house, which he would naturally have inherited in any case, to be converted into a church and monastery for the Oratorians. The church was consecrated in 1714. It was suppressed in 1798 and reopened as a theatre in 1801 by a society of amateur actors. It need hardly be said that it is now a cinema. The present large theatre of Cremona was not built until early in the nineteenth century.

Allacci's *Drammaturgia,* which goes down to 1755, does not mention a single opera that was performed at Cremona. Nevertheless there were occasional performances of Opera later on. A comic *intermezzo, la Donna Dottoressa,* by Pietro Chiarini, was acted in 1754, and in 1765 a comic opera, *La Sposa Fedele,* probably by Guglielmi, was given in a theatre described as the property of a nobleman. In 1794 another comic opera, *Gli Amanti della Dote,* by Silvestro di Palma, was given 'in the theatre of the noble association'. This may have been the Teatro Nazari, where Paisiello's *Il Sismano nel Mogol* was performed in 1785. The fact that the only operas traceable to Cremona were comic operas rather suggests that these may have been amateur performances. But by the middle of the eighteenth century travelling Opera companies, especially those of a light repertory, were not uncommon, and no doubt they visited Cremona, where we are told that managers all cultivated the favour of a certain Marchese Pier Francesco Araldi, an old gentleman who must have been a characteristic figure both in the theatre and outside it. Lancetti gives a delightful description of him, witty and amiable, the friend of everybody and the great leader of theatrical enterprise: a privileged character who could be seen any night in his box waving his hands to the actors and calling out to the audience to applaud. As Lancetti says, his behaviour was possible only in that century, and—it may be added—in a small provincial town like Cremona.

It is evident that Cremona's musical activities could hardly provide the livelihood of Cremona's violin-makers. It may even be doubted whether Cremona showed much appreciation of them. Arisi mentions Tarquinio Merula as one of Cremona's great men, but he says nothing at all about the violin-makers. It was in other countries that they were most appreciated. By the time that Lancetti began his *Biografia Cremonese* in 1819 even Cremona had realized their value. He describes the Amati brothers and the other great violin-makers with conscious pride, and tells us from his own personal recollection that when the general of the French armies passed through Cremona in 1795 (or, he says, General Masséna acting for him) he asked among other things for a violin of Amati and a viola of Stradivari, naturally imagining that in their own native city there would be an abundance of them. But there were none for sale, and such private persons as owned them refused to part with them at any price.

EDWARD J. DENT

Bird's-eye view of Cremona

CHAPTER I
ANDREA GUARNERI
(1626–98)

A thing shaped by the hand of Harmony;
To touch the finer movements of the mind.

THE name of Guarneri will ever hold high rank amongst the illustrious of the Italian violin-makers. It is true that it was destined, together with all other names, to be somewhat overshadowed by that of Antonio Stradivari—the greatest of makers for all time. But we recall with interest and gratitude that this Cremonese family gave to our art no less than five craftsmen who shaped instruments which, when at their best, proclaim an admirable individuality.

These five master-workers proved themselves to be well versed in their art, and all made use of their tools with ability. Yet not one of them showed that perfection of fitness for his calling which was made manifest in the more varied and skilled productions of their predecessors, the members of the Amati family.[1]

They were intimately connected with each other both by family ties and working traditions, but this close intercourse did not prevent each maker from contributing something purely of his own; and all have left us instruments which are distinctly personal.

Andrea, the pioneer, was to prove himself the most industrious of the family, Pietro of Mantua the least; the productions of the two Giuseppe, or of Pietro of Venice, were by no means numerous. In fact, with the exception of Andrea, they seem to have led working lives which were comparatively inactive, so far as instrument-making was concerned.

We learn from several sources that the Guarneri came of ancient lineage, the documents showing various ways of spelling the family name: Guarneri, Guarnero, Guarnerio, Guarnieri, Guerneri, and Guarnerius, the latinized form. Signor Livi cites a document bearing the date of 1209, in which mention is made of the brothers Oddolino and Guilielmino Guarneri. Among the ranks of the nobility, too, there existed branches of the family; and we reproduce on the cover and title-page of this book the coat of arms which they were entitled to bear. With the passing of the centuries the name spread to other cities of northern and central Italy, and to-day is to be found amongst those of the bourgeois class.[2]

Before taking up our direct subject, let us briefly consider the actual state of violin-making up to and during the first half of the seventeenth century, the period which marks the birth of Andrea Guarneri.

With the death of Maggini at Brescia in 1632 musical-instrument-making, which had flourished there for close upon two centuries, lay dormant for a time, to be revived later by the two Rogeri. During this interval the divers types of viols which several generations of Brescians had so successfully produced were slowly falling into disuse, and were being replaced by the true violin, viola, and violoncello.

Contemporaneously with Gasparo da Salò (1542–1609), who worked at Brescia, and in fact before Maggini was born, we find Andrea Amati, or Amadi,[3] as he

[1] The Amati made viols, violas, violins, and violoncellos.
[2] The present writers well recall, in the eighties of last century, passing frequently by the shop of a cabinet-maker, situated in

Bolsover Street, W., bearing the name of Guarneri.
[3] Probably Cremonese dialect.

himself inscribed the name on the manuscript labels inserted in his works, carrying on the craft of 'liutaro' at Cremona. Now was he the actual founder of the Cremonese School of violin-making? We believe so, for we can find no record of the name or work of any other contemporary or earlier Cremonese maker. Where and from whom did he receive his training? To neither question are we able to make a definite answer. At Brescia in all probability, for the city was comparatively near Cremona, and all that we can usefully add is that Andrea was a Cremonese[1] and that his few existing works give signal proof of a well-trained and accomplished worker who was ahead of his time both in craftsmanship and conception.

Notwithstanding repeated efforts, we have been baffled so far in our quest for the record of Amati's birth; but from evidence furnished by the labels of authentic instruments, we gathered that as early as 1560–70 he was making violins of two sizes, the one of small, the other of normal dimensions, and was embodying in them that remarkable charm of form and finish which his two equally illustrious sons were to continue and perfect. We have been unable to discover the date of the master's death, but we have found fairly definite proof that he had passed away before 1581, the year of Maggini's birth.

That Andrea owed his inspiration either directly or indirectly to Brescia is beyond question; and in seeking for his actual teacher it must not be forgotten that the Church had from early times brought into being men who were trained to be skilled wood-carvers. It is undoubtedly to this source that we owe a goodly number of the Italian instrument-makers.

Andrea Amati's calling was followed by the above-mentioned sons, Antonio and Girolamo, more generally known by their latinized names of Antonius and Hieronymus.[2] There is no reason to suppose that Andrea trained any other pupils.

These brothers remained in lifelong partnership; Girolamo alone signed a few instruments, Antonio never, so far as our experience goes. Their jointly signed works date from about 1590—possibly a few years earlier—until 1630, the year of the death of Girolamo; Antonio had predeceased him (date unknown). Both were most accomplished workmen; and the combined efforts of father and sons contributed materially to the laying down of the definite principles of violin-making from which no serious departure has since been made. Nor have their accuracy of finish

---

[1] We learn from a document existing in the Archives of Bologna, a contract drawn up there on 18th December 1268, that one of the witnesses was Bondatus de Amatis di Cremona.
[2] Their labels were invariably printed in Latin.

and beauty of contour ever been surpassed. Maggini never revealed himself as their equal in craftsmanship, though perhaps we might allow that he approached them when at his best. And no study is more illuminating than that of these three crafts men working for years, side by side as it were, drawing their inspiration from a com mon source, and yet imparting to their respective instruments a character of marked difference and originality.

Again we note throughout the brothers' lives the absence of any pupil other than Nicolò, son of Girolamo; and it is quite probable that both Andrea and his sons were jealously guarding their art and were unwilling to impart their knowledge to any one outside the family.[1] The many choice instruments they made testify in most eloquent manner to the favour they enjoyed; and no better endorsement of the unique position they held could be found than that furnished by the correspondence of Galileo-Micanzio given in our *Life of Stradivari*.[2]

With the tragic death of Girolamo—he, his wife, and two daughters fell victims to the ravages of the plague at Cremona in 1630—Nicolò, born in 1596 and generally known as Nicolaus Amati, became the Maéstro of the workshop, and he more than worthily upheld the prestige gained by his forebears during upwards of sixty years.

If we again pause for a moment to consider the state of instrument-making at this time—i.e. 1630—we recognize that the fame achieved by Cremona was a continu ously spreading one, and that the skill and industry of the Amati had borne abun dant fruit, with the result that an increasing number of orders was flowing to the city from the various Courts of Italy, and from still farther afield. A situation had thus arisen which called for greater production. So far the work had been kept strictly in the family, and we can imagine to ourselves with what thrill of pride Nicolò must have looked back upon the successful achievement of his father, uncle, and grandfather. But the master now stood alone, unaided in his work; and the demand for instruments had become imperative. So that the decision to take apprentices was inevitable—a decision fraught with the greatest importance, in that it led to the spread of violin-making among other Cremonese families, notably the Rugeri, Guarneri, and Stradivari.

[1] Extract from *La Provincia* of Cremona, December 1912: Giovanni Maria Cironi of Pozzaglio, who worked at Cre mona from 1590 onwards, applies for the right of citizenship for himself and family, which was granted to him in 1611. His will is dated 1630, in which year he is recorded as dead. He left three sons, Girolamo, Bernadino, and Florindo, who, like their father, made violins, guitars, and cithers, and one and all played.
(We have never seen, nor heard of the existence of any instru ment whatsoever, by a maker of the above family.)
[2] *Antonio Stradivari, his Life and Work*, p. 241. See Chap. VIII.

The first of this line of apprentices to be acknowledged was Francesco Ruger, born at Cremona in the year 1620. It is not very likely that there had been others at an earlier date, for no record of their existence or their work has been handed down to us.

Francesco[1] must have entered Amati's work-shop between the years 1630 and 1632, and was followed a few years later by the boy Andrea Guarneri, our first introduction to whom is effected by one of his violins bearing a label dated 1638, made evidently in his twelfth year (see illustration, facing p. 2). We then find his name given in the census returns of the house-hold of Nicolò Amati for the year 1641—the record of earlier years is non-extant. His age is here given as fifteen, and we therefore assume that he started his career not later than 1636. Andrea was the son of Bartolomeo Guarneri, and was born about 1626. We have failed to find his actual birth recorded; and in subse-quent references to the census returns his age is repeatedly subject to slight variations.

We learn nothing from our research respecting the occupation of Bartolo-meo, nor have we been more successful in discovering in which parish of Cre-mona he lived and died. The text of the first will of Andrea shows us that his father was no longer alive in the year 1687. Probably he had passed away some years earlier.

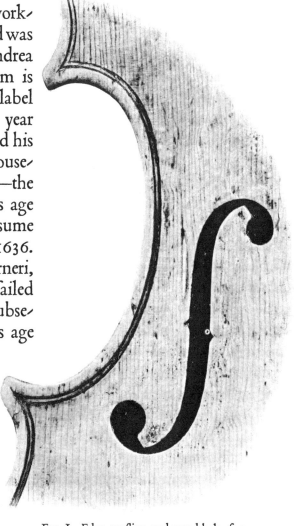

FIG. I. Edge, purfling, and sound-hole of an example of the period 1640-45.

Had Bartolomeo a large family? We think not, for otherwise we should surely have found some mention of them. We do know that in addition to Andrea, he had

---

[1] We assume that the absence of F. Ruger's name in the census returns was due to the fact that he was not resident in the house. The same reasoning applies with regard to Stradivari.

another son named Giovanni Battista, whose existence is attested by the will already referred to. It was likely enough that Bartolomeo was a close neighbour of Amati; he may have followed some calling kindred to viol-making—why not wood-carving? If this were the case, the impulse to place his son with a fellow craftsman would be natural enough. For we must not overlook the intimate link existing between the wood-carver and, let us say, the violin-carver. We repeat that there was a consider-able number of accomplished wood-workers throughout Italy. They were continu-ously engaged in carrying out the inspired work of the churches, or in embellishing the palaces of the noblemen. The viol-maker produced mainly for the same patrons. They fraternized, and we do not hesitate to reaffirm our belief that here we have the true source from which sprang many of the Italian violin-makers.

Signor Livi very appropriately draws our attention to the names of Cesare Cer-vato and Giovanni Battista Guerine, men described as 'intaliadori' (wood-carvers) who were living at Cremona in 1632, in close proximity to the house of Nicolò Amati.

Andrea Guarneri, then, was living with Amati in the year 1641, being instructed in the art of instrument-making, and quite probably working side by side with the fellow apprentice Francesco Ruger. We may conclude that he was in a friendly and congenial atmosphere under Amati's roof, for he is present as a witness at his master's wedding, which took place in 1645. In the following year his name dis-appears from the census returns of the household, and does not reappear until 1650, when he is designated as follows: 'Andrea, garzone anni 26', A (1). Two years later, in December 1652, while still living in Amati's house, he entered into marriage with Anna Maria Orcelli, daughter of Orazio Orcelli, A (2). Both Andrea's name and that of his bride are given on Amati's census return for the following year 1653 (see reproduction), B.

In 1654 Andrea took leave of the Amati household, and, we should imagine, at the same time severed his direct connexion with the workshop. We find him pro-ceeding to his father-in-law's house in the parish of S. Matteo, viz. the *Casa Orcelli*, which in due course became known as the *Casa Guarneri*. We have gleaned one interesting fact concerning the Orcelli family with whom Andrea had become allied. When searching the baptismal registers of the parish of S. Matteo, Signor Livi noted under the date 9th December 1620, the baptism of *'Franciscus filius Horatii de Orcellis et Johanni Juglium'* and on the margin of the register, in

A (1)

Census Return, April of the year 1650.

House of the Amati

Nicolò Amati	.	.	.	.	aged 52
Lucretia, wife	.	.	.	.	„ 27
Girolamo, son	.	.	.	.	„ I
*Elena Urbana	.	.	.	.	„ 14
*Valeria .	.	.	.	.	„ 11
*Anna Urbana	.	.	.	.	„ 9
Andrea, assistant	.	.	.	.	„ 26
*Giacoma, servant .	.	.	.	.	„ 13

* [Members of the household, not daughters]

A (2)

December 31st, 1652. Andrea, son of Bartolomeo Guarneri of the Parish of SS. Faustina and Giovita, and Anna Maria, daughter of the late Orazio Orcelli of this Parish, were joined together in Holy Matrimony, in the presence of witnesses, by me, Vulpio, Rector. The witnesses being Carlo Betta and Girolamo Collesio, of this Parish.

C.

Census Return of the year 1654

House of the Guarneri-Orcelli

Andrea Guarneri	.	. 27 Christened
Anna Maria Orcelli, wife	.	. 27 ,,
Angela Teresa, daughter		,,

of the year 1655

Andrea Guarneri	.	. 28 Christened, con-firmed and communicant
Anna Maria Orcelli, wife	.	. 28 Christened, con-firmed and communicant
Pietro Gio., son .	.	. 2 months.

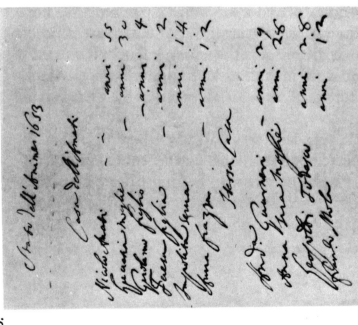

B.

Census Return of the year 1653

House of the Amati.

Nicolò Amati	.	.	. aged 55
Lucretia, wife	.	.	. ,, 30
Girolamo, son	.	.	. ,, 4
Teresa, daughter	.	.	. ,, 2
Impolita, servant	.	.	. ,, 14
Anna Frazza	.	.	. ,, 12

Same House
[Probably living on another floor]

Andrea Guarneri	.	.	. ,, 29
Anna, his wife	.	.	. ,, 28
Leopoldi, German	.	.	. ,, 28
Francesca Mola	.	.	. ,, 12

writing of the seventeenth century, was inscribed: *'fu gran musico e sonatore rarissimo di violino morto in Parma'* (was an accomplished musician and fine violinist, died in Parma). We here find the intimate relation between player and maker, inasmuch as this Orcelli was Andrea's brother-in-law.

Our interest in the census returns now shifts to those furnished by the *Casa Orcelli-Guarneri,* and we note living there under the date 1654, C:

Andrea Guarneri . . . . d'anni 27
Anna Maria Orcelli, moglie (wife) . . . . . „ 27
Angela Teresa, figlia (daughter)

In the following year 1655 comes an addition to the family, a son named Pietro Giovanni, the future violin-maker. His age is recorded as two months, C.

An additional reason for suggesting that 1654-55 marks the year when Andrea launched out upon his own is furnished by a label of more than ordinary interest, one that we found inserted in a violin dated 1655. It is of the first type of label, but differs from it in one important detail: the master says 'ex Allumnis Nicolai Amati'—in earlier years the similar label reads 'Alumnus', correctly spelt and without the prefix 'ex' (see reproduction of these labels (Chap. VII)). Now definite indications of the collaboration of the pupil with his master during the last fifteen to twenty years— the period in which we see Nicolò Amati at his zenith—are not frequent. We do, however, trace Andrea's hand in certain of the master's violins bearing his original label and dated from 1640 onwards to the fifties; and some of these instruments point clearly to the pupil rather than the master as their creator. But on reviewing the matter broadly, we assert that Andrea played a subordinate part only. He cer- tainly aided in the construction of the various instruments; but the master hand of Nicolò was rarely absent: it passed over all and gave the finishing touch. It was thus the exception for the 'alumni' to construct in entirety and finish off works which were subsequently to bear the signature of Amati—at all events at the period with which we are now concerned.

We are decidedly of opinion that long after they had severed connexion with their master, both Andrea and Francesco did occasionally make entire instruments for him, although these productions are to be met with bearing Nicolò's original labels. The fame of the Amati was widespread: Nicolò's choice instruments were more costly. And when asked to make at a lesser price he had recourse to his 'ex- Alumni'.

Now two questions very naturally arise in one's mind when reflecting on the outcome of Andrea's long connexion with Nicolò Amati. Had the pupil reaped full
advantage from this intercourse with his illustrious master? And do his productions
show relatively the same progress as that observed in those of his predecessors? In
the main we feel bound to answer both questions in the negative; and we do so
only after passing in review the whole of his life's work. Andrea was in no sense a
great craftsman; true, here and there he was not far behind the Amati, but he was
distinctly behind. We have never seen an instrument of his making in which the
conception and execution equalled the best work of his master. His originality was
only relative and generally found in the details; and the more closely we analyse his
work, the more firmly are we convinced that he was but a humble follower of the
Amati, and in the main pursued contentedly the path marked out by them. We do,
however, note two not unimportant deviations: firstly, his admirable conception of
a smaller-sized viola; secondly, his smaller proportioned violoncello, both representing progressive innovations.

Let us digress for a moment to make one point clear when we say that Andrea
Guarneri, with regard to his violins, simply followed in the footsteps of his master.

The Brescians, as exemplified by Gasparo and Maggini, had definitely decided
upon violins of two models, the one of large, the other of small form. Why these
two forms? Our reply is that in seeking to construct an instrument which would
respond to the musical requirements of the time—one producing a more soprano-
like quality of tone than that obtained from the existing viols—Gasparo learnt that *size*
played a predominant role. So feeling his way, he constructed the first true violin of
the large model; then continuing his efforts, he devised others of smaller proportions.
Examples of these different forms still exist to-day. When he found that the tone of
the smaller violin appealed more to some players, if not to all, he adopted these
different forms permanently. Maggini worked on the same lines, though he made
the majority of his violins of the large size.

Andrea Amati, with remarkable foresight, reduced his large model to approximately 14 inches, and the smaller form to about $13\frac{1}{2}$ inches. And we believe that all
his violins, without exception, were made of one or other of these two forms.

Thus we see that prior to 1600 it was an established practice to make two kinds
of violins, the one varying in length from 14 to $14\frac{1}{2}$ inches, the other from 13 to $13\frac{3}{4}$
and the widths of both varying correspondingly.

The brothers Amati adhered to their father's standard, Nicolò likewise. They never exceeded the 14-inch model, and many of their productions were of the smaller dimensions.

The earliest form of violin made by Andrea Guarneri (see illustrations, p. 2 and facing p. 24) reproduces strikingly the Amati characteristics, as one would naturally expect from the youthful pupil. We find the same outline of rounded bouts and slender corners, the lower curves terminating with a slight flatness. What more probable than that the pupil was utilizing one of his master's moulds to build up the sides, hence achieving the similar outline? The modelling is of moderate height, scooping gracefully towards the edge, and the sound-holes and head are of the Amati type. But the moment we scrutinize the instrument in detail, a different treat-ment is revealed. The purfling, the setting of the f-holes with a tendency to place the top holes too near each other, the carving of the head and other small points betray another hand. The truth is that these old masters always followed their own bent for better or for worse, and emancipated themselves from the past in a lesser or greater degree as the years sped on.

The general dimensions, however, remain the same, though we have never seen an example of Andrea's work belonging to this period which entirely succeeds in portraying that bold and masculine type of 'Grand Amati' with broad edge, characteristic of certain of the master's violins dating from about 1640–50.

This earlier form of Guarneri violin is comparatively rare; we ourselves have met with but few examples. It is obvious that the master found no difficulty in obtaining patronage, and that he settled down to a steady routine of work, the model most in favour being that of the small Amati type, with which all lovers of violins are familiar.

His modelling was generally full, hollowed around the edges—less so with the table—the sides were left low, the purfling more often was of full substance, and the mitres frequently turned somewhat abruptly across the corners: a feature quite his own. The edges were well rounded and on the light side, and the placing of the f-holes was generally towards the centre, thus narrowing the bridge platform.

The head was small in form, and the chamfer not clearly defined; the first turn of the scroll was flat, and the spiral less hollowed than that of the average Amati. Andrea's construction of the interior is again similar to the work of his master: the blocks and linings of willow are left roughly from the gouge or chisel, and the linings of the bouts are invariably mortised into the corner blocks. With regard to the thicknesses, the back at the centre is very full, diminishing to thin flanks; the table is worked to moderate proportions, and is of the same thickness throughout; there are no signs either in back or table of a desire to attain strict accuracy. The maple wood which the master generally used was of native growth and frequently of plain appearance. If at times it is more figured, we find it marked by that typically small curl with which the several generations of the Amati have familiarized us. Here and there Andrea, even as the Amati, utilized backs cut on the slab. This native wood was the least expensive then obtainable, but though at times quite exceptionally fine trees came to Cremona, it seldom fell to Andrea's lot to secure them.

The demand for a cheaper 'Cremona' was growing; the taste for instruments of Italian production was steadily being fostered in the musical centres of Europe. Their superiority was manifest; and the distribution of these instruments, other than by the Italian players themselves,[1] was made through the medium of the great fairs[2] held annually in many of the continental cities.

The Milanese makers, who specially responded later to this demand for cheap instruments, had not yet come into being; in the meantime Andrea Guarneri and Francesco Ruger were worthily filling the gap. But it must not be assumed that Andrea never rose, in favourable circumstances, to a higher level; on the contrary, we meet now and again with specimens which show him quite capable of greater achievements than his ordinary output when patronage encouraged him to give of his best.

The following are representative examples:

       1638. M. Franz Degen
Period 1640–45. Mr. G. F. Pettinos, ex Kahn
   „   1645–50. Lady Beauclerk, ex Langevin
   „   1660–70. Miss G. A. Oram, ex Seebeck
       1669. Hon. Mrs. Forbes, ex Dr. Webb
Period   1670. Mr. Charles B. Lutyens, ex Carl Maria von Weber
   „   1670. Mr. Geoffrey Lawrence, ex R. L. Harrison, ex Robert Bridges

---

[1] Rossini, writing from Italy in the early part of the last century, to his friend, Dragonetti (1763–1846), asks him to assist him with the sale of an Andrea Guarneri violin, the price of which was 600 frs. (£24).

[2] One of the writers recalls meeting in years gone by with Dr. Robatel, a distinguished doctor of Lyons, who was then in possession of a violoncello made by J. B. Guadagnini in 1777, which had been purchased by his ancestor when new at the Lyons Fair.

Andreas Guarnerius fecit Cremonæ 1638

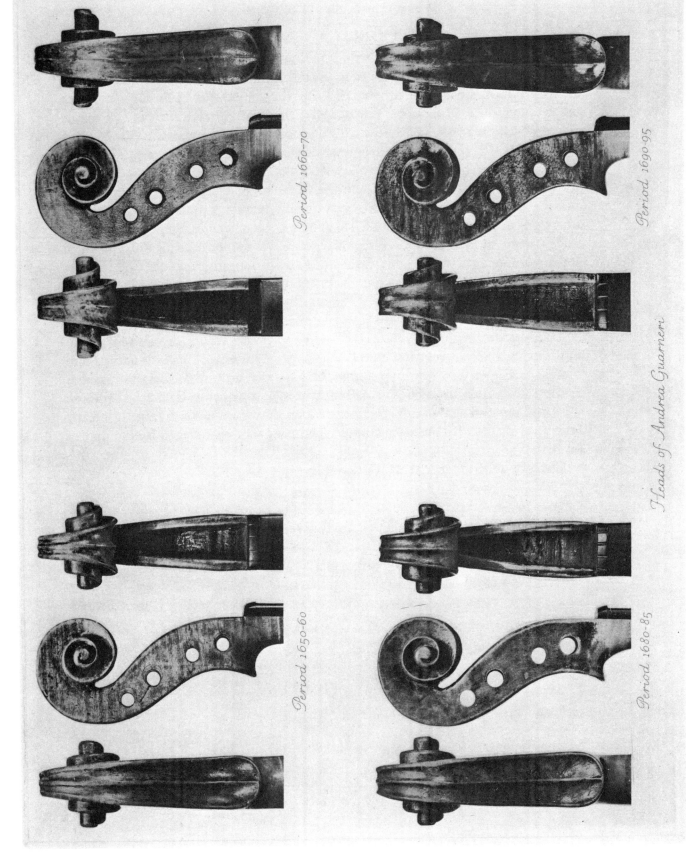

Period 1660-70

Period 1690-95

Heads of Andrea Guarneri

Period 1650-60

Period 1680-85

1676. Miss Miriam Lucas, ex G. Macmillan
1676. Lady Blanche Girouard, ex Squire
1676. M. Alfred Basset
1680. Mrs. Felix Schuster, ex Earl of Southesk
Period   1680. Miss Elsie Owen, ex Mylnarski
1687. M. Georges de Beristayn, ex Dr. Philips
Period   1690. Mr. Ernest A. Sandeman
1691. Mr. Rudolph H. Wurlitzer, ex Llewellyn Griffiths
1692. Mr. Hugh Rutter, ex van Welsenes
1694. Miss Mona Leigh, ex Read

Thus the master continued with but little variation until about 1680, engaged principally in the making of violins, at rare intervals a violoncello, and at still rarer intervals a viola. Actually we have never heard of or seen more than four violas and about fourteen violoncellos. Even the violins are not at all numerous. We compute after due consideration that the existing examples do not total above two hundred and fifty. Those of the last few years of his life are distinguished by a shortening of the corners, which are made broader and blunter. The edges are slightly heavier in substance, and the modelling remains full and is somewhat irregularly worked. The fluting around the edge is deeper in parts, especially at the corners. The mitres of the purfling are treated as usual; the f-holes stand up straighter and are cut well open with wings slightly hollowed. The head is neatly carved and the chamfer more defined; but at times the whole is lacking in finish; the back part being poorly shaped and narrow, and the fluting deeply cut in; and frequently traces can be seen of the fine gouge marks which the master failed to obliterate. In a word, the work is hasty. Or are these defects by any chance due to failing eyesight?

Throughout his life Andrea covered his instruments with an excellent oil varnish. It is exceptional to find it put on with the distinction of the Amati; but occasionally a charming example delights the eye. The colour is generally a light chestnut brown, at times an orange tint, and at rare intervals brown-red. This varnish has sometimes a dried-up appearance in places, caused by the use of dryers which were resorted to in order to hasten the hardening of the varnish. The earlier Amati[1] and Stradivari were more patient; they never added dryers to their varnish, but trusted rather to the strong heat of the sun to effect the purpose.

[1] Girolamo, the last of the family, at times made a similar use of dryers.

We have seen examples of Andrea's work where the wood has been subjected to treatment by acids before being varnished. Possibly these were isolated experiments, but incidentally they point a not uninteresting moral. Players were already in possession of instruments of old appearance; and we have no doubt that the newer-looking violin, then as now, proved less attractive to the eye; hence the experiment to obtain the more sober Brescian brown. Several of the Rugeri followed this practice, but fortunately it was soon discontinued.

FIG. II. Edge, purfling, and sound-hole of an example of the period 1670

We should not do Andrea Guarneri justice were we to omit making special reference to the admirable *viola* for which we are indebted to him. He embodied in it much that came from the brothers Amati, yet retained characteristics of his own, added to which he gives us a more robust construction. The model, placing of the *f*-holes, head, outline, all fit in with perfect harmony, and yield proof of a well-thought-out scheme; with the result that we see a finely proportioned instrument measuring just over $16\frac{1}{4}$ inches in length of body, and having a stop of $8\frac{1}{2}$ inches. In our opinion this viola is worthy of taking rank amongst the greatest, and it stands for Andrea's highest achievement.

The choice example (see illustration facing) which dates from the year 1676 and portrays the master's typical work remained over a hundred years in this country—at one period in the collection of Sir William Curtis.[1] It is now owned by Dr. Felix Landau of Berlin. A second example dated 1690 is most interesting when compared with the previous instrument. Made

[1] Sir Wm. Curtis, Bart. (1752–1829), a City Banker, Lord Mayor of London, and M.P. for the City during twenty-eight years.

of the same form it is of lighter build throughout; the model is fuller, the *f*-holes
are more open, the edges are neater, the fluting is deeper, and the head is carved
with Amati-like precision and finish. We could almost suggest Pietro as taking
a leading part in its construction, if that were possible. Or was it his younger
brother Giuseppe, and in that event obviously inspired by the character of the
work of Pietro rather than that of the father?

A third example of high merit dated 1697 was until recent times in the possession
of the Earl of Harrington. It had been purchased by the Earl who died in 1881, on
the advice of the father of the present writers, at the sale of the Gillott collection in
1872. But here, though the instrument bears Andrea's original label, we clearly
recognize throughout the touch of 'Joseph filius' (see illustration between pp. 24, 25).
The father was being helped by his sons. But of this we shall treat more fully later on.

We cannot indicate with certainty the exact period to which the master's first
violoncello of smaller dimensions belongs. The examples so far seen by us of the
smaller form can undoubtedly be assigned to the 1690 decade, though several now
bear fictitious labels, or else have had the dates falsified; but judging from the character of the work we suggest that it was only late in life that this change was evolved
from the instrument of traditional Amati form and size.

Whether we may definitely credit Andrea Guarneri with this innovation still
remains a moot point. Francesco Ruger undoubtedly did much in 'cello construction; and probably, as in the case of the viola, tentative experiments were made on
and off during the century. But on summing up our present information we are
disposed to cast our vote in favour of Andrea.

We are acquainted with an example of Andrea's work now in the possession of
Sig. Leandro Bisiach of Milan and dating from the year 1669—an example of surpassing interest inasmuch as it has remained uncut, and all its dimensions are therefore exactly as left by the maker. These dimensions are greater than those of any
existing Stradivari; and we never recall having seen another four-string violoncello
of similarly large size. Though quite impracticable for modern playing, it is worthy of
being permanently preserved in its present state as a relic of an age that is no more.
This specimen, the wood of which—i.e. back, sides, and head—is of poplar, was
probably abnormal as regards these extreme proportions; and the only other instrument which we believe was originally made somewhat on the same lines is that
formerly owned by Miss Theobald, but which has been reduced in length to 30

inches. (Let us add that this delicate operation was carried through with good judgement.) Here again the wood is of poplar, and it is dated from 1689. Both instruments bear the impress of Andrea's own characteristic work.

The few other examples which suggest the likelihood of having been made in these earlier years were all originally of large proportions.

In reality Andrea made few violoncellos, the total known to us not exceeding fourteen.

On examining a violoncello of the smaller form (see reproduction facing) the experienced observer is struck by the close resemblance in all its salient features to the master's viola. One might almost say that it represents a photographic enlarge- ment, so identical is the form of outline, model, f-holes, and character throughout. True, were Andrea to have added half an inch in length to the lower curves, correspondingly diminishing the width, flattening the model—especially that of the back—and raising the height of the sides, we should have gained in symmetry, but we should have lost touch with the Guarneri conception. On the whole we have nothing but praise to bestow on these violoncellos: the placing of the f-holes—an important feature which so many of the old makers bungled—is excellent, and the form of the head which he designed calls for special tribute. It forestalls Stradivari at his best, and possibly the great master recognizing its admirable fitness accepted it as his ideal when carving the heads for his own perfected form of violoncello. As in all things, the intellectual mind of the present drinks deeply of the past, and Stradivari formed no exception.

In addition to the above example which formerly belonged to a distinguished artist, M. Emile Doehaerd, we would cite the following:

Period 1690. Mr. J. H. Bowman
       1692. Mr. J. B. Smedley
       1693. M. Franz Fassbender
       1695. M. Hans Bottermund

The work of all these instruments is of the same character, but, in our opinion, they owe their construction more to the craftsmanship of the son, Giuseppe, than to that of the father. The example owned by M. Hans Bottermund stands out as a particularly fine specimen.

Now let us go back a few years and consider in their proper order the assistants who were aiding Andrea at his work. From an examination of the census returns furnished by the *Casa Guarneri-Orcelli* onwards from year 1654, *D, E,* we learn that Andrea Guarneri was blessed with seven children, three of whom were boys, viz. the eldest, Pietro Giovanni, born as already noted in 1655, the second, Eusebio Amati, in 1658, and the third, Giovanni Battista, in 1666; both the first named and the third followed their father's profession, the second choosing another calling; and beyond the interest evoked by his baptismal name—probably a member of the Amati family was one of his godparents—we do not again connect him with our subject.

We are more than justified in assuming that Pietro Giovanni—later to be known as Pietro of Mantua—was making his presence felt in the workshop by 1670-5; and we do perceive a change of character in the work of certain of Andrea's violins dating from these years. We see a violin of youthful mien (see reproduction of example dated 1676, between pp. 24, 25) light in build, of outline more Stradivari-like, the bouts less curved, the edges lightly worked, the fluting cut deeper, accentuating the rounding of the edge, the model full as usual, head and *f*-holes sharply cut, and the finish throughout indicating the handiwork of an accomplished craftsman. We have come across some particularly handsome examples of this type, and occa-sionally note the use of well-figured foreign maple. Additional interest attaches to this violin, inasmuch as it bears Andrea's original label dated 1676; yet it is unmis-takably the work of Pietro and reveals thus early the marked impress which we shall later see fully developed at Mantua.

Nothing could be more natural than this co-operation between father and son, but it was to prove of short duration. Pietro's name figures for the last time in his father's census returns for the year 1679. He had married in 1677 and in the eighties we come across him established in Mantua, where he was henceforth to spend his life; and we find no trace of his work in any of the productions emanating in the succeeding decades from Andrea's workshop.

But there were others, several of whom still remain in obscurity, ready to take Pietro's vacated place at the bench—first and principally the son born in 1666 and baptised under the names of Giuseppe Giovanni Battista, subsequently recorded in the census returns as Giuseppe only, sometimes spelt Gioseppe, and later to be known in the violin world as Joseph Guarnerius, filius Andreæ. As in the case of Pietro we have no exact information as to the actual year when Giuseppe entered on

D.

Census Return of the year 1667

House of the Guarneri

Andrea Guarneri	.	.	.	.	aged 41,	Christened,	confirmed,	communicant
Anna Maria, wife	.	.	.	.	„ 40	„	„	„
Pietro, son	.	.	.	.	„ 12,	„		„
Angela, daughter	.	.	.	.	„ 11,	„		„
Eusebio, son	.	.	.	.	„ 9,	„		
Elisabetta, daughter	.	.	.	.	„ 7,			
Anna, daughter	.	.	.	.	„ 4,			
Gio. Batta, infant-son								

E.

Census Return of the year 1672

House of the Guarneri

Andrea Guarneri	.	.	.	.	aged 46,	Christened,	confirmed,	communicant
Anna Maria, wife	.	.	.	.	„ 45	„	„	„
Pietro, son	.	.	.	.	„ 17	„	„	„
Angela, daughter	.	.	.	.	„ 15	„	„	„
Eusebio, son	.	.	.	.	„ 14	„	„	„
Elisabetta, daughter	.	.	.	.	„ 12	„		„
Anna, daughter	.	.	.	.	„ 7	„		„
Gioseppe, Gio. Batta, son	.	.	.	.	„ 5			

his apprenticeship, but probabilities point to about 1680; and within the next few years we discover traces of his participation in the making of Andrea's instruments, a participation which steadily increases as we pass on towards the end of the master's career.

We are the more disposed to assert that Andrea had other assistants, because in certain of his productions we fail to recognize the orthodox 'Guarneri touch'; and we have found some of these instruments bearing a label on which the master states: *'Sotto la disciplina'*, &c. (see reproduction, Chap. VII). This clearly proves that he himself sought to draw a distinction between the works of the family and those of outside pupils or workmen; and it is of interest to note that he was the first of the Cremonese makers to record this difference on the inserted labels. The Amati never did so; but Stradivari followed Andrea's example.

That there were men living in Cremona who never rose to the dignity of master-makers is conclusively demonstrated by referring to the census returns furnished by Nicolò Amati: we note amongst others the following, who were at different periods inmates of his household:

Giacomo Gennaro,[1] 1641–46.   Girolamo Segher, 1680.
Francesco Mola, 1653–54.   Bartolomeo Cristofori, 1680.
Leopoldo (Tedesco), 1653.   Guiseppe Stanza, 1680–82.
Giorgio Staiber? (Tedesco), 1665–67.

Probably these men were pupils or assistants on the respective dates given, yet with the exception of Gennaro and Cristofori, who have both left signed works, nothing whatever is known to us of any of them. The German, Giorgio Staiber, also figures in the return made by Andrea Guarneri for the year 1665; but in both the census entries the writing of the surname is not clearly decipherable. There exists one other name, Paolo Grancino, the alleged work of whom bears, so we find, relationship to Andrea. But in reality we have no absolute knowledge of this particular Grancino, have never seen an instrument with his original label, and so far have not met with any responsible expert who has done so.

We do recognize the existence of 'Grancino' instruments, both violins and violoncellos, earlier and more distinguished than those of the well-known type bearing the label of Giovanni Grancino, and dating from about 1680 to 1730. We refer to instruments covered by a fine oil varnish, the general character of which bears

---

[1] Gennaro states on his labels, 'Alumnus Nicolai Amati'.

analogy to that of Andrea Guarneri. They are found as a rule inscribed as the work of one or other of the good Cremonese makers. We are also acquainted with the instruments made jointly by the Fratelli Giovanni and Francesco, which date from Milan about 1670–80.

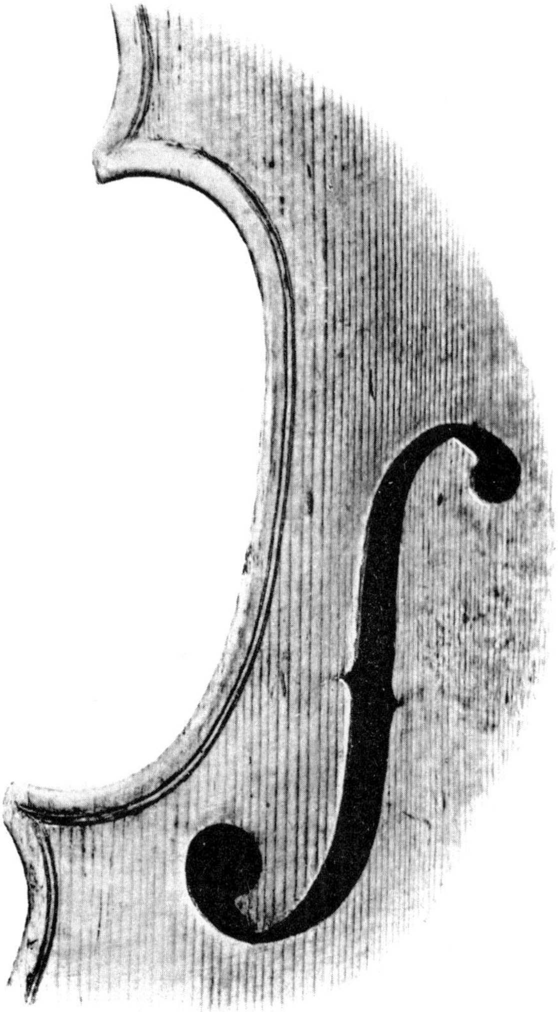

To resume, we should say that if Paolo Grancino[1] really existed, he was a pupil of Andrea and consequently must have worked at some period in Cremona.

From about 1685 onwards it is clear to us that the son Giuseppe was taking the leading part in the workshop. Occasionally we get glimpses of the father's orthodox style, but we see with ever increasing frequency a more youthful mind at work. Giuseppe was decidedly inspired at this period by his brother Pietro of Mantua: we note the same full model, similarity of outline, and light and raised edge, the f-holes and head forming a blend of father and brother. The general finish of the work is excellent, though not equal to that of Pietro.

The hand of the master was stayed. He had given of his best during upwards of fifty years, and realizing that the call of the workshop was over, he decided to make disposition of his worldly belongings. His will was drawn up at Parma by the Notary Venusto Coruzzi, and is dated 15th June 1687. The testator is designated as follows: 'Il Signor Andrea de Guerneri filo del fu Sigre. Bartolomeo ch'habitta nella città di Cremona, nella vicino di S. Matteo, sano per gracia di Iddio, di mente intelletto et di corpo.' ('Signor Andrea di Guerneri son of the late Signor Bartolomeo residing in the City of Cremona, in the Parish of San Matteo, sound, by the grace of God, in mind, intellect, and body.')

FIG. III. Edge, purfling and sound-hole of an example of the period 1690.

[1] Fétis says he was the father of Giovanni (Antonio Stradivari).

He desires to be buried in the Church of S. Domenico in the Chapel of the Rosary, in the vault on which are inscribed the names of Sig[ri.] Giov. Paulo Orcelli, Anna Maria Orcelli, and Andrea Guernieri.[1] His heirs named are: li Sig[ri.] Giovanni Giuseppe, Giovanni Pietro, et Eusebio Amati, his legitimate sons by his wife Sig[ra.] Anna Maria Orcelli de Guarnieri. All his property was to be divided into four portions, two parts of which were to accrue to Giovanni Giuseppe '. . . *per la buona servitù e compagnia che fa al detto Sig. testatore. . . .*' ('. . . in return for the good and faithful services rendered to the testator. . . .') The remaining two parts were to be divided between the said Sig[ri.] Giovanni Pietro and Eusebio Amati, his heirs. After his death L. 100 was to be paid to the Sig[ra.] Lucia de Guernieri, niece of the testator and daughter of his brother, Sig. Giovanni Battista Guernieri.

The testator further ordains that should the impending law-suit concerning his property at Parma—Villa di Costa Mezzana[2]—be decided in his favour, it was to be at once sold and the proceeds devoted to Masses for the repose of his soul.

The executors of the above will were the Marquis Antonio Maria Pallavicini[3] and Signor Andrea Clerici.

Five years elapse, and Andrea then decides to supersede this will by a new one, drawn up this time by the Cremonese Notary, Giulio Cesare Porro, and dated 11th July 1692. The master is again designated as in the previous will which he now annuls; he names as his heirs the three sons, Pietro, Eusebio, and Giuseppe, adding two daughters, Angela Teresa and Anna Maria, all born of his wife Anna Maria Orcelli: he confirms the marriage portions assigned to his daughters, adding L. 1,500 to the second who is still unmarried; and furthermore:

'*ha lasciato e lascia che detto Giuseppe suo figlio minore debba avere avanti le divisioni da farsi con li detti suoi fratelli de' beni ereditari di detto testatore, tutti li ferri, legni et altri istrumenti concernenti l'esercizio di liutaro, violinaro e chitarraro esercito da detto testatore i quali lascia al medesimo Giuseppe oltre della portione che gli competisce nella sua eredita, atteso che egli e sempre stato obbidiente e non l'ha mai abbandonato, ed ora nella sua vecchiaia lo aiuta e soccorre nel detto esercizio. . . .*'

('He has willed and wills that the said Giuseppe, his youngest son, is to have, before the division of the hereditary effects of the said Testator between him and his brothers, all the tools, wood and

---

[1] We see here, as with Stradivari, his tomb was prepared and his name inscribed in advance.

[2] Owing to the fact of this will having been drawn up at Parma and the reference to Andrea's property there, Sig. Livi suggested the possibility of finding some connexion with Orcelli, the violinist and his brother-in-law, and with a view to elucidation proceeded to Parma and there made diligent research but

with negative results.

[3] The Pallavicini were amongst the oldest and most distinguished of the Italian noble families. They held sway in the districts about Piacenza from the twelfth to fifteenth centuries, and a branch had long been settled in Cremona. (*History of Cremona*.)

other utensils connected with the craft of the lute-maker, violin-maker and guitar-maker practised by the said Testator, these being in addition to the portion which accrues to Giuseppe by way of inheritance, in consideration of his always having been obedient, not having abandoned him and having helped and stood by him in the said craft in his old age. . . .')

Nevertheless, should there be any completed violini, violoni, chittare, or other similar instruments remaining, they shall be divided equally between the said Giuseppe and his brothers. Nothing more is added of sufficient importance to call for further comment.

Now the contents of this second will are of extreme interest; we learn definitely what we had surmised from our repeated examination of Andrea's instruments. Pietro had early left the parental workshop and gone to Mantua, and for this act he was but partially forgiven. On the other hand, the touching reference to the devotion of Giuseppe confirms the important part taken by him in the construction of instruments during the latter part of his father's life.

Two more years pass and Andrea determines to make yet a third will, dated 28th October 1694, this time in conjunction with his wife, 'Domina Anna Maria de Orcellis, filia quondam Horattii.' He annuls all former wills, and again names the same children as heirs, adding, however, Giovanni Eusebio, son of the above Eusebio, and leaves to his niece Lucia, daughter of the late Giovanni Battista, his brother, the sum of L. 50. This will contains no allusion to instruments, nor does it mention Andrea's calling. But the master still refers with bitterness to his son, Pietro Giovanni, who has been living apart from his parents for about sixteen years, stating that it is his wish that he shall not inherit from them more than that share to which he is legally entitled, in view of the fact that he has never contributed anything to their support since he left the parental roof, and was ungrateful to them even before that time: furthermore, that he had taken away various articles of considerable value, of which they themselves had kept no account.

In the following year, 1695, on the 11th day of January, Anna Maria Orcelli died, and was buried in the tomb already prepared for her and her husband in the Chapel of the Rosary (S. Domenico), F.

The burial extract reads as follows: '12 Januar 1695. Datto sepoltura alla moglie di Miser Andrea Guarneri che fa i violini, Capella del Rosario' ('Interred in the Chapel of the Rosary, the wife of Master Andrea Guarneri, maker of violins.')

Note that in the census returns for that year the wife's name is omitted.

F.

January 12th, 1695.

*Anna Maria Orcelli, wife of Andrea Guarneri, about 68 years of age, fortified by the Last Sacraments of the Church
and commending her soul to God, departed this life on the 11th day of the above month and year, her body
being borne to the Church of S. Domenico.*

G.

Census Return of the year 1695

House of the Guarneri. 2nd Floor

Andrea Guarneri	. aged 70,	Christened,	confirmed,	communicant
Giuseppe, son	. „ 28	„	„	„
Barbara, wife	. „ 25	„	„	„
Andrea, son	. „ 3			
Elisabetta, daughter	. „ 2			
Barbara Maria, niece	. „ 10			„
Gio. Batta., brother	. „ 7			

H.

December 8th, 1698.

*Andrea Guarneri, about 76 years of age, fortified by the Last Sacraments of the Church, Penance, Holy Eucharist,
and Extreme Unction, commending his soul to God, departed this life on the 7th day of the above month,
his body being interred in the Church of S. Domenico, on the above date.*

The master survived his wife nearly four years, dying on the 7th day of December 1698, and the extract from the Register of Burials in S. Domenico under date 8th of December, states: '*Datto sepoltura a Andrea Guarnero Par*ª· *di S. Matteo posto nella sepoltura nella Capella del Rosario.*' ('Interred in his tomb, in the Chapel of the Rosary, in the Parish of S. Matteo.') *H.*

In the Register of Deaths of the Parish of S. Matteo it is noted that Andrea Guarneri was about seventy years of age.

Notwithstanding prolonged research by Signor Livi in the Burial Registers of S. Domenico, no later entries concerning the descendants of the master are to be found. We therefore conclude that the tomb was not reopened until the time of its desecration in the year 1869. Readers of our *Life of Stradivari* will recall the account we give of the demolition of S. Domenico, which contained the Chapel of the Rosary where the mortal remains of Antonio Stradivari rested; and nothing is more probable than that the bones of the Guarneri and Stradivari were mingled together and finally reburied in an unknown grave. The tombstone of the Guarneri was not preserved as was the case with that of the great master.[1]

Thus passed away Andrea Guarneri, the pioneer of the family with whom we are concerned. He had lived a useful life, and contributed to the spread of violin-making then taking place, not only in Cremona, but in various other cities of northern Italy.

Had he obtained a modest competence from his industry? We should say so, and as a result left his family in comfortable circumstances. Before his death, living as he did, in close proximity to Antonio Stradivari, he must have frequently seen and marvelled at the consummate productions coming from the great master's hands. He must also have vied, in intimate rivalry, with the several members of the Rugeri family and with Girolamo Amati, who were all working steadily to supply the demands for her musical instruments, which were brought to Cremona from far and wide; for the city was now approaching her zenith. The succession to the workshop of the Casa Guarneri had passed to the youngest son Giuseppe, who in 1698 would be aged thirty-two.

Let us leave him there for the moment, and proceed to the consideration of Pietro, his eldest brother, who had settled permanently in Mantua.

[1] We learn with interest that the descendants of these two families have intermarried; on a *faire-part* received by the present writers on the occasion of the death of Giacomo Stradivari in 1901, we read the name of Arturo Guarneri of Lucca and Cremona, who is mentioned as a nephew of the deceased.

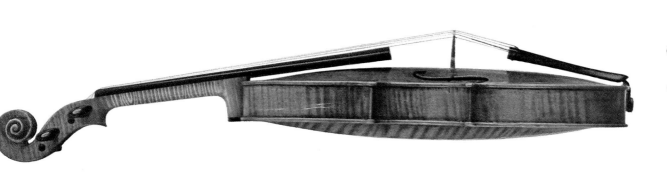

Andreas Guarnerius fecit Cremonæ 1680

Andreas Guarnerius fecit Cremonæ 1676

Andreas Guarnerius fecit Cremonæ 1691

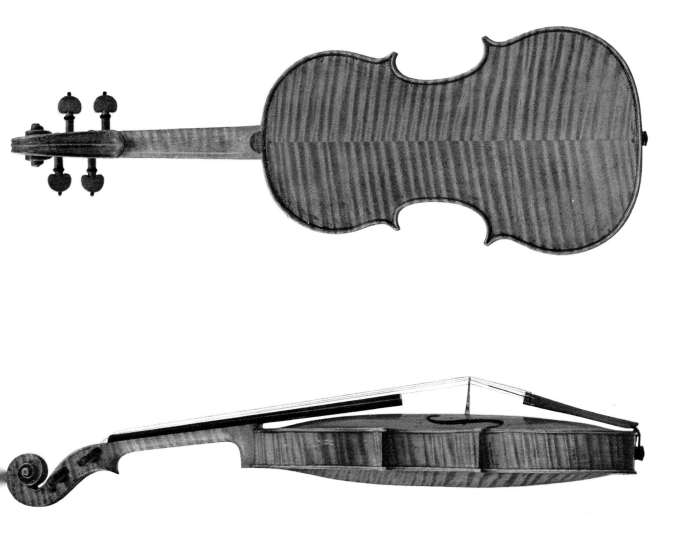

Petrus Guarnerius Cremonensis fecit Mantuæ 1703

Petrus Guarnerius Cremonensis fecit Mantuæ 1707

Joseph Guarnerius filius Andreæ fecit Cremonæ (period 1705-10)

Joseph Guarnerius filius Andreæ fecit Cremonæ (period 1710–15)

Joseph Guarnerius del Gesù fecit Cremonæ 1733

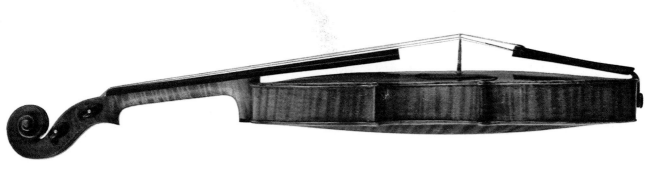

Joseph Guarnerius del Gesù fecit Cremonæ 1735

Joseph Guarnerius del Gesù fecit Cremonæ 1735

Joseph Guarnerius del Gesù fecit Cremonæ 1738

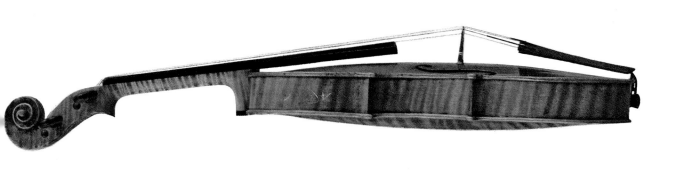

Joseph Guarnerius del Gesù fecit Cremonæ 1742

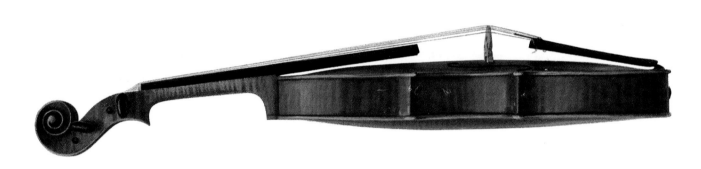

Joseph Guarnerius del Gesù fecit Cremonæ 1742

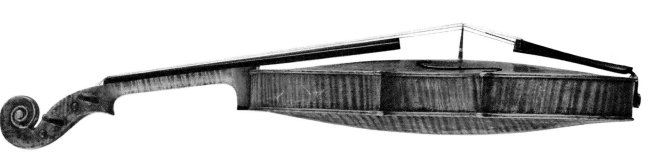

Joseph Guarnerius del Gesu fecit Cremonæ 1744

Andreas Guarnerius fecit Cremonae (period 1640-45)

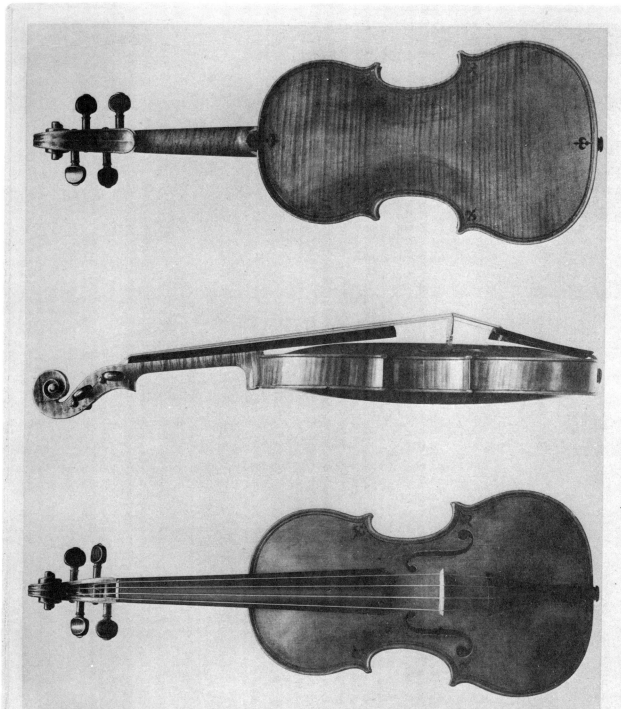

Andreas Guarnerius fecit Cremonæ 1676

Andreas Guarnerius fecit Cremonæ 1687

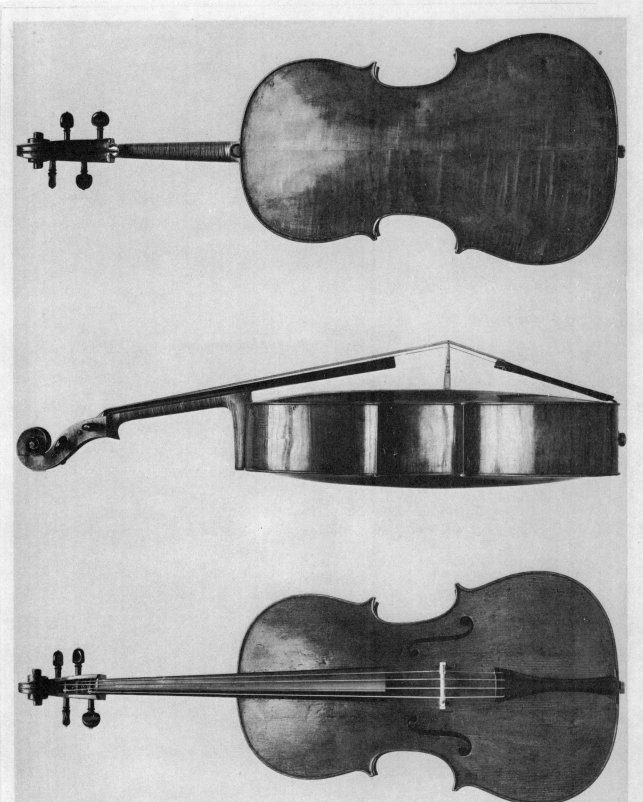

Andreas Guarnerius fecit Cremona 1697

Prospetto della Citta di Mantoua e suoi forti 1735.

CHAPTER II
PIETRO GUARNERI OF MANTUA
(BORN 1655, DIED 1720)

*Dwells within the soul of every Artist
More than all his efforts can express
And he knows the best remains unuttered
Sighing at what we call his success.*

(ADELAIDE PROCTER)

PIETRO GIOVANNI GUARNERI, more generally known as Peter Guarnerius of Mantua, was born at Cremona on 18th February 1655, the eldest son of Andrea Guarneri and Anna Maria di Orcelli. We reproduce the baptismal certificate, *A.*

Of the master's early working life we know little, nor have we ever succeeded in meeting with an instrument of his making, one bearing his own label and dated from the city of his birth. We are fully aware of his co-operation in some of the works signed by his father, instruments dating from the years 1670–78; in fact, we recognize that certain of these violins were entirely made by Pietro. But he does not, in contradiction to his brother Giuseppe, appear in a single instance to have inserted his own distinctive label.

These youthful works reveal, not only his acquired skill as a craftsman, but that he was equally possessed, thus early in his career, of that decidedly personal touch so distinctively his own—those unmistakable f-holes, accurately shaped corners, skilled purfling, full modelling, and deep fluting—all these features are present.

We have already pointed out that the master ceased to figure as a member of Andrea's household later than the census returns of the year 1679, and we find no mention of Caterina Sassagni, to whom he was married in 1677. In this connexion we obtain confirmatory evidence from Andrea's will of 1694, in which he says that Pietro had been living a separate existence for about sixteen years—'ab annis sedecim circiter'—i.e. since 1678 or 1679. Did the master, on quitting the paternal home, depart at once to Mantua? We do not know. It may have been so, but then we are faced by our failure to find any trace of him either working or living in that city prior to the year 1685.

What could he have been doing in the interval? Certainly he was not at work shaping violins. But we are in a position to state what we believe to be the chief reason of Pietro's departure from his native city; for we learn, as a result of the researches carried out by Signor Livi in the Archives of Mantua, that the master was a cultured musician, playing both viol and violin. We reproduce the very interesting petition dated March 1685, presented to the Marquis Cavriani, Chamberlain to the Duke of Mantua, asking to be appointed as one of the Musicians attached to the Court, B. A second document dated 1st May 1690 attests that Pietro had been duly appointed, eulogizes his talents, and names the sum of four doppie[1] which he is to receive monthly for his services, C.

We thus discover that the master had devoted his early years to becoming skilled in music as well as in violin-making; and we have here the only instance yet

[1] Approximately equivalent to £5 per month in money of to-day, i.e. prior to 1914.

Die 19 februarij 1655

Petrus Joannes filius Andreæ de Guarnerijs, et Annæ Mariæ de Orcellij coniugum huiusmod. uic.ⁱ S.tⁱ Matthæi [...] fuit baptizatus a me Don Clemente Flammeno Præposito, patrinij existentibus Ill.mo Marchione Mutio Pallauicino uic.ⁱ S.tⁱ Bart.ⁱ et D. Camilla de Ferrarij uic.ⁱ S. Ceciliæ

February 19th, 1655.

Pietro Giovanni, son of Andrea Guarneri and Anna Maria de Orcelli, his wife, of this parish of S. Matteo, Cremona, was baptized by me, Clemente Flammeno, Rector. The godparents present, the Illustrious Marquess Muzio Pallavicini[1] of the Parish of S. Bartolomeo and D. Camilla de Ferrarii of the Parish of Sta Cecilia.

[1] The Marquess Antonio Maria Pallavicini was one of the executors of Andrea Guarneri (see Chap. I, p. 21.)

B. ...che Guarnieri   Lunedi. 1 Maggio. 1685.

Ill.mo et Ecc.mo Sig.r Marchese Ferdinando Cauriani Cavag.re
dell'Ordine del Redentore, Maestro di Camera di S.A.S.
e del Consiglio, ritrovato della med.ma A. S. stando
nel suo solito Pallaggio com.se à me infrascritto No=
taro di far nota come

Essendo stato supplicato humilmente il, ecc.mo Prone da
Pietro Guarnieri di Cremona Fabricator d'Istro=
menti Musicali, e particolarmente di Violini
di poter non solo essere aggregato per hora al
numero degli altri suoi Musici suonatori attuali
per sonar egli la Viola e Violino sopra le carte
mie della sourauicenza ancora di Francesco
Malfoni suonator di Viola, quando ne seguisse
col tempo la mancanza con tutte le prerogatiue
e stipendio che di presente gode. L'A.S. è beni=
gnamente condescesa à fargli l'una e l'altra
gratia, commanda perciò à me med.mo Altezza sia uiu=
tù di queste, che il sudetto Guarnieri uenga di
presente posto al ruolo degli altri suoi Musici
suonatori attuali con le prerogatiue solamente
che essi godono, e che dopo la morte poi di Frances=
co Malfoni, succedeui nel di lui posto, con la pro=
uigione ch'egli hora gode. Altro in contrario non
ostante, tale essendo la mente di S.A.S.

Pietro Guarnieri   Monday, May 1685

The Most Illustrious & Excellent Marquess Ferdinand Cavriani, Knight of the Order of Our Holy Redeemer, Chamberlain of His Serene Highness, and of His Privy Council held in His own Palace, bids me, the undersigned Notary, make known the following :

Pietro Guarnieri of Cremona, Maker of Musical Instruments, and of Violins in particular, having humbly supplicated His Serene Patron to be admitted to the number of His Musicians as player of the Viol & Violin, and to be appointed successor to Francesco Scalfoni, viol-player, with all the stipends and privileges enjoyed by him: His Highness has benignly condescended to grant both favours &, in virtue thereof, ordains that the name of the above-mentioned Guarnieri be added to the Roll of His actual Musicians and that he be made participator of all the privi-leges enjoyed by them, & after the death of Francesco Scalfoni, succeed to the post vacated thereby & receive the same salary as his predecessor, this, notwithstanding anything to the contrary, such being the will of His Highness.

[Unsigned]

recorded of one of the great Italian violin-makers engaged in this dual calling. It may well be that he owed his musical attainments to his maternal uncle, the Orcelli previously mentioned,[1] who was a gifted violinist and musician.

The question naturally arises, what was there in the past and present state of music in Mantua to attract Pietro Guarneri to that city?

An 'Accademia' for the study of poetry and music had been founded at Mantua in 1568 by the ruling Duke Gonzaga (1536–89) who was himself a composer; and subsequent members of this family proved to be generous and wise patrons of the sister arts, particularly in the form of Opera. Their enlightened support brought about the production of Monteverdi's opera of *Orfeo* during the marriage festivities of the reigning Duke's son in 1607—a momentous event in the annals of music, and one which placed Mantua at the height of her reputation as a seat of musical culture and advancement. A Cremonese by birth and training, Monteverdi, while still a youth, had joined the Mantuan Court Orchestra about 1583 as a talented violist, from which position he rose to that of 'Maestro di Capella', and became the most remarkable composer of his time.

A hundred years later, between 1680 and 1685, Pietro Guarneri follows the example of his illustrious fellow citizen, and leaves Cremona for Mantua, also to play the viol in the same orchestra—an interesting parallel. Pietro's admission into an orchestra of such long-standing excellence speaks convincingly for his skill as a performer on viol and violin (see warrant of appointment), C.

Although this is the first instance brought to light of a fine Italian violin-maker carrying on simultaneously the correlated branches of playing and making, we regard it as certain that many of the makers who settled in the smaller musical centres could play well enough to take the minor parts in orchestras, and indeed would need to do so to supplement their earnings as makers. These were the days of many-sidedness, when makers of the highest standing, the subject of our memoir, and even Stradivari made various kinds of lutes and guitars, viols and violins and violin bows, and even cases and fittings. The player needed also to be resourceful; for Mace instructs the lutenist very thoroughly how to adjust his instrument and

[1] Cremona in the sixteenth century, anterior to its violin-making, gave birth to other notable violists and musicians besides Monteverdi, of whom we note specially the following: '*Jean Maria da Cremona*, violist attached to the Court of Henry VIII, in 1540' (*Audit Office Accounts*, Sandys and Forster, p. 102); '*Cristoforo de Cremona*, contrabasse de viole'; '*Marsolini de Cre-* *mone*, organiste et homme de grand talent.' Among the performers attached to the Bavarian Court in 1568 were Orlando de Lassus, and Pallavicino, native of Cremona, who became Maestro di Capella at Mantua in 1596, preceding Monteverdi in that post.

C.

Ferdinando Carlos. Wishing to avail Ourselves of the services and the virtuoso's talents of Pietro

Guarneri and taking into account his upright conduct and great skill in playing the

violin, we are pleased to honour him by conferring on him our Warrant of Appoint-

Warrant of   *ment, by virtue of which we elect, and promote him to be Our Master of the Violins*

Appointment   *with all the honours, benefits, privileges & prerogatives attached to the position,*

as   *which, Our other, similar Servants are accustomed to enjoy, and with a stipend*

Violinist   *attached thereto of four doppie per month, according to a special order confirmed by us.*

Commanding Our Musicians and other Officers whom it may concern, that, as they

value Our good will, they observe and do, worthily honouring the aforesaid Guarneri,

the holder of this Appointment.

Given at Mantua, May 1690

Ferdinando Carlos

Righius

Petrus Galliardus, Chancellor by order of His Excellency & according to

the report furnished by His Excellency's notary and secretary, Count Maria Vialardi.

carry out difficult repairs: 'As also, that many times you living in the country, far from Work-men may either Your self be able to mend such Faults, or give Direc-tions to some Ingenious Country Work-men to assist You Therein.' [1]

Thus we see that the Court of Mantua offered greater scope to the musician than was attainable at Cremona, and we suggest that this fact furnishes a reasonable ex-planation of the master's decision to leave his home and his father's workshop and apply his energy to playing on, rather than to making, violins. He thereby incurred the displeasure of his parent, for it will be recalled that Andrea very feelingly alludes in his wills of the year 1692 and that of 1694, to Pietro's indifference and, as a result, altered the wills in favour of the younger son, Giuseppe. [2] Pietro, apprised of the situation and finding that his father was only leaving him the portion to which he was legally entitled, decided in August 1698 to come to an agreement with Giuseppe whereby the latter undertook to compensate him on the death of their father with the sum of 600 lire, [3] *always provided that Andrea himself was willing to give his consent to the agreement.* Strangely enough, the consent of the father having been obtained, this stipulation forms part of the actual Deed. We learn further that in August of the year 1700, a second legal document was drawn up embodying the above conditions. Pietro Guarneri is therein described as a public merchant (*publicus mercator*) of Mantua, and he pleads that he is in a position to make profitable use from day to day of the above stipulated sum. Giuseppe accordingly grants him interest at the rate of 5 per cent. until the money is paid.

Here then is the master established at Mantua between 1680 and 1685, occupying the position of a Court Musician and, when free from his duties, turning his atten-tion to the making of violins. There had never been a violin-maker working at Mantua prior to Pietro Guarneri, though, judging by the records of the past splen-dour of the city, there were doubtless lute and viol makers attached to the Ducal Court.

The rarity of his productions is proof that the master's time was not mainly devoted to instrument-making. He appears never to have made either a viola or violoncello; we doubt whether more than fifty of his violins are at present in exis-

---

[1] *Musick's Monument, 1676,* p. 54.
[2] See the second and third wills of Andrea Guarneri, Chap. I, pp. 21 and 22.
[3] The Mantuan lira varied in value between the years 1665–1733; we can, therefore, form only an approximate estimate of

the equivalent value of the above-mentioned sum, viz. £30, the purchasing power of which would, to-day, be at least four times greater. (See also footnote, p. 40.)

Both these contracts were drawn up by the Cremonese notary, Giulio Cesare Porro.

tence; and with the exception of several five-string viols (one of which made in 1689 we possess), we are acquainted with no works to which his name can be rightly ascribed. His time was evidently spent in the service of the Court, possibly to his gain at the moment, but eventually to our unquestionable loss; for he proved himself to be an accomplished workman, distinctly superior to his father. And if we judge him purely from the craftsmanship point of view we should say that he surpassed all the others of his family, not excepting Giuseppe del Gesù.

His work is full of originality, bold of design, and dexterous of finish, and he frequently clothed his violins with a superb varnish worthy of the greatest—in this direction nothing finer exists. If with the advent of the new century Pietro had come into intimate contact with Stradivari, and had shown appreciation of the trend of his teaching, then indeed the violin world would be the richer by some great works. It would have proved a noble combination. But it was not to be; for from the start the master was inspired by the full modelling of the Amati, at times emphasized by a touch of Stainer, and from that ideal he never once departed.

There is no doubt that Stainer had as early as 1680—he died in 1683—influenced the work of the Italians. Players were returning to Italy from their foreign tours bringing with them Stainer instruments, and they were evidently impressed by the easy emission and more piercing quality of tone to be obtained from these violins of full model and light construction. The inventories of the Medici family at Florence give proof that the Court was in possession of Stainers prior to 1700; possibly the Mantuan Court also possessed similar instruments. It would not in our opinion be far-fetched to imagine Pietro playing upon a Stainer and allowing himself to be somewhat captivated by its undoubted charm; for the master was not alone among the great to be thus captivated.[1] Even Guarneri del Gesù and Carlo Bergonzi were at times caught up in the vogue. The only maker who consistently throughout his life would have none of it was Antonio Stradivari.

The sense of beauty, the rare accomplishment displayed in the work of Pietro Guarneri, and his proficiency on the viol and violin which enabled him to hold a permanent post in a notable orchestra—these endowments make him in our study of violin tone a subject of unusual interest. The dominance of the Amati design and principles is clearly shown in Pietro's working out of violin form; and consequently

[1] In the inventory of the possessions left by Bach, who died in 1750, we note a violin by Jacob Stainer and a second example in bad condition, the former is valued at eight thalers, the latter, at two. (No instrument of Italian make is mentioned.) (*Life of Bach*, by C. S. Terry.) The equivalent purchasing value to-day of eight thalers would be about £9.

we find the tone of his instruments similar in character to the tone which we should anticipate from that of his model. But we can trace the inclusion of a foreign element in his tone-scheme, which is derived from another source, that of the Stainer violin.

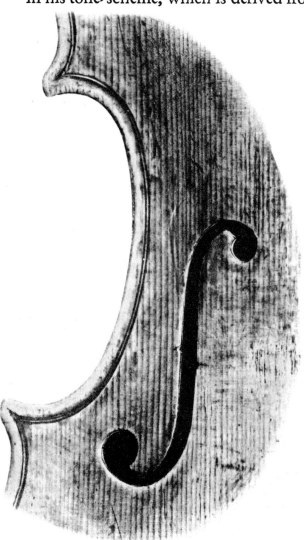

And now to touch briefly on the causes which placed the Stainer tone in the fore-front and straightway brought it into popu-larity. The labours of the brothers Amati had contributed to settle the main prin-ciples of violin tone, a tone in closer affinity to the fine voice of a soprano singer than to that of the treble viol, and which in its capacity for variety of expression, quality, and expansion, quite surpassed the earlier instrument. It is conceivable, then, that during the latter part of the seventeenth century when the viol players were still numerous, the Stainer tone, with its timbre of acid-sweetness which responded to the least touch, and held back no reserve—features all reminiscent of viol tone—should appeal to ex-violists, who saw with regret the passing of their earlier choice, the 'generous viol', to quote Mace.

Himself a viol player, and attached to the Ducal Orchestra as such, Pietro must have shared, at least partially, the views of other violists, and also, in his capacity of violin-maker, observed the success of the Stainer violin, and studied the qualities to which it was due. Setting himself to retain

FIG. I. Edge, purfling, and sound-hole of an example of the period 1690-98.

those distinctive properties which had gained the Amati tone its position—the beauty of sound in its entirety, the charm of the round and limpid quality, backed by some reserve to draw upon—the master mingled with them some of that 'penetrat-ing bite', to which the Stainer violin owed most of its vogue: for it conveyed to the performers an illusion of carrying power of tone, which experience has proved to be fallacious.

The Pietro Guarneri violin has held its own better than the Stainer in the esteem of makers and players. This statement receives some confirmation by the fine reproduction of a Pietro Guarneri, made by Lupot in 1810;[1] whereas we cannot recall any maker of equal distinction producing a copy of Stainer since the opening of the nineteenth century. Violinists of note have continued to use the instruments of our gifted Mantuan player and maker, thus proving that their tone is quite capable of responding to the demands of modern music.

Fortunately Pietro rarely departed from the more robust Cremonese principles of construction; the back and table, especially the former, were left sufficiently thick in wood, taking into account the strong arching of the model, and the linings and blocks were stoutly proportioned.

The earliest violins of the master which we meet with dating from about 1685 and bearing the Mantuan label are in form suggestive of Amati plus a slight lengthening and stiffening of the curves of the bouts which savour of Stradivari; their total length is of the normal 14 inches; the widths are narrow, and this feature, together with the longer bouts, gives to the whole an elongated appearance. The corners and edges are delicately cut and lightly formed; the fluting of the latter being deeply cut in; the f-holes, Amati-like in aspect, are throughout more open in treatment, both top and bottom holes larger and the nicks more pronounced. The head charmingly shaped and again of pronounced Amati character, the volute deeply cut, the bevel or chamfer lightly made, nor, as with the mitre joints of sides, were they ever picked out in black; Giuseppe filius practised this Stradivari innovation occasionally, Guarneri del Gesù omitted it but rarely.

To resume, we see violins of a technical construction, obviously superior to that of his father, reproducing characteristics of the Amati yet with an added personal touch and conception distinctly Guarnerian.

We find Pietro before leaving Cremona, and while still, in fact, working with his father, seeking to ornament certain of his violins by adding a fleur-de-lis inlay at the corners and, at times, a second line of purfling (note the illustration of an example dated 1676, between pp. 24, 25, Chap. I). This innovation was scarcely his own, for it was clearly inspired by a somewhat similar design which had been carried out with

---

[1] Sold by our firm to the late D. J. Partello of Washington, U.S.A.

exceptional charm by Nicolò Amati, notably in one of his violins dated 1656. We are acquainted with several other examples similarly ornamented and dating from Mantua, in the years 1685–86; another violin (see illustration, between pp. 46, 47) is still more elaborately treated. We cannot add our meed of praise in favour of this additional embellishment; the design of ivory was clearly borrowed from Stradivari, but Pietro failed to impart that sense of grace and proportion rarely absent from the work of the great master. The ivory diamonds are slightly exaggerated and equally so is the triple fleur-de-lis design inlaid at both top and bottom of the back.

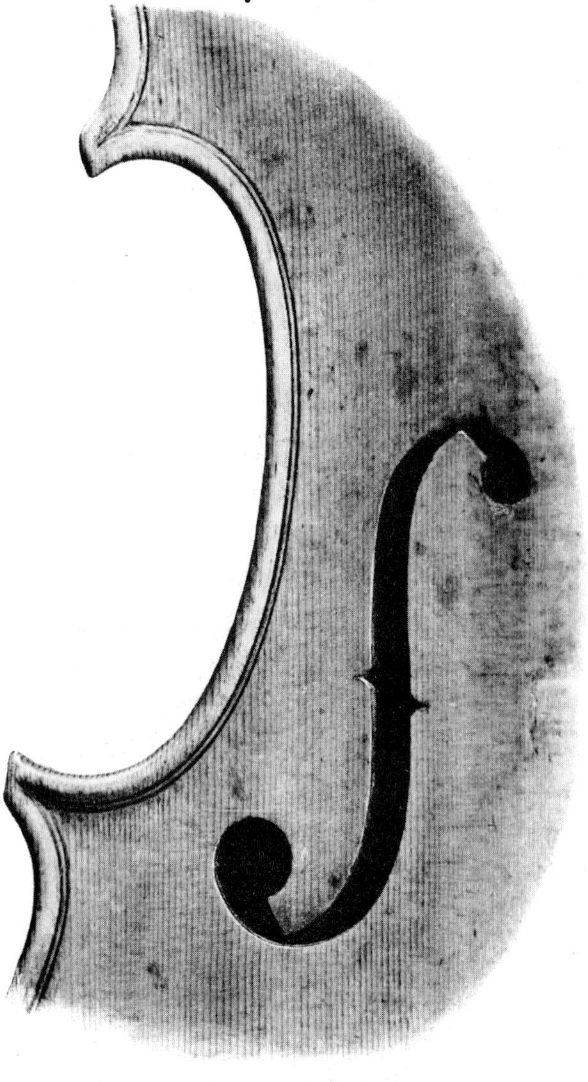

From about the year 1700 we begin to perceive a broadening of his style throughout the whole. He was abandoning the delicate Amati-like touch and replacing it by work of a more solid build. His model and form remain the same, the dimensions being increased in width, edges, corners, purfling, f-holes, and head are all bolder in treatment; the deep fluting around the edges is even more pronounced, and the sides are set with full margin and kept low to accord with the design of his generous model. The more massively carved head and manly cut f-holes are full of character —observe that the master when carving the volute now leaves the first curve of the spiral abnormally high, so much

FIG. II. Edge, purfling, and sound-hole of an example of the year 1703.

so, that, when the head is viewed from the frontal aspect, the tips appear to be dwarfed. (See illustration.)

None, not excepting the greatest, proved more fastidious in the choice of material, both as regards pine and maple, the last-named wood frequently of foreign growth and attractive appearance. In a word, the master produced a violin the ensemble of which conveys the impression of real charm and originality.

We have already commented upon the superb varnish which he used, now of a golden-brown, or an orange tint, again of a fascinating red—a varnish both in texture and colour impossible to surpass. Broadly speaking, Pietro owed but little to his forebears. He was endowed with a real sense of beauty and the cultured environment of the Court of Mantua must have both inspired him and afforded scope for the exercise of his talents. We admire the more his steadfast consistency; and the few choice examples of his work which have been handed down to us will ever prove of absorbing interest to the true connoisseur of old violins.

The following are fine and representative examples:

    1685. Mr. Rudolph Wurlitzer
    1685. M. Sigmund Keller
    1698. Miss Diana Cator, ex Teetgens
    1701. Madame Franceschi, ex Cte Baldeschi
    1703. Mr. Richard Bennett, ex Austin
    1704. Mr. F. Lingard, ex Brichta
    1707. Mrs. Bingham, ex Jeffreys
    1707. Mr. Frederick Popple, ex Baron Heath
    1708. Mr. A. C. Marshall, ex Marquise de Sers
    1710. Mr. Nathan E. Posner, ex Mme von Fritze
    1714. Mr. Géza de Kresz, ex Caressa.
    1715. Miss H. White, ex Cte de Chaponay

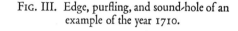

FIG. III. Edge, purfling, and sound-hole of an example of the year 1710.

Now according to various writers of the past Pietro Guarneri worked at Cremona and Mantua from about the year 1698 to 1725-28. Piccolellis[1] even goes so far as 1740, making mention of a violoncello bearing the master's label so dated. Our own conclusions, founded upon examination of labels seen in authentic violins, had led us to the belief that he did not work later than the years 1715-18. Several exhaustive researches in the Archives of Mantua undertaken by Signor Livi had proved, up to June 1922, fruitless in unearthing the desired information. But a final effort made in that year crowned our friend's work with success, and as a result we are not only able to give the exact date of Pietro's death—March 26th of the year 1720—but we have also learned various interesting details concerning the master's life.

Let us briefly recall that he was married at Cremona to Caterina Sassagni in 1677, and a son Andrea Francesco was born in the following year. In 1679 he quits his father's house; but though we have reliable evidence that he was living in Mantua from 1685 onward, we do not succeed in locating his actual home prior to the year 1694. We have been fortunate enough to trace him as living in that year in the Parish of S. Lorenzo—Contrada Monte Negro—and the following extract is taken from the census return:

Pietro Guarneri
Lucia Guidi, sua moglie (his wife)[2]

Teresia ⎤
Pavola ⎥
Angela ⎬ Suoi figliuoli,
Alovisio ⎥ (his children).
Alessandro ⎦

The census returns of the following years, 1695 and 1696, are to the same effect with the one exception of the son Alovisio, who falls out; those of the years 1697, 1698, and 1699 are missing, and that of 1700 reads as follows:

Signor Pietro Guarneri
Signora Lucia, moglie (wife)
Anna Maria Borani, madre di Lucia (mother of Lucia)

---

[1] *Liutai Antichi e Moderni*, Piccolellis, 1885.

[2] It will be noted that the wife is no longer Caterina Sassagni; apparently she had died, and her first-born child, Andrea Francesco, is not of the present household. The master had married again on the fourth day of May 1694, his second wife being Lucia Guidi Borani. We have reason to believe that she came from Guastalla (Province of Reggio).

Pavola ⎫
Angela ⎪
Francesco ⎬ figli (children).
Alessandro ⎪
Caterina ⎪
Isabella ⎭

Regular returns continue up to the years 1707 which call for no special comment, and in 1708 we find two fresh names introduced: Dionisio, liutaro;[1] Giuseppe, figlio.

Belonging to this same year 1708, and dated 27th September, we find an interest‑ing document drawn up by the Notary Giovanni Cotti of Mantua between the two brothers, Pietro, 'Civis Mantuae per decretum', and Giuseppe of Cremona, 'so‑journing at the present time at Mantua in the house of the said Pietro his brother', in which they state that they have made an amicable division of all the goods, house, furniture, utensils, and fixtures bequeathed to his heirs by the late Signor Andrea Guarneri their father and the late Anna Maria Orcelli their mother, and declare themselves satisfied with the division thus made.

We glean nothing of further interest from the census returns before the year 1714, when we note the master described as Pietro Guarneri, chitarraro (guitar‑maker), and in 1718 we see, for the first time, that the age of the respective inmates of the household is given:

Pietro Guarneri, aged 63.
Lucia, wife,   „   41.
Anna Caterina,   „   22.
Isabella Clara,   „   19.

In 1719 Caterina is absent from the household, and we learn from another source that she was given in marriage on the 5th day of October 1718. The year 1719 furnishes the last census record of the family; and we can only assume that on the death of the master in 1720 the widow and surviving children moved away to another part of the city, the house probably being disposed of.

The burial certificate of Pietro Guarneri taken from the register of deaths of the Parish of S. Lorenzo, Mantua, reads as follows, D: 'In the year of Our Lord, 1720, March 27th, Dom. Pietro Guarnieri, the husband of Lucia Burana, of this Parish,

[1] Possibly the Christian name of an apprentice or assistant, but we would add that no such name has come down to us as a violin‑maker.

aged 66, fortified by all the last Sacraments and in communion with Holy Mother Church, yesterday gave up his soul to God; his body was interred to-day, in the Church of the Fathers of S. Francis Paula, in this city, with the usual ceremonies.'

Among the various documents found by Signor Livi at Mantua we have several, notably the master's will together with an inventory of the contents of his workshop, which are of considerable interest.

The will, which was drawn up on the 25th of March 1720, the day before his death, by the Mantuan Notary, Ludovico Mozzi, makes various bequests, but contains nothing directly touching on our subject. It reads as follows:

'*Testamentum domini Petri Guarnerii.*

'Signor Pietro [son] of the late Signor Andrea Guarneri, native of the City of Cremona, at present residing at Mantua, Contrada del Monte Negro, sane, by the Grace of God, in mind, senses, sight and intellect, though infirm in body, disposes of himself and goods as follows:

'He desires that his body shall be buried in the Church of S. Francesco di Paola.[1]

'He leaves to the Hospital of Mantua the sum of twelve lire.[2]

'To Sister Maria Caterina, his daughter, of the Convent of SS. Annonciade, an oil painting framed, representing the Dying Jesus.

'To Sister Clara, another daughter, a second oil painting representing S. Anthony of Padua.

'To the Fathers Bonaventura and Alessandro, his sons, Friars of the Order of S. Francesco di Paola, he leaves all his books.

'He leaves to Lucia Burani his wife, and to Isabella his marriageable daughter a life-interest in all his property personal or otherwise, and he desires that the aforesaid Isabella and Caterina, his daughters, shall finally inherit his property in equal portions.'

In the margin of the will is written: '*Actum, quia decessit 26 martii 1720.*' ('Registered, after death, 26th March 1720.')

The inventory of the contents of the house, both movable and immovable, situated in the Contrada del Monte Negro, was made by the same Notary Ludovico Mozzi, and at the request of the Executors and Legatees.

[1] This church for all practical purposes exists no longer; during the Austrian occupation of Mantua (1815–66) it was used as a military store-house.

[2] Approximately in value of to-day, i.e. prior to 1914, £8–10.

D.

Anno Domini millesimo septingentesimo vigesimo, die vero
vigesima septima martii, dominus Petrus Guarnieri,
maritus Luciæ Burana huius Parochiæ, ætatis suæ
annorum sexaginta sex, omnibus sanctis munitus
sacramentis in communione Sanctæ matris Ecclesiæ
animam heri Deo reddidit, cuius cadaver huma-
tum fuit hodie in Ecclesia Patrum Sancti Francisci
de Paula huius civitatis, more solito, &c.

E.

Due basseti di venere con suoi archi e corde
Due chitare senza corde
Tre tiorbi, due liuti e tre viole diverse.

Quatro rapparelle di ferro per lavorar violini

Dieci archi da violino di pelegrino parte finiti e parte
di finire.
Una cassa di arpa senza corde.

Quindeci violini fornicii fatti dal Sig.r Defonto con dominici
Un altro simile senza dominici.

Otto violini di diversi autori parte novi, e parte usati
Un altro violino novo mà non finito.

After enumerating various articles found in the shop *(botega)* of the said house such as tables, benches, armoires, chests, tool-rack, &c., we note the following items of more especial interest, *E*:

Two violoncellos *(bassetti da sonare)* with their bows and strings.

Two guitars without strings.

Three theorbos, two lutes, and three viols of divers types.

Sixteen bows *(da violino)* of snake wood *(di serpentino)* some finished, some partly finished.

The body of a harp *(una cassa da arpa)* without strings.

Then follows a list of ordinary tools which includes most things which would be found in a violin-maker's workshop of to-day, i.e. planes, knives, files, saws, and even scrapers.

We then find a list of pictures, mostly of religious subjects; these were in two upstairs rooms *(camera di sopra)*, and finally we come to the following items:

Fifteen violins finished, made by the late master *(fatti del signore defonto)* and with their varnish.

One similar violin without varnish, i.e. in the white.

Eight violins by various makers, partly new, partly old *(parte novi e parte usati)*.

One other new violin unfinished.

We learn from the above that the master thus made bows, as was the case with Stradivari, and in all probability he also made all the other accessories.

It is with more than ordinary interest that we read of the violins, the work of Pietro, some of which are unfinished, and find no mention whatever of a violoncello or viola; and this fact does strengthen our conviction—the result of lifelong observation—that he probably never made either the one or the other. Our conviction is somewhat strengthened by the words of the deed of appointment (see page 28), 'Maker of Musical Instruments, and Violins in particular'. We would add that the earlier entry of 'due bassetti' refers, in our opinion, to instruments not made by him.

How illuminating when we ponder over these items of the inventory, and allow our thoughts to revert to that other great master of Cremona, who still in this year 1720, at the age of 76, continued with unflagging zeal to add to his already over-generous legacy to futurity. He, too, must have required an inventory drawn up of his possessions at death; and although we have hitherto failed to come across such

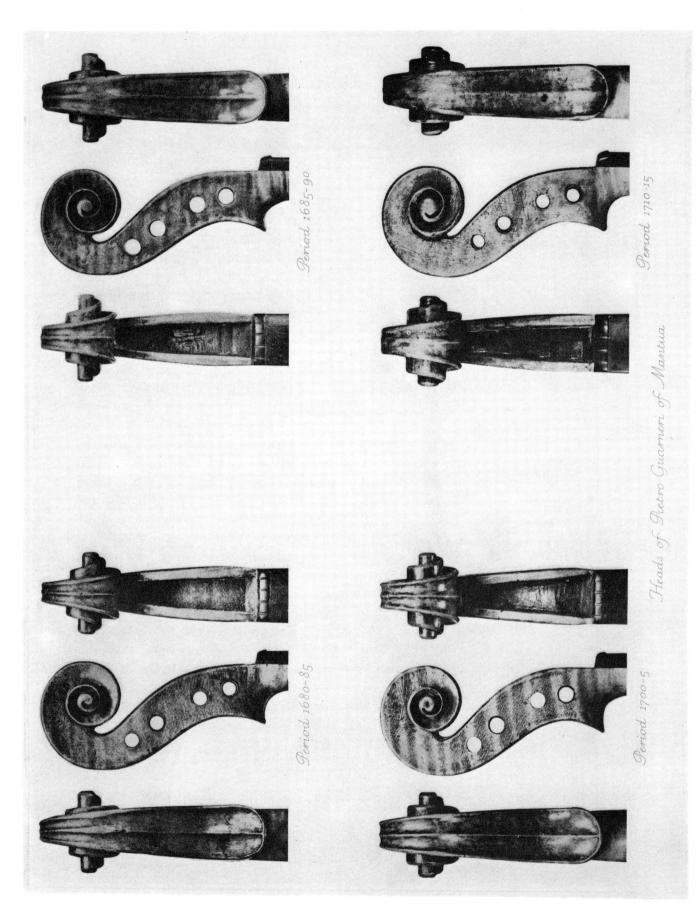

Period 1685-90

Period 1710-15

Period 1680-85

Period 1700-5

Heads of Pietro Guarneri of Mantua.

Corso delle Barche di Paolo

...ERI WAS BURIED, (2) THE PARISH OF S.LORENZO, WHERE HE LIVED

a document, we do know, on the authority of Count Cozio di Salabue, who obtained his information from the sons of Stradivari, that the total of the instruments left amounted to the large number of ninety-two. A contrast indeed. The respective numbers of the works of these two masters as computed to-day testify to the industry of Stradivari and the slackness—whatever the cause—of Pietro.

Besides the pictures, of which there were quite a number (no names of the painters are in any case given), we note several items of jewellery, including a ring with a small diamond, and other worldly goods; and the general impression we obtain from studying the inventory is that the master was living, to say the least, in quite comfortable circumstances. Nor ought we to be surprised when we realize that not only had Pietro obtained and held the Court appointment as Musician, but he was also accorded other prerogatives such as the decree issued in 1690, and again in 1692, conferring the monopoly for the sale of harmonic strings *(corde armoniche)*. Moreover, such a monopoly probably covered other articles and accessories as well as strings. Why not violins? For we can affirm that no other violin-maker was working at Mantua at the same time as Pietro.

In the year 1694 we find that the brothers Sigismondo and Alassio Bianchi sold to '*Domino Petro fili Domini Andrea di Guarnerius Cremonensi cive tamen Mantua per ducale decretum ut dixit.*' (to 'Dom. Petro, the son of the late Dom. Andrea Guarneri, a Cremonese, but by virtue of a Ducal Decree a citizen of Mantua . . .') for the sum of one thousand écus[1] a piece of land in the city of Mantua with a house and shop situated in the Via Monte Negro, otherwise called Via della Cicogna.

In the year 1717, 31st March, Pietro Guarneri enters into an agreement with the Monks of S. Francesco di Paola, by which he renounces in their favour all claims to the property hitherto belonging to his son Alessandro,[2] who eight years previously had entered the said Monastery.

And lastly we have the fully detailed marriage contract drawn up in August 1718 by the Mantuan Notary Muti, on the occasion of the betrothal of Signora Caterina, the master's daughter, to Signor Gaetano, son of Signor Antonio Vernizze of Guastalla. The contract fixes the marriage portion accorded by Pietro to his daughter at two hundred and fifty Mantuan crowns, at the rate of exchange of six lire apiece; and the master also agrees to endow her with effects of an equivalent value.

[1] Approximately £150.
[2] Alessandro was one of the executors named in Pietro's will.

Signor Antonio Vernizzi also binds himself to settle on the bride a similar sum of money, and effects of like value, but stipulates that the dowry shall be duly valued by experts to be chosen by both parties to the contract, and that the valuation thus arrived at shall be registered in the documents relating to the marriage settlement. Various other precise conditions are added to the contract; and finally the three interested parties, namely the bridegroom, his father, and Pietro Guarneri append their signatures together with those of five witnesses. We thus obtain and are able to reproduce the actual signature of Pietro himself, F.

F.

I, Pietro Guarnieri, acknowledge and accept the above.

We furthermore learn that the marriage was solemnized on the 5th day of October 1718 at the Church of S. Lorenzo. And in the inventory of the marriage portion made over to the father of the bridegroom we have a list of the linen, clothes, and other effects, beside various articles of jewellery, the whole of which is valued at 1,500 lire (about £40).

This series of documents shows that the master not only held a sufficiently good position financially, but also as a citizen of Mantua by Ducal decree—an honour which carried with it a certain distinction. We are disappointed at finding no reference whatever to his brother Giuseppe, nor to either of the nephews Pietro and Giuseppe del Gesù, more especially the last named, who, as we shall later learn, was the master's godchild.

We have no evidence allowing us to assert that Pietro Guarneri at death left either a pupil or a direct successor to continue his work; he had sons, but apparently they showed no desire to carry on the family tradition. And here again we note that same reluctance to take pupils other than members of the family.

The work of these master-craftsmen was above all personal. Did they carry it on for material gain? Doubtless, since they had to live. But we see these simple violin-makers as men inspired by love and reverence to serve the Church through music—and assuredly the master was no exception.

We suggest that the nephew Pietro (son of Giuseppe) may have spent a short time in Mantua after his uncle's death engaged in clearing up the contents of the workshop, prior to his departure for Venice. But whether or not that was the case we assert that the several liutari who continued to make instruments in this city during the eighteenth century were in a large measure inspired by the masterful creations left by Pietro Guarneri.

The names of the men we have more especially in mind are Antonio Zanotti,[1] Camillo Camilli,[2] and Tomasso Balestrieri,[3] all of whom have left us meritorious work—instruments which at times are strongly tinged by features reminiscent of the late master. But none of these makers were possessed of his superb varnish, nor did they in common with the growing number of their colleagues throughout Europe appear to recognize any practical reason for making use of a varnish other than one of a spirit basis.

No, with the passing of Pietro Guarneri in 1720 Mantua suffered the loss of her one really distinguished violin-maker; he was not to be replaced. And in order to study the higher traditions we must again turn our vision to Cremona—still the Mecca of our art—where we shall once more pick up the Guarneri threads, see the brother, Giuseppe, peacefully carrying on, and, what is more interesting, giving rein in due course to his two sons, one of whom is to prove himself a close and worthy disciple of his Mantuan namesake, and the other to stand out as the great genius of the family.

---

[1] *Antonio Zanotti* was born at Ceretto in the province of Lodi about 1690–5, and he states on one of his labels that he was a pupil of Geronimo Amati, son of Nicolò; he worked in Mantua from about 1724–50.

[2] *Camillo Camilli* was born at Mantua about 1704, and died on the 21st of October 1754; aged, so the death certificate adds, about 50 years. He was an excellent maker, and we believe him to have been a pupil of Zanotti. His work shows considerable affinity with that of Pietro Guarneri.

[3] Tomasso Balestrieri (1735–40 to 1790) states on his labels that he was of Cremonese origin; and we must assume this was the case, although we have failed to find any trace of the name in the Cremonese annals. At times his works reflect Stradivari's teaching, but he was equally influenced by Pietro Guarneri.

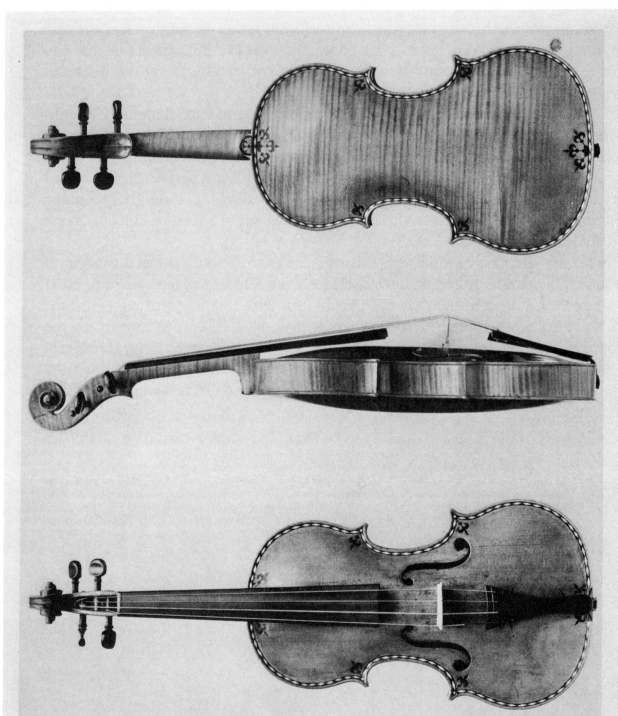

Petrus Guarnerius Cremonensis fecit Mantuæ 1686

Petrus Guarnerius Cremonensis fecit Mantuæ (period 1698-1700)

CHAPTER III

GIUSEPPE GUARNERI, SON OF ANDREA

BORN 1666, DIED 1739-40

Oh, the little more, and how much it is!
And the little less, and what worlds away!
(BROWNING)

LEAVING Mantua, we retrace our steps to Cremona and there throw our minds back to the year 1698 and to the Casa Orcelli-Guarneri, where we shall find Pietro's younger brother, Giuseppe, from whom we then parted.

Giuseppe, who had rendered diligent and faithful service to his father in the declining years of his life, now found himself, as a reward for his filial devotion, in the possession of the parental home and the contents of the workshop. His past furnishes testimony of a skilled worker well able to sustain the reputation which Andrea had gained by a lifelong application to violin-making. But above all posterity, now enlightened as to the true facts, will no longer withhold its tribute both to the master and Barbara Franchi for that son, born to them in this very year, 1698 —the boy who was destined to shed the greatest lustre on the Guarneri name.

A.

November 26th, 1666. Born on the 25th of the above month, the son of Dom. Andrea Guarneri & Maria Orcelli, his wife, was baptized by me, Giacomo Filippo Porro, Rector of the Church of San Matteo, the names of Giovanni Battista Giuseppe being conferred upon him, the Very Rev. Dom. Ortensio Bonetti, priest residing in the Palace of the Illustrious Marquess Giovanni Battista Ariberti, in the parish of SS. Vito & Companions, standing proxy for the god-parents, the Illustrious Marquess, & Anna Trompelli of the old parish of San Michele.

Let us briefly recall that Giuseppe was the third and youngest son of Andrea, born in November 1666, and commonly known as Joseph Guarnerius filius Andreæ, A. He figures in the census returns up to the year 1671, as Giuseppe

Giovanni Battista, and afterwards as Giuseppe only. He was married to Barbara Franchi in 1690, whose presence in the household of Andrea is noted for the first time in 1692.

Here is the exact extract:

Andrea Guarnieri, aged 67
Gioseppe, figlio (son), aged 25
Barbara, moglie (wife), „ 22
Andrea, figlio (son), „ 5 months

It is of interest to consider for a moment the environment of Giuseppe at Cremona, as far as violin-making was concerned, in the year 1698. In reality there were members of but four master families at work—namely the Amati, in the person of Girolamo, figlio Nicolai, the Guarneri represented by himself, the Rugeri by the three sons of Francesco—for we doubt whether Francesco was alive at the above-mentioned date, as our latest record of his work is 1694—and lastly, Antonio Stradivari. There were a few stray workers in addition to these master makers, but some of their names are scarcely recorded.

Had Giuseppe already signed instruments with his own name previous to Andrea's death? Unquestionably so; in fact we have as early as the year 1690 records of existing instruments thus labelled, but whether these particular examples were inscribed in every case by Giuseppe himself is open to some doubt. A good deal of labelling and relabelling was practised during the early half of the nineteenth century, and the 'Guarneri' possibilities were not overlooked. Numbers of Andrea's violins were renamed 'Amati', certain of those of Giuseppe also; others of the master's were transformed into 'Bergonzi's'; and even to-day experts fail to distinguish between the one and the other. Anything at all roguish in the work of either Giuseppe or of Pietro of Venice was immediately rebaptized 'Giuseppe del Gesù'. Pietro of Mantua stood apart; his clear delineation did not admit of disguise.

The proof of the separate identity of the master's work prior to 1698—the year of Andrea's death—is established by his authentic label dated 1696 (see reproduction, Chapter VII). It represents one of two labels met with by us, concerning which we have no misgivings. Giuseppe himself placed it in the violin, every feature of which bears the stamp of absolute purity (see illustration, facing).

The second, still earlier example, is dated 1690, and, here again, we are able to affirm the absolute authenticity of both violin and inscription.

Joseph Guarnerius filius Andreæ fecit Cremonæ 1696

The death of Andrea brought no immediate change to the character of the instruments emanating from the workshop. It remains much the same as that to which we
have been accustomed during the last ten years; but henceforth we shall miss that
orthodox 'Andrea Guarneri' of small Amati form, with its light edges and corners,
f-holes of small design, full breasted model, and low sides, covered by a varnish of
light chestnut brown colour.

As we pass onward in the new century towards 1710 we perceive modifications
taking place from year to year. Giuseppe remains notwithstanding singularly faithful
to the Amati ideals as transmitted by his father; throughout his work we sense that
very distinct 'Guarneri' touch in all its main characteristics. During these years we see
certain violins which are clearly inspired by the work of his brother Pietro of Mantua
—the same outline, a form measuring 14 inches in length, widths 8 and $6\frac{9}{16}$ inches respectively; the edge and purfling fairly bold, model full, and fluting moderately deep.
Nor should this resemblance cause surprise, for the two brothers appear to have lived
in friendly intercourse, and Pietro when visiting his native city probably took interest
in Giuseppe's work, and submitted to him some of his own superb productions. We
see some examples more Amati in type, though the bouts are less curved and tend to be
longer, the form full 14 inches in length, the width as usual, the top corners long and
slender, the others shorter, the edge small, and fluting slight. The purfling is of good
substance, and, generally speaking, made from wood which was not carefully prepared—neither the black nor the white colour standing out distinctly. In other words
it was but indifferently stained, and was not evenly drawn prior to its insertion. The
model is gracefully shaped, now of full proportions, now quite moderate. We notice a
tendency to place the f-holes somewhat low; and frequently they are shortened in design,
otherwise they are happily posed. The sweep of the top curves is distinctly personal,
and the wings are slightly hollowed. The heads are of typical Guarneri touch as
carved by Andrea, but are rendered with more truth and vigour, are more accurately
finished, and often of bolder design. At times we find the chamfer picked out in black.

All the Italian makers were to a considerable extent creative in the details of their
work. Their very free method of working fostered the spirit; hence we see example
after example, each one differing from the other. Never do we find stereotyped reproduction. Giuseppe was no exception; we should be inclined to say that he varied
more than his father.

We perceive the growing influence of Stradivari reflected in his work—no matter for surprise seeing that he was living and working under the shadow of S. Domenico—in close proximity to his great neighbour.

Like his father, he also must have marvelled at the ever-increasing number of masterpieces, the production of the genius of the Piazza, but he must have viewed them with that added advantage of youth —the more receptive mind. And dull indeed would be the craftsman who would not have been impressed by their mastery of design, unsurpassable workmanship, and splendid material.

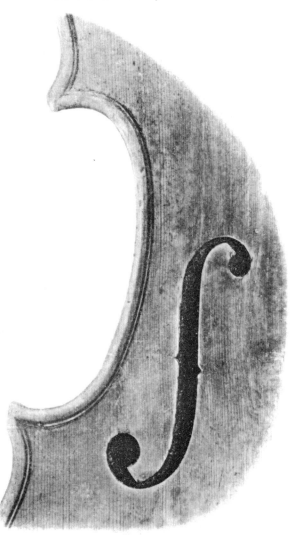

FIG. I.   Edge, purfling, and sound-hole of an example of the period 1710.

Surely no vain imagining to picture Stradivari himself at times submitting these fruits of his labour for the approval, nay, the admiration of his fellow workers.

The really surprising thing is that such an environment did not give much greater results. Perhaps, however, in the long run the violin lover has been the gainer. For which of us has not sensed both charm and gratification as a result of playing on and examining these very distinctive productions of the Cremonese master?

We note violins generally dating from about 1700–10—we have seen an example dated 1696—which were obviously inspired by the 'Long Stradivari', though Giuseppe made them of ordinary length, i.e. here $13\frac{7}{8}$ inches bare, there 14 inches and 14 inches bare; otherwise the outline of top curves and bouts follows the Stradivari with considerable exactitude. The f-holes, head, modelling, treatment of the edge and corners, in fact the whole of the work forms a blend of Amati-cum-Guarneri-cum-Stradivari character, yet lacking the stronger virility of the last. The varnish is at times of superb colour and texture, superior to anything left by Andrea, and at its best rivalling that used by his brother Pietro. On the other hand, we occasionally come across a varnish distinctly dry in texture, and of uninteresting appearance; so much so as to cause us to doubt whether it be of an oil basis.

The wood varies a good deal; in some instances we see maple—more frequently of native growth—of quite handsome appearance, with the backs cut on the slab, and the sides the right way of the grain; at other times wood of plain figure, neither sides nor head matching. Giuseppe also made use of poplar, lime, and kindred woods; and we have seen beech used by him. His pine is generally of excellent quality. To sum up, we should say that his material was more varied than that of his father; and taking into consideration both wood and varnish, we would add superior. But it is evident that the choicest wood coming to Cremona generally fell to the lot of the great master of the Piazza and to none other.

We have previously pointed out that the output of instruments by the Guarneri does not appear to have been at all generous, although both Andrea and Giuseppe passed the allotted span of life, three-score years and ten. But we must remember that no member of the Guarneri ever occupied the unique position held by the Amati, and later by Stradivari. The material they made use of, and the average standard of their craftsmanship, always excepting that of the elder Pietro, clearly proclaim that their productions were sold at a relatively cheap price; and during the eighteenth century their works were not prized to any appreciable extent. As a result they fell into less careful hands; and, in consequence, the past had already dealt harshly with many a Guarneri long before the dawn of the nineteenth century, when a quickening of the appreciation of the better Italian instruments was fast taking place.

We would cite the following violins as representative examples of the master's work:

	1690.	Capt. H. de Broen.
	1696.	Mr. Sidney Wright, ex Wedekind
	1699.	Miss Elizabeth Chapman
Period	1700.	M. Martin Schiff
	1700.	Mrs. Carolou, ex Col. Nolloth
	1703.	Mrs. Francis Forbes
	1705.	Miss Fish
Period	1705–10.	M. Julio de Igartua, ex Paul Deschamp

1707. Hon. Mrs. Ponsonby
1710. Lady Maxwell, ex Bonynge
1710. Mr. Jules Falk, ex Barton Willing
Period 1710-15. Mr. Pierre Goodrich, ex Daniel Herrmann
1711. Rev. M. F. Coates, ex Merton
1714. Dr. H. Kühne
1714. Hon. Mrs. Walsh, ex Col. H. F. Makins
Period 1715-20. Mr. John F. T. Royds, ex Hudson
„ 1715-20. Miss Bacon, ex Boyd
„ 1719-20. Miss Marian Jay
„ 1720. Mr. Sigmund Beel, ex Harold Joachim
„ 1720. Miss Dorothy Ewens, ex Bennett
„ 1720. Mme Samuel, ex Ysaÿe
„ 1720. Mr. R. M. Tobin, ex Rayner
„ 1720. Mrs. Cook, ex Sellon
„ 1720. Miss Florence Field, ex Derenburg

We estimate that Giuseppe made quite as many violins as his father,[1] and a few more violoncellos. We have so far searched in vain for a viola bearing his original label—strange indeed when we recall the example previously mentioned (p. 15) which is undoubtedly his work. The only explanation we can offer is that the demand for violas was more than satisfied by the existing old ones—the work of the Amati and the early Brescians—which were numerous.

Did the master make violoncellos of the large Amati type? We think not, though possibly there may be found an isolated example hitherto unseen by us. By 1700 an instrument of more manageable proportions was from time to time required, especially one which could be more easily held between the knees, for the violoncello leg was then unthought of; and Giuseppe, taking his father's modified form as a guide, made to that pattern. He then reduced his dimensions both in length and width; and at times we even see a form measuring but 28½ inches in length with corresponding widths: in fact, a comparatively small instrument.

When considering Giuseppe's efforts in this connexion, one's mind involuntarily reverts to Stradivari, who during these very years under review was giving to the world his perfected form of violoncello. Giuseppe was apparently not at all impressed

[1] See Andrea Guarneri, Chapter I, p. 13.

by it, for he plodded on in his own way; nor were his modified forms symmetrical —the lower curves, i.e. those below the bridge, lacking breadth when viewed in relation to the upper part. This was a weakness shown by various subsequent Italian makers, notably the Guadagnini. His general principles of construction were excellent, and the finish of his work was good. Like Andrea, when giving of his best, he appears to have been a sufficiently skilled craftsman. His modelling was usually less full than that of his father. The f-holes, of distinctly smaller design and elegantly cut, remind us of those of J. B. Rogeri and are well set upon the table, and permit of a stop of $15\frac{3}{4}$ inches, similar to that of Stradivari. The heads, boldly carved, sometimes with a broad chamfer picked out in black, are inclined to a certain squareness in design; they lack that perfect throw of the volute which we see exemplified in the superb head previously commented on—the work of his youth.

The fine violoncellos dated 1710 and that of the period 1710-15, of which we give illustrations between pp. 64, 65, are typical examples, the back and sides of the latter specimen being made of well-figured poplar.

Giuseppe's material was seldom handsome or very happily assorted; for instance, we see a back of maple, and sides and head of beech, or the beech used for the latter part only; again, the back and sides may be of wood cut on the quarter, and a head cut on the slab, or arranged vice versa. In addition to maple and beech, the master used, as for his violins, both poplar and lime.

Thus worked Giuseppe Guarneri, obviously not in the running with his great contemporary, yet fulfilling the same useful part as his father before him. He was Andrea's superior as a craftsman, but not greatly so; and he continued to produce a thoroughly serviceable violin and violoncello, one answering to the requirements of the times, and at a relatively moderate cost.

Other than the above-mentioned violoncellos, the following are representative of the master's work:

<pre>
Period 1695-1700. Dr. Price Jones, ex Ker
           1707. Russell B. Kingman, ex Beal
           1709. M. André Levy, ex Delsart
Period   1710. M. Hammig, ex Kummer
           1712. Miss May Fussell
           1712. Mrs. Snelling
           1731. Mr. James Messeas, ex Pendarves
</pre>

Of his life outside the workshop we have gleaned but little; the census returns reveal him throughout his career under the same roof where he was born. From year to year we note the arrival of fresh inmates, or their departure. Reverting to 1692, we see no change before 1695, in which year we learn of the birth of a second son, baptized under the name of Pietro and born on the 14th of April, *A* (2). This son was destined to follow the career of his father. Andrea, the firstborn, was not; nor have we any knowledge concerning his later life. Continuing onward we find nothing calling for comment until the year 1699, when we note the birth of a third son to Giuseppe and Barbara Franchi. The exact extract, a facsimile of which we reproduce together with that of the following year, reads as on p. 56, *C*.

This birth of a son bearing one of the Christian names of his father naturally arrested our attention, and as a result of our examination of the baptismal records we found that the child was actually born on the 21st day of August 1698, and baptized under the name of Bartolomeo Joseph, and that the godfather was none other than his uncle Pietro of Mantua. We give the facsimile of this interesting extract on p. 55, *B*.

Nothing of exceptional interest is revealed in the following years. We reproduce the extract from the year 1713 in order to show that Andrea, the eldest son, had then left the paternal home; but what is of infinitely more importance, we learn that both the other sons—namely Pietro and Giuseppe—were still alive and living with their father, *D*.

Five more years pass without any notable change, but in 1718 the name of the son Pietro is missing from the household returns; he would then be aged twenty-three, and apparently had gone to live elsewhere. We know, however, that he was still working in Cremona in 1721, and that his marriage took place at Venice some few years later.

No fresh item of importance presents itself before reaching the year 1723, when we mark the absence of Giuseppe, the third son, from the family record; he too had followed the example of Pietro and abandoned the paternal roof, *E*.

Marriage seems the most probable explanation of his departure; but whatever the cause, we shall pick him up again within a few years, living in close proximity to his previous home, and married.

Continuing to the years 1738 and 1739 we find the census returns only recording one name, that of the master himself, and the age 71 and 72 respectively is correctly given, *F*.

A (2)

On April 17th, 1695

Pietro, son of Dom. Joseph Guarneri & Barbara Franchi his wife, who was born on the 14th day of the above month, was baptized by me, Francesco de Arquatis, Rector of S. Matteo: the godfather being Dom. Andrea, one of the clergy of the parish of S. Nicolò.

B.

On August 21st, 1698

Bartolomeo Joseph, son of Dom. Joseph Guarneri & Barbara Franchi, his wife, was born &, on that same day, baptized by me, Francesco de Arquatis, Rector of S. Matteo: the godfather being Dom. Pietro Giovanni, son of Dom. Andrea Guarneri, living at Mantua.

C.

1699.

2ᵃ Casa Guarneri
Giuseppe Guarneri an. 32. ch. c. c
Barbara Franchi moglie an. 29. ch. c. c
Andrea figº. an. 7.
Pietro figº an. 4
Giuseppe figº. in fte
Barbara Maria nip. an. 14. ch. c.
Giº Battᵃ fretto an. ii ch. c.

1700

1ᵃ Casa Guarneri vuota
2ᵃ Casa Guarneri
Giuseppe Guarneri an. 33. ch. c. c.
Barbera Franchi moglie an. 30. ch. c. c.
Andrea figº an. 8.
Pietro figº an. 5.
Giuseppe fyº an. 1.
Barbara Maria Nip. an. i5. ch. c.
Giº Battᵃ fretto an. i2. ch. c.

1699

House of Guarneri, 2nd floor

Giuseppe Guarneri, aged 32. Christened, confirmed, communicant

Barbara Franchi, wife, aged 29. Christened, confirmed, communicant

Andrea, son, aged 7

Pietro, son, aged 4

Giuseppe, infant son

Barbara Maria, niece, aged 14. Christened, confirmed

Gio. Battista, brother, aged 11. Christened, confirmed

1700

House of Guarneri

1st Floor, vacant,

2nd occupied by

Giuseppe Guarneri, aged 33. Christened, confirmed, communicant

Barbara Franchi, wife, aged 30. Christened, confirmed, communicant

Andrea, son, aged 8

Pietro, son, aged 5

Giuseppe, son, aged 1

Barbara Maria, niece, aged 15. Christened, confirmed

Gio. Battista, brother, aged 12. Christened, confirmed

D.

1713. House of Guarneri

Giuseppe Guarneri, aged 46. Christened, confirmed, communicant
Barbara Franchi, wife, aged 43. Christened, confirmed, communicant
Pietro, son, aged 18. Christened, confirmed, communicant
Giuseppe, son, aged 12.[1] Christened, confirmed, communicant
Barbara Maria Guarneri, niece, aged 28. Christened, confirmed, communicant

[1] It will be observed that the age of the son 'Giuseppe' as recorded in 1700 and 1713 is incorrect (see certificate of birth) but, as pointed out in the next chapter, p. 73, such errors are not infrequent. Several of the later census returns do, however, give the correct age. (See Chap. IV, p. 86.)

E.

Census Returns for the Current Year. 1723. Piazza S. Domenico.

House of the Guarneri, occupied by them

Giuseppe Guarneri, son of the late Andrea—paterfamilias—56 years. Christened, confirmed, communicant.
Barbara Franchi, daughter of the late Giovanni and wife, 53 years. Christened, confirmed, communicant.

House of the Steffanoni, let

House of the Stradivari, half occupied

F.

1738

House of Guarneri

Giuseppe Guarneri (son) of the late Andrea, aged 71. Christened, confirmed, communicant.

1739

House of Guarneri

Giuseppe Guarneri (son) of the late Andrea, aged 72. Christened, confirmed, communicant.

G.

On January 1st, 1738

Dna. Barbara Franchi, wife of Giuseppe Guarneri, fortified by the Holy Sacraments of the Church, died yesterday, being about 67 years of age, and to-day her body accompanied by funeral rites was taken to the church of the Dominican Fathers and there interred by me, Domenico Antonio Francari, Rector of the church.

In 1740 we draw a complete blank, nor do we again succeed in getting in touch with the master elsewhere. The explanation was soon forthcoming, for we found the certificate of death of Barbara Franchi under date 1st January 1738, G: and in two instructive documents dating from May 1740, of which we shall speak more fully later, the master is spoken of as the late Giuseppe. He had thus died after the completion of the census of 1739 and before that of 1740, and was therefore aged about 72 years.

Barbara Franchi was buried in S. Domenico, but, strange to relate, we can find no similar record concerning the master. Possibly he had died away from his native city. Maybe after the death of his lifelong companion he had joined his son Pietro, who had been established now for some years in Venice, or had even gone to live with another of his relatives no longer residing in Cremona, and had there died. Certain it is that his body was not laid to rest in the tomb of the Guarneri in the Church of S. Domenico.

We now return to the Casa Guarneri and assume ourselves to be in the year 1715. From that year to about 1725–30 another and final type of violin emerging from the workshop arrests our attention. It represents a certain break with the past in the sense that we have here an instrument of stronger design and build measuring in length $14-14\frac{1}{16}$ or even $14\frac{1}{8}$ inches ; widths respectively $8\frac{1}{8}-8\frac{1}{4}$ and $6\frac{5}{8}-6\frac{11}{16}$; height of sides more frequently $1\frac{3}{16}-1\frac{3}{16}$, here lower, there normal. Features reminiscent of Stradivari are found at this time, though the character as a whole still continues to be that of the 'Guarneri'. Perhaps the most noticeable characteristics are the elongated bouts, the form of which is distinctly less curved at the top corners—a treatment which imparts a certain squareness to their appearance—and the decidedly narrow aspect of the waist (i.e. the width across the bouts)—which in reality measures from $\frac{1}{16}$ to $\frac{1}{8}$ inch less than the average Amati or del Gesù violins. The lengthened bouts are gained at the expense of the bottom curves, which are, so to speak, foreshortened: in other words, the sweep of the outline referred to is somewhat out of balance with that of the top part. Carlo Bergonzi has strongly accentuated these features in most of his violins.

Now the question as to who were the actual workers employed in making these examples is a particularly interesting one. They certainly stand apart from the master's earlier works; and the vigour of treatment found in them suggests to our minds that they were being shaped with the assistance of other hands than his own.

May not this type of violin have sprung from the younger mind of those now as-sociated with the workshop, who, stimulated by the sight of the splendid contem-porary productions of Stradivari, sought to emulate his example? The edges and corners are more broadly treated; the *f*-holes are heavier and more open in design, but still set low down on the table; the model has a full swell; the head is more masterful and vigorously carved; the varnish is of fine quality, the colour varying from an orange-brown to brown-red, at times a fine deep-red colour of real beauty.

We have here a subject which permits of much speculation; and let us start by stating our belief that these particular vio-lins did not originally, with possibly rare exceptions, bear any label. Consequently we are not in a position to assign defi-nite dates of production; but we have no doubt that the period 1715-30 is correct. Needless to add, they have since been labelled, and with no special accuracy; at times not even their authorship has been correctly assigned, and they are accepted as quite the orthodox Carlo Bergonzi!

In the year 1715 the master was still under fifty, and we should imagine in possession of his full vigour. He had trained apprentices, for we know that both the sons, Pietro and Giuseppe, aged respectively twenty and seventeen, were in the workshop. Then there is another name

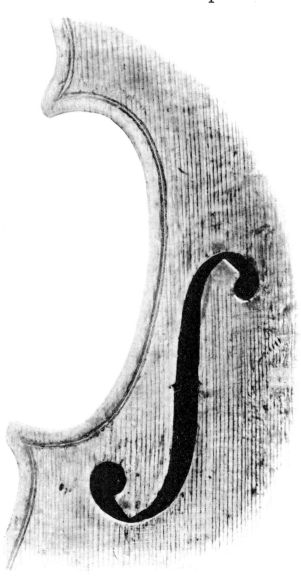

FIG. II. Edge, purfling, and sound-hole of an example of the period 1720

which has not hitherto been in any way connected with that of the 'Guarneri'—namely Carlo Bergonzi, who was born, as we learn from our Cremona researches, in December 1683 (and not as hitherto recorded).[1] He would thus be thirty-two years of age at the above date.

The accepted dictum that Bergonzi was a pupil of Stradivari—a dictum to which we ourselves subscribed at the period when our *Life of Stradivari* was written, though even then we had a vague feeling that it might in the course of time prove incorrect—is one which has never been supported by any evidence. And the more we have been given the opportunity to reconsider the point, the less are we disposed to allow it to continue unquestioned.

Nor are we to-day in a position to offer any positive evidence connecting the master with either of the Giuseppe Guarneri; yet, when in searching for proof of affinity of workmanship, we do find that there exists much to connect the three men. The assumed relationship with Stradivari rests on conjecture only; and as we shall learn later, in the case of Guarneri del Gesù, statements were light-heartedly made at the beginning of last century, accepted and repeated as time sped on, without any attempt being made to verify their correctness either by the light of experience or renewed research.

It is quite possible that Carlo Bergonzi was now simply an assistant or workman with Giuseppe; but then the pertinent question arises, from whom did he learn his calling? Seeing the date of his birth, 1683, we should fix about the year 1695 for the starting of his apprenticeship, certainly not later than 1697; and if he had been in Stradivari's workshop it is difficult to believe that his very striking impress would not have occasionally revealed itself in some part of the work of the great master at that, or a later time—say between 1695 and 1715. We can only affirm as the result of prolonged scrutiny that we have never found the smallest vestige of proof of his co-operation with Stradivari at this period—years, we repeat, when in the natural order of things we should be entitled to find it.[2]

And what of the great master when in his old age? Was there co-operation then? Again we do not hesitate to answer in the negative, and to give voice to our belief that his real and only assistants at that period were the sons, who from 1720 to 1725 upwards contributed much more towards the output of the workshop than has hitherto been credited to them.

On the other hand, we see Bergonzi working to the same general dimensions as

---

[1] The working years generally assigned to Carlo Bergonzi by writers of the past are 1716–47.
[2] Bergonzi does not even refer to Stradivari on his labels.

those of the Guarneri, with a marked similarity in the form, curves of outline, and placing of the sound-holes—placed by Bergonzi, with rare exception, low down. Purfling, mitres, edge, blocks, linings, interior thicknesses, and other small points all show affinity; then again the character and texture of his varnish is infinitely more like that of the Guarneri (Giuseppe filius Andrea and del Gesù) than that of Stradivari; equally so the material, more especially his pine. Why not an earlier pupil of the same master as that of del Gesù? We make bold to throw out the suggestion, feeling it to be far more probable than the accepted belief that he was indebted for his training and knowledge to Antonio Stradivari.

If both the Giuseppe and Carlo Bergonzi had produced more, and had consistently labelled their instruments, as Stradivari did, we should be in a position to affirm their working relationship without the shadow of a doubt.

The smallness of Giuseppe's output during the last twenty years of his life—i.e. 1720-40, is really astonishing. What could he have been doing? Certainly not making instruments. If he had been, then we are reduced to the conjecture that they have not survived. But this we do not accept; firstly, because the hand of destruction works impartially: secondly, because we are aware of the survival and present existence of a considerable number of contemporary Italian instruments. We have no serious number of recognizable works of either Pietro the son, Carlo Bergonzi, or Giuseppe del Gesù—instruments made between 1720 and 1730—which would fill in the gap. We are therefore brought to the conclusion that not one of these four makers was producing with an activity in any way comparable to that of the illustrious veteran of the Piazza S. Domenico.

The latest dated example of the work of Giuseppe so far seen by us is of the year 1731, a violoncello, and made quite in the style of the contemporary violins. It is of the smaller form; the wood of the back is of poplar, and the sides are of beech—a choice of material not suggesting opulence. The label, the reproduction of which we give, is beyond question original, and the interesting alteration of the third printed figure 1 into 3, is to be noticed. We have never come across a violin of these years bearing a similarly dated label, and we repeat that we have so far not succeeded in tracing a single specimen of his work between the years 1731 and 1740. It is obviously possible that human frailty in some form may furnish the true explanation, indeed, we have good reason for suspecting that happiness no longer reigned in the Guarneri home and, the master-mind failing, the guiding hand of the workshop passed away. It is conceivable that the patronage of Giuseppe had been falling off for some years—beaten in the race, completely outdistanced by his more skilled and versatile colleague of the Piazza, he had more or less abandoned his work.

Consider for a moment these words culled from the deed registering the contract of sale of the Casa Guarneri, sold in May 1740, after the death of Giuseppe:

'Cum sit quod defuncto domino Josepho Guarnerio superstitibus et post se relichi Petro et Josepho eius filiis ac filiis etiam et heredibus domine Barbare de Franchis illius uxoris, hi cum agnoverint patris hereditatem pluribus onoratam esse debitis abea se abstinere debberaverint, credentes magis eis convenire in ea consequi dotale creditum matris quam in illa se immiscere;

'Cumque sit quod nil aliud in paterna hereditate compertum fuerit quam una domus sita in vicina Sti Matthei cum uno oculo appotheca, quam itaque vendere statuerunt. . . .'

'Seeing that the deceased Josepho Guarnerio left behind him Petro and Josepho, his sons, also sons of theirs, of the lady Barbara de Franchis, his wife, and that they, when they knew that their father's estate was loaded with debts, determined to abstain from any claim on it, thinking it more to their interest to claim in their mother's right for her dowry, and, as in the father's estate there was only one house situate in the Parish of S. Matteo with a small room, or shop which they decided therefore to sell. . . .'

To what cause could we attribute this lamentable state of the worldly affairs of the master? Vice, we fear, in some form, and one of the resultant effects would be this dearth in the production of instruments. This, too, would furnish the explanation of the non-burial of Giuseppe in the same tomb as his wife, Barbara Franchi; leading a dissolute life he had died elsewhere, neither loved nor cared for!

Pietro had very wisely turned his footsteps towards Venice, and the man who we shall presently learn was to continue the succession to the family calling at Cremona, will prove to be no other than the youngest son, Giuseppe, later to be known as Giuseppe del Gesù.

In reviewing the result of the life-work of the master and contrasting it with that of his father, it would seem that, on the whole, he has left us a violin representing a slightly higher conception, but violoncellos less so. The earliest violin followed Amati lines pure and simple, then we trace the influence of Stradivari of the nineties, equally that of his brother, Pietro of Mantua, and, lastly, we come to those interesting specimens which undoubtedly came from the workshop, beginning about 1715. Weigh matters as we will, we do feel, and feel very strongly, that their real authorship lies between Carlo Bergonzi and Giuseppe del Gesù.

To sum up, we judge the master's skill, as a craftsman, to have been superior to that of Andrea, yet we frequently detect in his work the same lack of real precision and the same somewhat hasty production, and we estimate that the remuneration received by him for his instruments approximated to that obtained by his father. In reality, he was throughout his life in large measure overshadowed by the ascendancy reached by Antonio Stradivari.

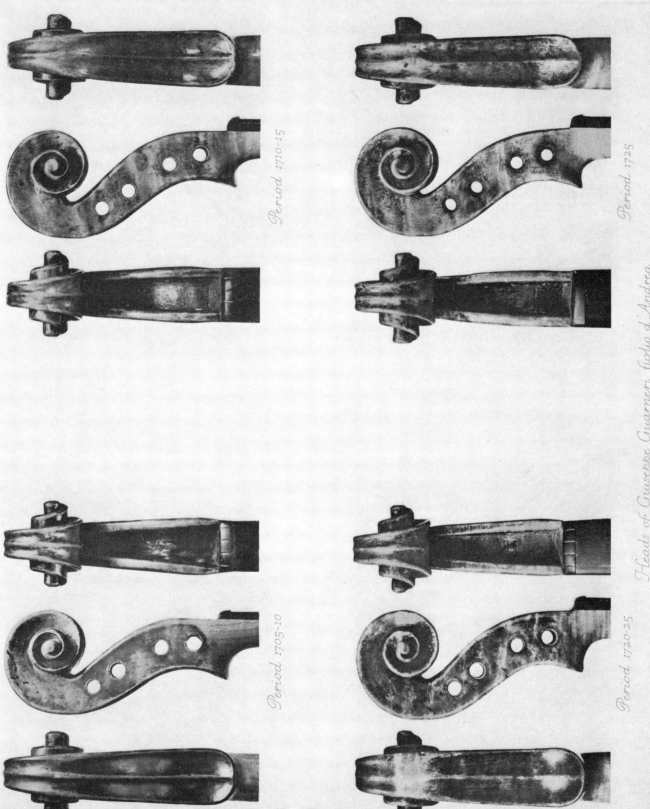

Period 1710-15

Period 1725

Period 1705-10

Period 1720-25

Heads of Giuseppe Guarneri figlio d'Andrea

Joseph Guarnerius filius Andreæ fecit Cremonæ (period 1700)

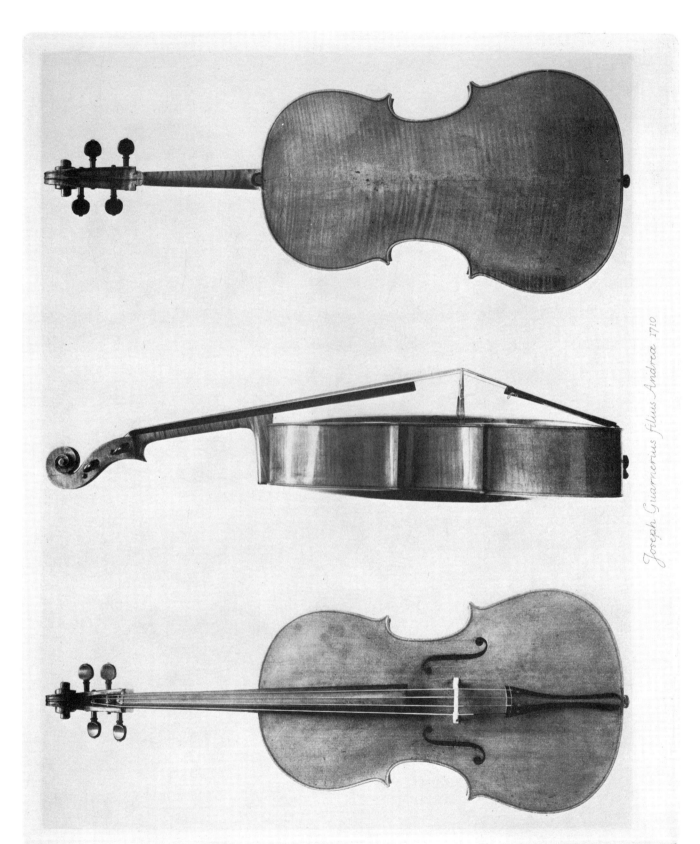

Joseph Guarnerius filius Andreæ 1710

Joseph Guarnerius filius Andreæ 1710

Joseph Guarnerius filius Andreæ fecit Cremonæ (period 1710–15)

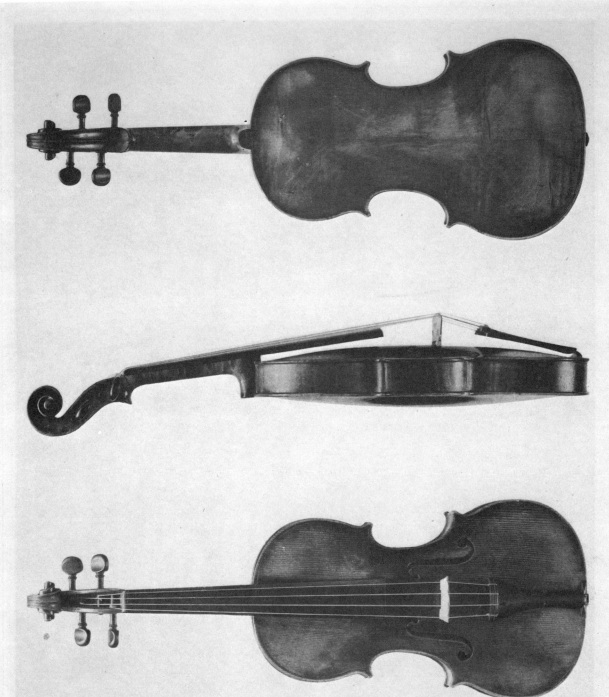

Joseph Guarnerius filius Andreæ period 1715-20

Joseph Guarnerius filius Andreæ period 1715-20

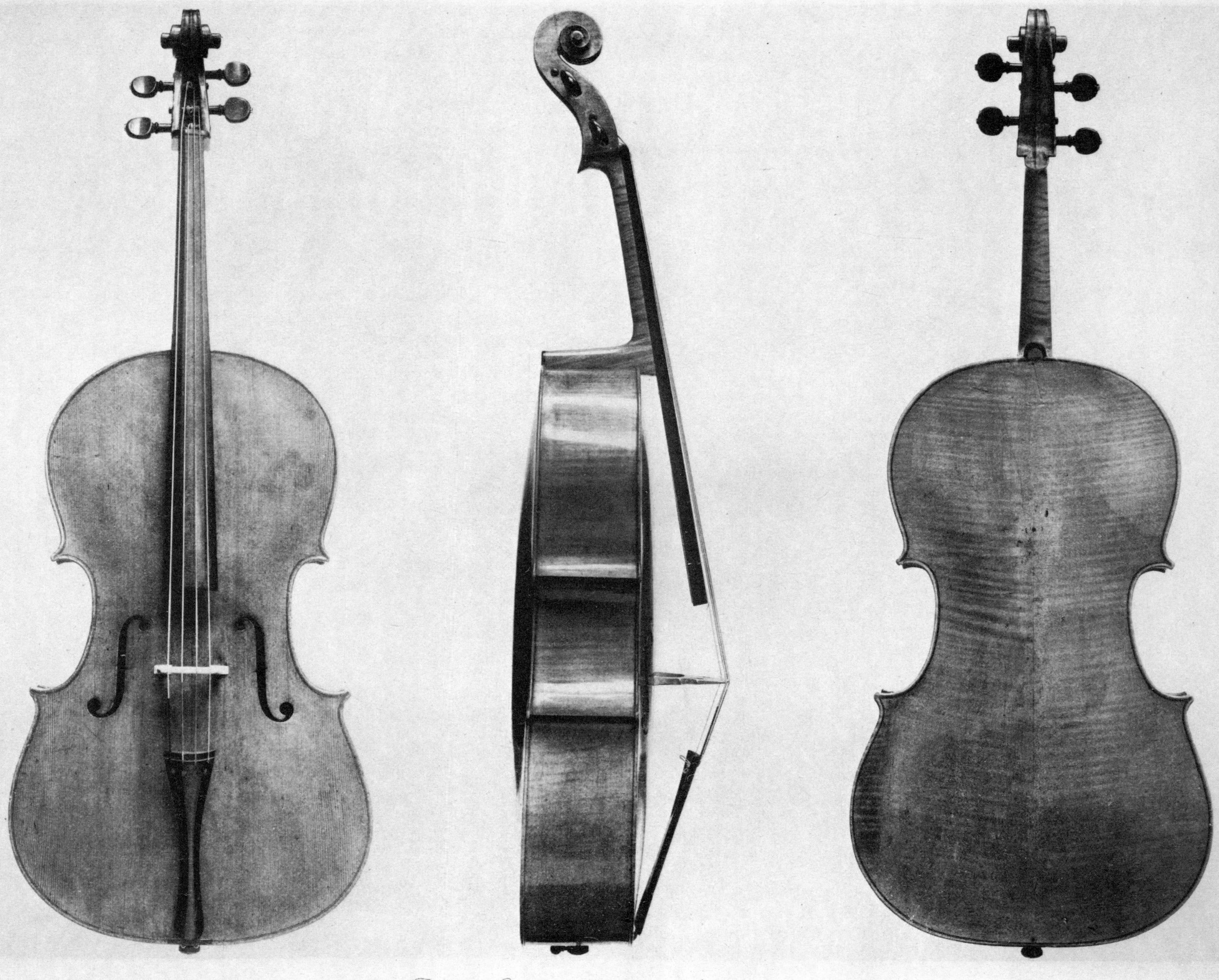

Joseph Guarnerius filius Andreæ 1710

CHAPTER IV
GIUSEPPE GUARNERI DEL GESÙ

BORN 1698, DIED 1744

Some are born great, some achieve greatness and some have greatness thrust upon them.

WE now turn to the consideration of the most illustrious of the Guarneri, Bartolomeo Giuseppe del Gesù, to whose reputation the halo which surrounds the family name is mainly due, and permits of it taking rank side by side with that of Antonio Stradivari. No name has ever evoked greater enthusiasm amongst true violin-lovers, no maker been more commented upon and discussed, yet, withal, there has hitherto survived a touch of mystery and romance concerning both the man and his works. The master's ability was striking; his craftsmanship excellent, though at times erratic; his conception wholly admirable, and, when we realize how doggedly, even through chequered days, he held to this conception of his own, although it was here and there but a burlesque of his better self, our admiration of his productions is whole-hearted, mingled, alas! with deep regret for what he might have achieved, in more fortunate circumstances, for the benefit of posterity.

The master's life was a brief one, whether due to the consequences of crime, as has been suggested, or to some less sinister cause, we shall probably never learn. But that he was born to his calling and started on its threshold with a real love for his art is writ large on the works which he has left to us. To assert that he was not indebted to his predecessors and contemporaries would be, obviously, absurd, for, after having mastered the rudiments in the workshop of Joseph filius Andreæ, he turned to the fountain's source, Brescia, then gazed, and not infrequently, at the productions of the Veteran of the Piazza, and, finally shaking himself free from them all, gave to the world, during fifteen to twenty brief years, violins—violins only, we believe—which will ever be acclaimed by the lover of our subject as instruments of unsurpassable charm and originality.

Who was, in reality, this remarkable man, now universally known as Joseph[1] Guarnerius del Gesù,[2] this maker whose works, honoured by few at the time of their birth, were ultimately to challenge, and at times to challenge successfully, the

---

[1] Joseph is the Hebrew form of the name and was frequently used in Italian.
[2] See explanation of term del Gesù, p. 71.

supremacy of the greatest? Who was this man, destined to prove himself possessed of unrivalled fertility; here and there rising to great heights, yet leading a life marred to a great extent by ill fortune, which his admirers would fain believe was not of his own creating?

> 'Whether men think well or ill of thee, thou art not therefore another man.'
>
> THOMAS À KEMPIS.

The hitherto accepted belief is that first recorded by Fétis,[1] on the authority of J. B. Vuillaume, who caused researches to be made in the Archives of Cremona in the year 1855—viz. that Giuseppe Antonio was the son of Giovanni Battista Guarneri and Angiola Maria Locadelli, born on the 8th of June 1683, and baptized on the 11th of the same month. Fétis adds that the master himself inscribed on certain of his labels 'Joseph Guarnerius, Andreae nepos', thus indicating that he was a nephew of Andrea.

Neither of these statements is correct, no *original* Guarneri label so worded has ever been seen by the present writers, and we can only suggest that Vuillaume must have been misled by some fabricated inscription of early origin,[2] or by erroneous information obtained from Italian sources. That the Cremonese researches should prove to be equally incorrect was due, we believe, to the inexperience of Paolo Lombardini, the Cremonese priest who carried them out. The old priest simply sought in the Parish Registers for the birth of a Giuseppe Guarneri towards the end of the seventeenth century. His task was stimulated, so we learn, by Vuillaume's signed photograph only! And coming across a branch of the 'Guarneri' to whom a son was born named 'Giuseppe', he assumed that the infant in question must be the 'Simon Pure'. Thus matters remained until the year 1886, when the Marquis de Piccolellis[3] published the results of more thorough research then recently made in Cremona by the Rev. Gaetano Bazzi. These researches furnished not only the proof that the above-mentioned 'Giuseppe' had died in infancy, but that a second son had been born to the same parents on the 11th of October 1686, who also was christened by the name of Giuseppe. Piccolellis therefore concluded that this second son was the future celebrated violin-maker. Later writers have all accepted one or other of these versions. As to the exact date of the master's death, nothing quite definite had hitherto been known. The statement of Fétis, recording the tradition handed down

---

[1] *Antoine Stradivari*, by F. J. Fétis, Paris, 1856.
[2] We have seen fictitious labels so worded.
[3] The late Marquis was an ardent amateur and student of the violin and its makers. We are indebted to him for *Liutai Antichi e Moderni*, Florence, 1885.

in Cremona and related by the last of the Bergonzi, who died in 1838, that 'Guar-neri del Gesù died in the year 1745', has invariably been accepted. So much for tradition, and as we shall later see, it was not far wrong.

Now for the real facts—and we will first take up the question of birth and identity. Repeated examination of various instruments, the work respectively of Giuseppe filius Andrea and Giuseppe del Gesù, had long convinced us of the working inti-macy which existed between the two men; hence, we reasoned that a thorough scrutiny of the census returns relating to the household of Giuseppe filius might possibly throw some light on the identity of Giuseppe del Gesù. We had noted, as first recorded by Piccolellis, the birth of a third son to Giuseppe filius, who was christened by the names of Bartolomeo Joseph,[1] but the significance of this fact only dawned upon us when Signor Livi pointed out that this child figures in all the subsequent census returns without exception as 'Giuseppe' alone.

Why, we then asked ourselves, should not this son prove to be the true 'del Gesù' rather than another Giuseppe coming from an assumed collateral branch of the family? We say 'assumed', because no proof of relationship has been cited by either Fétis or Piccolellis. 'Why not?' we repeated to ourselves, and the more we considered all the circumstances the stronger became our convictions. This child was baptized in the names of his paternal great-grandfather and father on the day of his birth—21st August 1698, the same year that marked the death of Andrea; he figures (as will have been noted in the preceding chapter, page 56) for the first time in the census returns for the year 1699; and onwards up to and including the year 1722 he is regularly to be found a member of the household of Giuseppe filius, A.

In 1723 his name disappears from the family census, nor is it again to be found in the returns by the father to the end of his life. We dismissed the idea of death, for the very obvious reason that we were fairly convinced that he and none other was the real 'del Gesù', and therefore we were aware of his later existence. We considered that the most reasonable explanation of his departure was that of marriage, and that possibly, as in the case of his grandfather Andrea, he had gone with his bride to live at the house of her parents. In any case the problem confronting us was to find which of the thirty-seven parishes of Cremona he had chosen as his home.

Let us here pause for a moment in order to clear up the history of the two hitherto accepted claimants to the name of Giuseppe del Gesù. We start by ruling out the

---

[1] See baptismal certificate, Chap. III, p. 55.

A.

Stato dell'Anime p̃ l'Anno Corrente 1722.

1.   Casa parrocchiale
2.   Casa Soccini
3.   Casa Rossi
4.   Casa Aselli
5.   Casa PASQUALI

6.   Casa Guarneri
    Giuseppe Guarneri an· 55· ch· c· c·
    Barbara Franchi mog.ᵉ an· 52· ch· c· c·
    Giuseppe fig.° an 21 ch· c· c·

7.   Casa STEFANONI
8.   Casa Rolla
9.   1ª casa di S. Domenico
10.   2ª Casa di S. Domenico

11.   Casa Stradiuari

12.   Casa Meschieri &c. &c.

Census Return for the Current Year 1722

Piazza S. Domenico.

1. Parish House.
2. House of the Soccini.
3. House of the Rossi.
4. House of the Aselli.
5. House of the Pasquali.
6. House of the Guarneri.

Giuseppe Guarneri, 55 years, christened, confirmed, communicant

Barbara Franchi, wife, 52 years, christened, confirmed, communicant.

Giuseppe, son, 21 years, christened, confirmed, communicant

7. House of the Stefanoni.
8. House of the Rolla.
9. 1st house belonging to S. Domenico.
10. 2nd house belonging to S. Domenico.
11. House of the Stradivari.
12. House of the Meschieri.

B.

July 16th, 1683[1]

Joseff Antonio Guarneri died on the 7th day of the last named month & rests in communion with the dead reposing here in S. Donato. He was the son of Giovanni Battista, of this Parish.

C.

October 20th, 1686.[1]

Giuseppe Guarneri, the son of Giovanni Battista, passed, yesterday, the 19th, from this, to a better life, aged 5 days, and was buried in the Parish Church of S. Donato, on the 20th, as above.

D.

October 27th, 1702.[1]

Joseph Antonio, the two-day-old infant son of Joannes Baptista Guarneri, died and was buried, the same day, in this Parish Church.

[1] The above entries are taken from the Register of Deaths of the Parish of San Donato.

child accepted by Fétis and other writers, for we are able to produce the certificate of death proving that he died on the 7th of July 1683, *B*. We are then faced by the second son, whose birth was first revealed by Piccolellis, born to the same parents on the 14th day of October 1686, and baptized on the 17th in the name of Giuseppe. But here again death stole into the household; and this second son of Giovanni Battista Guarneri and Maria Locadelli was buried, as the certificate records, on the 20th of the same month, *C*. Thus the second Pretender is disposed of.

Here we might very well have left matters, for we repeat that no evidence has ever been brought forward—nor have we succeeded in finding any—in support of the claim that this branch of the Guarneri was even connected with the violin-makers. But we decided to continue a close scrutiny of the later census returns, and curiously enough we see recorded a third son of the family bearing the name of Giuseppe, though we have failed to find the date of his birth. In 1702 he disappears, and no doubt had died, otherwise another son would not have been given the same name; for on the 25th of October of the same year a fourth son is born, yet again to be christened Giuseppe Antonio, and fated to survive only two days, *D*. For the year 1703 no 'Giuseppe' figures in the census returns; and in the following year the family leave the Parish of San Donato to disappear into the unknown. And we have not thought it necessary to seek to follow them.

After thus eliminating this branch of the Guarneri we will get back to the man of our choice, and the year 1723 in which Bartolomeo Giuseppe takes leave of the paternal home. He was then twenty-five years of age. Had he really decided upon marriage and a life separate from his father?

In order to clear up the former point, we requested Signor Livi to make a thorough examination of all the Cremonese marriage registers of the period. His researches on this occasion, we regret to say, proved in vain, a disappointing result, but understandable when we bear in mind the obvious possibility that Giuseppe had chosen a bride living elsewhere than in the city or its vicinity.

We have some evidence, though slight, in favour of the separate existence. The earliest dated violin of Giuseppe del Gesù hitherto seen by us is of the year 1726,[1] that is, within three years of leaving his father. And we note that the text of this label never varies in any detail whatsoever throughout the master's whole career; he abandons the tradition of his predecessors who worked under the auspices of the

---

[1] It is interesting to compare this date with that suggested by Charles Reade. (See footnote, p. 87.)

patron Saint Teresia, and adopts instead the cipher 'J.H.S.'[1] surmounted by the Cross; hence his Italian designation of 'Guarneri del Gesù'.

Observe also that the master, unlike the other three members of the family, makes no mention of his parentage. Perhaps he himself wished to avoid having his instruments confused with those of his father. Both bore the same Christian name, both were unquestionably working for some few years contemporaneously; and we suggest that these facts would supply a practical explanation for the omissions in the text of the label which he inserted in his violins.

These points, small though they be, do rather encourage us to think that their lives were spent apart. The master's work certainly indicates that of a man of independent ideas. Perhaps he was equally of independent character, and not imbued with that filial affection to which Andrea, the grandfather, makes touching allusion in the wills of 1692 and 1694.

Did Giuseppe receive a rudimentary education? The position occupied by the family would justify us in thinking so. We see that the figures added to his labels are as a rule excellently formed, but more than this we cannot say, for so far not a scrap of his handwriting, not even a marginal note added to one of his labels, has ever come to light. It is quite conceivable that he owed his education to the Jesuits; no doubt there were members of that great teaching Order settled in Cremona, and here perhaps is a further explanation of the adoption of the cipher on his labels.

We were in no sense daunted by our failure to find the master's marriage record, and year in year out Signor Livi followed up with indomitable perseverance any clue likely to lead us to the footsteps of Giuseppe after the year 1723. At one time, in the early days of our Cremona researches, we thought we had unearthed him living as late as 1773 in retirement at the Convent attached to S. Domenico; for Signor Livi came across a Notarial Act of that year in which there figured as a

---

[1] This appellation is no doubt due to his veneration of the Holy Name, to which his labels with the monogram JHS (the Greek abbreviation of Jesus, Italian Gesù) bear testimony. The practice of inscribing this monogram on private and public buildings, yea, even on streets and corners, was very prevalent in the north of Italy in the fifteenth, sixteenth, and seventeenth centuries, and owes its origin to the preaching of S. Bernardino of Siena, a Franciscan Friar, who designed the monogram in 1410, at Camaiore, where, for the first time, holding it up to the veneration of the faithful, he exhorted his hearers to keep this Holy Name constantly before them to remind them of their Saviour (the name Jesus signifying Saviour). It was the favourite subject of his discourse, and we learn that at Bergamo, which at that time was torn by rival factions, he persuaded the citizens to live in peace together, to remove party emblems that had been set up over every door and window and even on Church furniture, and to replace them by the sacred Name of Jesus. One of the most interesting portraits of the saint is that depicting him bearing the sacred monogram in his hand, by Pietro di Giovanni Ambossi, Sassatta's assistant, in 1439. S. Bernardino was connected with many of the fascinating Sienese artists of his day, who, at his bidding, painted the sacred monogram on thousands of buildings. (See *Life of S. Bernardino of Siena*, by A. G. Ferrers Howell.)

witness *'Josepho Guarneri f.q. Johannis Baptiste degente in dicto venerando Conventi'* ('Joseph Guarneri, son of the late Joannes Baptista, residing in the said venerable Convent'), but later inquiries proved him to be the 'ex portinaio' of the Convent, and not the real 'Joseph'. Quite possibly this man was directly connected with the branch Guarneri-Locadelli.

In resuming our quest we reasoned thus: Stradivari was still living under the shadow of S. Domenico, where he had passed a long and successful career devoted to our craft. Would not the knowledge of his presence there serve as an attraction to any of his fellow workers to settle in more or less close proximity? We thought it would, and therefore determined to focus our attention on the houses radiating around the Piazza S. Domenico. We recalled that the Casa Orcelli, situated in the Piazza, had finally passed to Andrea Guarneri, and from him to his son Giuseppe, in whose hands it had remained until death. What then was its subsequent history?

With a view to solving this question Signor Livi decided in the autumn of 1917 to make a renewed effort of research in the Notarial Archives of Cremona, and to devote special attention to the contracts drawn up by the Notary Giulio-Cesare Porro, who had acted for the Guarneri family in the past.

Now we will let our friend speak for himself. He writes: 'I examined contract after contract; many of them were not indexed, and in vain did I cast about for the name "Guarneri", when as by a miraculous impulse I took up a deed indexed out in the name of Galanti and Arrighi—nothing to suggest connexion with Guarneri. Curiosity, and curiosity alone prompted my perusal of the deed, and great was my joy on scanning it through to find the very name I had been so vainly seeking. The deed bears the date May the 24th of the year 1740, and I found it to be the contract of sale of the house known as the Casa Guarneri situated in the Parish of S. Matteo, entered into *by Josepho Guarneri son of the late Josephi, living in the Parish of S. Prospero, and Petri Guarneri brother of the said Josephi, living in the City of Venice,* and one Antonio Arrighi[1] through the intermediary of Antonio Galanti.'

The deed, drawn up in Latin and Italian, consists of some six or seven pages, the gist of which is as follows: firstly, by an Act of Procuration, Dominus Pietro Guarneri, son of the late Giuseppe, does appoint, depute, and elect as his legitimate procurator and administrator, one Dominus Giovachino Botte, who in the former's absence is authorized to sell in his name and hand over to others, the half-share

---

[1] Giacomo Antonio Arrighi was the 'Maestro di Capella' of the Cathedral of Cremona. He was born in 1702 and died in 1746.

accruing to him of the maternal dot consisting of half a house, the dowry of the late Signora Barbara Franchi, his mother, situated in the Parish of S. Matteo in Cre-mona. Apparently the house was mortgaged for 1,000 lire of Cremonese money, and stipulation is made that no binding agreement be made before this mortgage be repaid. Especially interesting is the further paragraph mentioning that the pur-chaser has bought from Dom. Josepho Guarnerio, *son of the late Josephi* and Dom. Joachina Botti acting as procurator for *Dom Petri Guarneri, brother of Dom. Josephi,* living in the State of Venice. A description of the house follows. The sum of 3,000 lire imperiali[1] is named as the purchase price; and it is stated that the house is an inheritance from their *late father Josephi* (see Chapter VI).

Here was indeed a fortunate find; the goal of many and persistent efforts was at length reached, for not only were we obtaining absolute confirmation of the identity of Giuseppe del Gesù, but further, and equally important, we were learning the name of the parish where he was then living—exactly as we had surmised—within a stone's throw of his great compeer.

The next step was to turn to the records of S. Prospero[2] and search for the census returns; and our readers may imagine the elation of Signor Livi on discovering the returns made by Giuseppe del Gesù beginning with the year 1731 and continuing without one single interruption until the year 1744, which, as we shall learn later, was that of his death.

The exact entry of the first census return, a facsimile of which we reproduce, p. 86, reads as follows:

Casa di S. Bernardo.

Giuseppe Guarneri of the late Giuseppe, aged 34.
Catterina Roda, wife of Giuseppe,   „   30.

It will not escape notice that this census extract of the year 1731 speaks of the father of del Gesù as the late Giuseppe; obviously incorrect as the similar returns furnished by the 'Casa Guarneri' prove the contrary. Signor Livi by way of ex-planation points out that these returns were with few exceptions made out by the

[1] The Milanese lira imperiale (the Milanese provinces being then under the sway of Austria) was reckoned at 14½ to the gold sequin, the approximate value of which at this period was 8s. 4d. of our money; consequently the price paid for the house amounted to about £86–7, and its purchasing power prior to 1914 would be from three to four times greater. (See value of money given in *Life of Stradivari*, p. 249.)

[2] The Parish of S. Prospero was suppressed in 1788, and the church itself, which dated from the thirteenth century, was closed for public worship in 1796, then used for secular purposes, and finally transformed into ordinary dwellings; consequently no vestige of the tombs or monuments which it contained are now to be seen, nor have we succeeded in finding either drawing or illustration of the church. The Registers were transferred to the Archives of the Cathedral.

parish priest; and it is not rare to find them unreliable in minor details. We are unable to throw any light on the identity of Catterina Roda, or *Rota* as suggested by Livi, the latter being a name not unknown in Cremona, and one actually borne by a Cremonese violin maker, Joannes Rota, who was working there at the beginning of the nineteenth century, and who migrated later to Mantua. Fetis,[1] on the other hand, gives credence to the tradition that the wife of del Gesù was a native of the Tyrol.

We are nevertheless conscious of having achieved substantial progress, for the true identity of Giuseppe del Gesù stands revealed once and for all time, as well as the correct dates of both his birth and death. This last point we shall deal with later.

Would that it were possible to clear up in the same satisfactory manner the mystery as to the activities of the master between the year 1723, when he left his father's house, and 1731, when his presence in the Casa S. Bernardo is first noted. The record of his age and that of his wife certainly tend to confirm our belief that marriage was one of the reasons of his leaving the paternal home; but when we turn our attention to his working career we have to confess that we still find ourselves groping vaguely in the dark. Now we must remember that from 1720 onward the workshop of Giuseppe filius Andrea shows but small signs of activity. Probably, as already suggested, the master had in great measure abandoned his work, but even then, what of the two sons? The fact that Pietro left Cremona about 1722–24 to settle in Venice points either to an insufficiency of orders for instruments at home, or to the fact that life under his father's roof was no longer congenial. The more con-vivial life to be found in a famous city like Venice may be the true explanation, and let us add that there was a continual demand there for instruments which were the work of the famous Cremonese makers. Much playing was going on, and the city's exports were considerable.

Pietro thus disposed of for the present, what then was del Gesù doing? We have previously recorded that he did sign a violin in 1726 with his own distinctive label. Where was he actually engaged in his work, and where was he living up to the year 1731? Both queries offer matter for speculation, and are incapable of clear explana-tion with our present knowledge. But one thing is quite evident, and that is that the violins which the master was presumably making are for the most part now non-existent; further, the relatively few examples of this period which do exist were not, with possibly rare exceptions, labelled by him.

---

[1] *Antonio Stradivari*, Fétis, p. 109.

Two highly instructive documents have recently come to our knowledge which touch incidentally on this very question about Giuseppe living his own life apart from his father. Their contents shed a flood of light on the point, and actually confirm what has hitherto been only conjecture on our part.

These deeds, the one drawn up by the Cremonese Notary, Nicolò Porro, dated 10th May 1738, the other by Bernardino Vardelli, dated 11th December 1739, are concerned with the raising of a mortgage of 330 lire in the then current Cremonese money, on the security of the parental house, the Casa Guarneri.

The first deed speaks of '*Domini Joseph filius quondam Andreae vicinie Sti. Matthei et dominus Bartholomeus vicinie Sti Prosperi presentis civitatis pater et filius.*' ('Dom. Joseph son of the late Andrea living in the Parish of S. Matteo, and *Dom. Bartolomeo*[1] living in the Parish of S. Prospero of this city, *father and son.*') The house is referred to as of the dowry of the late Signora Barbara Franchi, mother of the said Bartolomeo *living apart from his father and carrying on his business independently of the said father since over seventeen years.*

The second deed speaks of '*Joseph Guarnerius filius alterius Joseph, vicinie Sti Prosperi huius civitatis, separatim tamen vivens a dicto eius patre negotiaque sua de per se et independenter ab eo gerens tamquam Paterfamilias ab annis decem et octo citra.*' ('Joseph Guarnerius, son of the other Joseph, of the Parish of S. Prospero of this city, nevertheless living separately from his said father, and carrying on his business by himself and independently of him as the head of a family since eighteen years.')

The master affirms having received the amount of the loan, and states that it was used by him in settlement of a debt of similar amount to Georgius Plainer, who had threatened him with legal proceedings.

Here then we have real enlightenment. Giuseppe del Gesù had left home in or about the year 1722–23, set up a separate establishment, and was actually working as a liutaio apart from his father. His brother had previously done the same. Neither was apparently willing to continue the family tradition of dedicating his work to the patron Saint Teresia; and the fact that both the sons abandoned the parental workshop does undoubtedly suggest that their presence there was either unnecessary, or, what is the more probable, uncongenial.

Apparently the past was to repeat itself; for had not Pietro of Mantua suffered the

---

[1] It will be recalled that the master was baptized in the names of Bartolomeo Joseph (see Chapter III, p. 55).

reproaches of his parents for having similarly left home and workshop some forty years earlier? Were father and son nevertheless in touch with each other? We do not

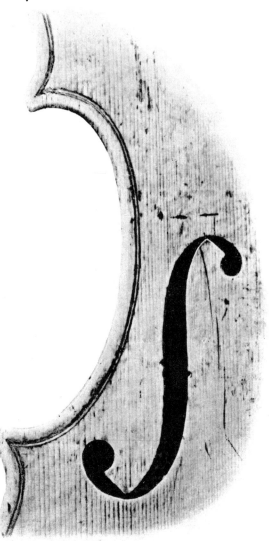

FIG. I. Edge, purfling, and sound-hole of an example of the period 1730-33.

know, but we do observe that the block or type utilized by del Gesù to print his labels was identical with that made use of by the father and grandfather in the latter years of their lives. (See labels, Chapter VII.)

Only after long observation do we venture to state our conviction that most of the instruments of the last period of Giuseppe filius, and also a considerable number of those of del Gesù—notably his earliest works—were sent into the world without labels, and the labels which these instruments bear to-day were inserted during the nineteenth century,[1] in the main with honest intention. But more frequently than not they were dated inaccurately, and no care was given to ensure quite correct reproductions of an original.

We must conclude that a spirit of nonchalance had invaded the 'Guarneri' environment. Working more, so to speak, from hand to mouth, they frequently did not trouble to sign their productions unless asked to do so. Another solution of this problem occurs to us when seeking the reason for the scarcity of del Gesù's early works. May he not, following in the footsteps of his ancestor Orcelli, and his uncle and godfather, Pietro, also have been both a player and maker of violins, a player of more ordinary capacity than his relatives, possessed of no desire to be attached to one of the Ducal Courts?

Singing and dancing to the accompaniment of music was much favoured by the

---

[1] Taking 100 Guarneri del Gesù violins of all periods we find only 60 bearing original labels; in the case of Stradivari the similar percentage works out at 90.

mass of the people throughout Italy; and Cremona, the seat of instrument-making, must from this very fact have inspired some members of her craftsmen families to become players. We have no doubt that such was the case; and supposing it in the case of del Gesù, his double calling would in the circumstances seem to fit in with the tradition handed down to us by the last of the Bergonzi.[1]

Having now dealt fully with the master's identity we will take up the direct subject of his violins, starting with the recognized examples of his early years—i.e. those made previous to and during the year 1730.

All, without exception, are instruments of finished work, and reveal the master as an experienced workman; there is nothing to suggest the impulsive genius stepping into the arena, and producing examples of startling originality. On the contrary he had been correctly trained in the workshop of his father, where we have already suggested he had as fellow workers Carlo Bergonzi and his brother Pietro.

He started life, then, as a good and well-trained craftsman. Let us analyse a violin typical of these years, which stands before us.

First note its dimensions:

Length	.	14	inches bare	
Width	.	$8\frac{1}{8}$	,,	
,,	.	$6\frac{9}{16}$	,,	
Sides	.	$1\frac{1}{4}$	,,	,,
,,	.	$1\frac{3}{16}$	,,	,,

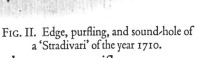

FIG. II. Edge, purfling, and sound-hole of a 'Stradivari' of the year 1710.

The outline is distinctly founded on Stradivari, the bouts are a trifle more curved, the shoulders less square, the lower curves if anything lacking in breadth, the corners

[1] Carlo Bergonzi (1758–1838) (son of Michel Angelo and grandson of the first Carlo) is stated to have said that Guarneri del Gesù had led an irregular life, was lazy and negligent, and addicted to drink and the other pleasures of this world. His wife, born in the Tyrol, had not found happiness with him, yet notwithstanding helped him with his work. *Antonio Stradivari*, Fétis, p. 109.

of moderate length, cut without striking precision. The edge is of excellent aspect, its thickness regular, and the margin around the sides normal. The modelling of both back and table is noticeably flat, inspired more by Maggini than anybody else, rising with modest fluting immediately, though not precipitately, from the purfling. The *f*-holes are of Stradivari form,[1] cut more open, and less refined; the wings are heavier and barely fluted, with holes of full size; and we see a Bergonzi-like touch about the shape of the bottom ones. The nicks are fully pronounced. The head is of sober proportions, the throw of the volute of good breadth; the first spiral is kept low and the tips are carved on the small side, nor do they protrude when viewed from the front. The fluting is flat and not remarkably true, with the mortice roughly cut but well open—a most useful feature and one from which the master with all his vagaries but rarely departed. The irregularly formed chamfer of the head and the mitre joints of the sides are picked out in black, an unvarying characteristic of his work.

His oil varnish, both soft in quality and light in texture, is excellently put on, with the colour varying between a pale orange, orange-brown, and occasionally a tint approaching red.

To sum up, we have in this and other contemporary examples violins constructed on thoroughly sound principles, and showing true and well-finished work, comprising qualities reminiscent of his father, something of Stradivari, and a touch of Bergonzi.

They are not the work of a consummate craftsman whom we should rank with the foremost of the Amati, or with Stradivari; yet, whatever their shortcomings, we get more than due compensation from their marked virility and individuality.

The following are characteristic examples of the early years:

1726. Mrs. Stretton, ex Chas. Finch
Period 1726–30. Mr. W. W. Cobbett, ex Downs
1729. Mr. T. D. Brown, ex Heath
Period 1729–30. Miss Chapman, ex Bennett
1730. Mr. A. Payne, ex Ferdinand David
1730. Frl. Rode, ex von Heyder
1732. Mr. T. Spiering, ex Pixis

Now, who were the patrons of the master? Assuredly not the Church or the

[1] See Figs. I and II.

nobility. It is far more likely that his productions passed into the hands of those who played hard and earned little. And may not this early wear and tear in their exis⁄ tence account for the relatively fewer surviving finely preserved examples, when compared with those of Stradivari?

The next ten years, 1730–40, proclaim the master's rise, his zenith, and if not the decline, yet the beginning of the end. True, the four years which followed this period were still to prove fruitful; yet, if we contrast this brief term of life's labour with that of Stradivari, now passing on to the final haven of rest, we find in the one case the man's lifework practically crowded into a quite short span; in the case of the other, decade following decade, Stradivari still hale and well in 1730 at the advanced age of eighty⁄six, and continuing with unflagging vigour to shape vio⁄ lins which future generations were to gaze upon with intense admiration and profound respect.

In December of the year 1737 the great master passed away at the ripe old age of ninety⁄ three. He had nobly upheld and carried onward the widespread fame of Cremona as the home of violin⁄making; and his unrivalled gifts, his intense personality, had in a sense cast a spell over the 'Guarneri' for upwards of fifty years. That domination was now to cease.

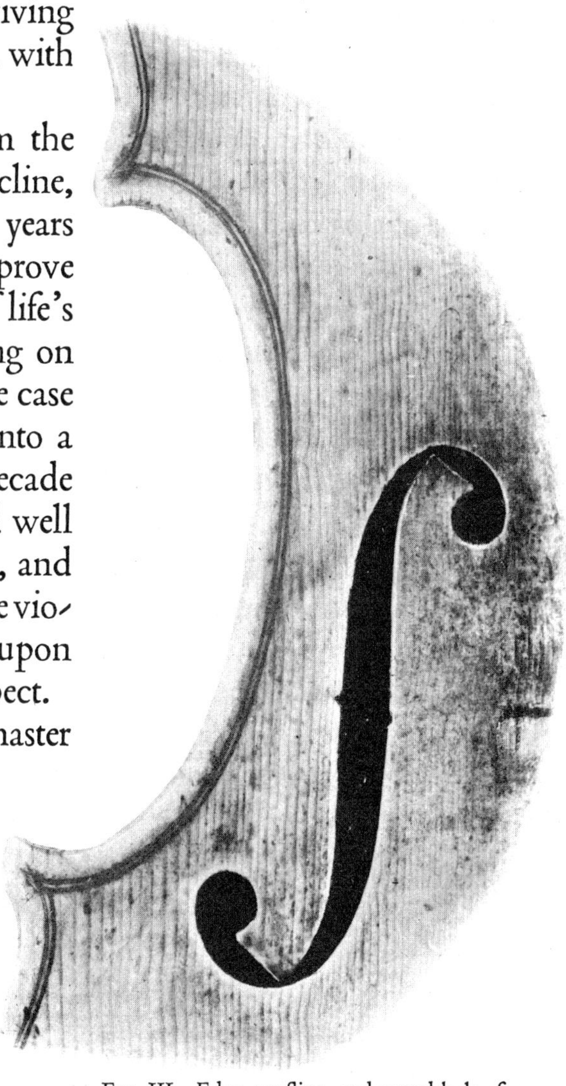

Would that we were possessed of the

FIG. III. Edge, purfling, and sound⁄hole of an example of the period 1734–35.

power to divine the thoughts of del Gesù on that December day as he followed the mortal remains of his venerable colleague across the Piazza to their resting⁄place in the Church of S. Domenico. Would that he had realized that now was the supreme moment of his life: that he and he alone of Cremona's sons was sufficiently well endowed to safeguard the prestige of that splendid heritage of the city's past.

But it was not to be; and we can only conclude that the master neither sought nor heeded the call.

After 1730 del Gesù soon gave proof of his matured ability; and now let us try to convey to our readers a pen picture of the man at his work. Haste, relatively speaking, was ever present throughout all he touched; we can trace no loving pauses to admire the beauty of the material which he was shaping into life, for there was no reason to pause and wonder how his productions would be received by the Musician of this or that Ducal Court. No, he was working for the peasant rather than the noble, the itinerant musician rather than the wealthy dilettante; and the price received when his violin was finished and sent forth on its career was repre-sented by a modest number of lire imperiali. If we were asked to hazard a figure we should answer about half the remuneration paid to his greater contemporary.[1]

The material selected for his instruments was usually of quite good acoustical quality—what one would in fact expect from a trained maker; but the maple was rarely cut from an exceptionally fine tree as regards the figure; and we have not in a single instance met with a choice of maple of arresting appearance utilized for the whole instrument, back, sides, and head alike, as in Stradivari's productions in certain years. Del Gesù made use of wood of either foreign or native growth, the backs at times sufficiently handsome, with sides and head plain, or vice versa. In the majority of instances the sides were made from plainly figured wood; it is obvious that his selection was somewhat limited, doubtless on account of the cost; though on the other hand we have to place on record the fact that, unlike the other members of his own family and even Stradivari himself, we have never seen nor heard of his having made use of the cheaper woods such as poplar, willow, or beech. His pine was excellent from the start—a stiff and vigorous type of wood; and it has been pointed out by past writers that many tables cut from this particular pine-tree show a sap-mark running down on either flank. This is found in a good many of the violins, but it is not always the case. It is instructive to see that Carlo Bergonzi at times utilized pine cut from this self-same tree! Did both men obtain their wood from the same source, and is this not a further indication of working intimacy?

The Italian free and easy method of construction was admirably suited to a man possessing the temperament of del Gesù; he had fixed his mind upon a model of the length of $13\frac{7}{8}$ inches—at times a trifle longer or shorter, the more often shorter—a

[1] See *Antonio Stradivari*, Chap. XI.

model of small dimensions, relatively little it is true, but under the normal if we accept the average 14-inch Stradivari as our standard. Quite three-fourths of his instruments were made to these proportions; and we cannot call to our remem- brance a violin of the full 14-inch model plus the respective standard widths of $8\frac{1}{4}$ and $6\frac{11}{16}$ and sides of $1\frac{1}{4}$ and $1\frac{3}{16}$. A few examples do exist of the normal 14-inch size; in these the widths are invariably narrow, compensated for in certain instances by sides of abnormal height. The master fixed the position of his sound holes with a view to the bridge being placed so as to give a body stop of $7\frac{1}{2}$ inches in length— Stradivari$=7\frac{5}{8}$—at times they were set to give a stop of $7\frac{3}{8}$ only; and one finds generally in these latter cases that the nicks of the f-holes have been filled up and recut lower down in order to preserve the harmony existing between the bridge and nicks when the stop was thus lengthened to suit the normal player.

Once the approximate form of outline decided, and the primitive mould made in accordance, we see del Gesù starting to fix on it the six blocks—note that they were invariably of pine—then shaping them (he probably considered the use of a square superfluous) and proceeding to bend and glue the sides to them. The corner blocks were not left true by the gouge—the only tool he made use of—nor were the sides quite accurately bent. One of the obvious reasons why these latter were more often made from plainly figured wood was because such material presented less trouble in the process of bending. If, as from time to time was the case, handsomely figured wood was utilized and the strong curl resisted the bending process, then we see a series of flats in place of the perfect curve, or even splits on the interior sides; and the work was left thus. And we cannot say the master was over particular in making his sides conform quite accurately to the mould. Approximately correct was in all cases sufficient unto the day!

After deciding the height of the sides—here left too low, there above the normal— the master proceeds to glue to them the linings—again invariably of pine—roughly mortising those of the bouts into the corner blocks, and then trimming away in a similarly hasty manner. The sides finished, the next step was to form the approxi- mate outline of both back and table, done by placing the sides alternately on the chosen and prepared slabs of pine and maple, and then passing a tracing point around their contour, allowing an extra margin for the formation of the outer edge. At times this margin was very meagre, never over-generous as was frequently the case with Stradivari in pre-1690 years; nor was much time spent in rounding accurately the under-edge; in fact, at the corners, it was left in most cases fresh from the chisel or flat file.

Del Gesù shaped his corners on the small side, short in his early years, then longer and hook-like in appearance—very rarely all in agreement. Once the outline sawn out and roughly trimmed up, he proceeds to model the surface; and here we find him fairly consistent for some years; the model was kept flat, rising gently from the purfling, and either that of the back or the table being left the higher, with the edge more deeply fluted.

Then he turns to the thicknessing, and we note a continuation of Amati principles with his own modifications. He adheres to the principle of a back left thick at the centre, in some instances abnormally so, but more generally we find the back varying from a centre of $1\frac{4}{64}$–$1\frac{2}{64}$ to flanks of $\frac{1}{8}$–$\frac{6}{64}$ or $\frac{7}{64}$. The thickness of his tables also varies a good deal, here $\frac{6}{64}$–$\frac{7}{64}$ all over, there $\frac{1}{8}$, and in parts as much as $\frac{1}{8}$ and $\frac{1}{64}$ or $\frac{2}{64}$ and more.

Reviewing his methods as a whole, we find that irregularity in the adjustment of his thicknesses which our knowledge of the master's work would cause us to anticipate; yet, generally speaking, he left more wood in both back and table than did Stradivari. (See Appendix, Chap. IV.)

In deciding upon the position and cutting of the sound-holes we perceive a tendency, in a good many instances, to place them too high in relation to the curves of the bouts and the relative position of the bridge; in fact, it is apparent to the experienced observer that del Gesù both placed and cut them without any close adherence to fixed principle or pattern. He simply relied upon a rough-and-ready determination of the position of top and bottom holes, and the rest depended upon the fancy of the moment. And what an astonishing result! Sound-holes of diverse form and varying length, some cut very open, others moderately so; some placed upright, some slanting; yet, however cut, shaped, or placed, we never fail to recognize that strong impress of the man. Nothing could be more fascinating to the true connoisseur than this entire freedom from restraint so admirably shown in this feature of the master's work.

And the carving of his heads, how varied do we see them! When well disposed he carved with a superb dash—nor was he lacking in precision, though his work was rarely of high finish; here, bold of outline to a marked degree, accompanied by a free treatment of the volute of surpassing charm; there, marred by some touch

Joseph Guarnerius del Gesù fecit Cremonæ 1726

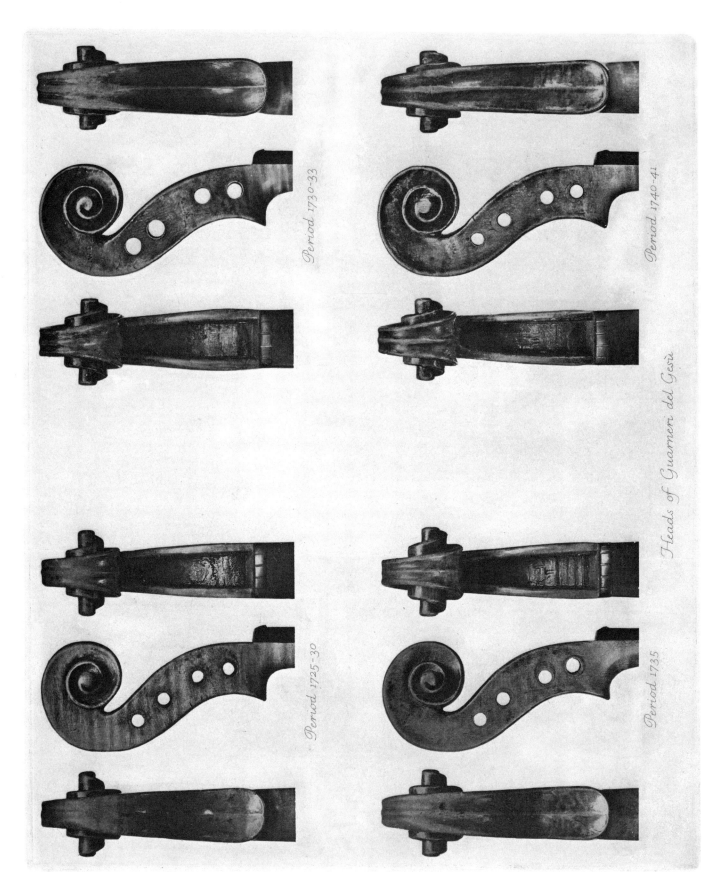

Period 1730-33

Period 1740-41

Period 1725-30

Period 1735

Heads of Guarneri del Gesù

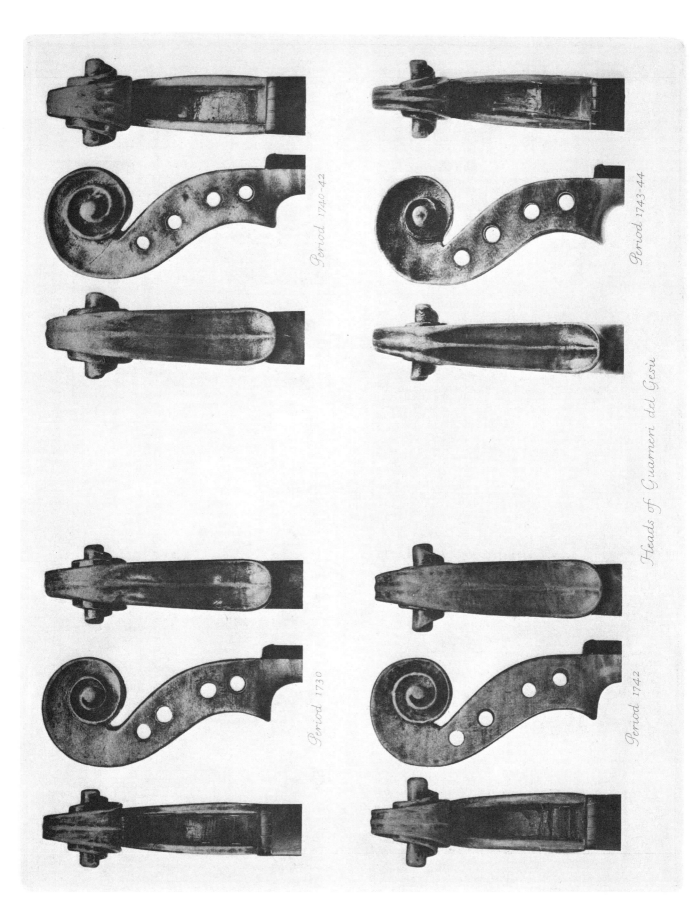

Period 1740-42

Period 1743-44

Period 1730

Period 1742

Heads of Guarneri del Gesù

Joseph Guarnerius del Gesù fecit Cremonæ 1740

betraying meanness or the result of careless work; yet, in spite of these lapses, we invariably find that the strict essentials, such as the well-shaped peg-box, are always present. As with the sound-holes so with the heads; beyond outlining the necessary dimensions, the master trusted entirely to his mood at the moment, again never failing to impart with hasty strokes of the knife, gouge, or file, features revealing true Guarneri characteristics.

So too with the purfling and the fluting around the edges; in early years he took care to thin down correctly the three separate strips of black and white—neither colour well pronounced—to a moderate substance. The trench for its insertion was accurately chiselled out, and the well-formed mitres pointed straight up the corners.

The fluting, at first shallow, became deeper as the years passed; it was now neither deep nor shallow, and gouged out by a hand not always steady. The tendency to dig in the gouge viciously at corners was a fairly early and cultivated habit, quite one of the master's pronounced mannerisms, and one which grew upon him as time sped on.

Thus, as we have tried to show, worked Giuseppe del Gesù, and now let us turn to the more intimate consideration of his violins made between the years 1730 and 1735. Certainly some of the most seductive examples date from these years, violins embracing features reminiscent of the dulcet-like Amati combined with a flatter

FIG. IV. Edge, purfling, and sound-hole of an example of the year 1742.

model and closely knit construction throughout. It is now that we find the sides set on the back and table with a margin of edge around reduced to the utmost limit. Made invariably of a form the measurements of which are on the small side, one would hazard the belief that the master was seeking to combine the finer lines of the Amati model with those found in the broader build of Stradivari, that is, as he himself conceived the blending of the two should be done. Their principal characteristics consist of a $13\frac{7}{8}$ model, frequently $\frac{1}{16}$ less—with lengthened bouts, gained at the expense of the bottom sweep of the outline, more elongated f-holes, model flat—that of the table here and there noticeably so—but above all a neat and correct finish of edge, corners, f-holes, head, in fact of the whole throughout.

This is the master's golden period if we wish to see him behaving at his best in the handling of his tools; and it is now that we sense the full charm of his conception, enhanced by the use of a lustrous varnish of soft texture combined with a colour of orange, orange-red, which at times out-rivals all that has gone before. There is nothing in the work of these years which suggests exaggeration, though now and again we note a sound-hole of extra boldness, a head with an extra vigorous throw of the volute, an edge and a purfling of broader aspect, features combined, perhaps, with a back in one piece of broad curl wood, which lead us to imagine that we are at last faced with an example of greater proportions, yet, the moment we take a measure in hand, we find the eye has been deceived.

Amongst others we would cite the following as typical examples of this period:

1730. Mrs. Frances G. Lee, ex Baron Vitta
1731. Mr. Felix Kahn, ex Cte de Chaponay
1732. M. Blanco, ex Armingaud
1732. M. Plotenyi, ex Remenyi
1732. Mr. Ferencz Hegedus, ex Lord Dunmore
1732. Baron Erlanger, ex M. de Brabandière
1732. M. Zlatko Balokovic, ex Becker
1732. Mr. Sascha Colbertson, ex Carolina Ferni
1733. M. Jaroslav Siskovsky, ex Deichmann
1733. M. Fritz Kreisler, ex Mountford
1733. M. Duchamp, ex Alday
1734. M. H. Grohmann, ex Pugnani
1734. Miss May Harrison, ex Lord Amherst of Hackney
1734. M. Harry Wahl, ex Rode
1734. Mr. Richard Bennett, ex St. Léon
1734. M. Bronislaw Huberman, ex Alfred Gibson
1735. Mr. Eric H. Rose, ex Goding

1735. Prince Wilhelm of Prussia, ex d'Egville

1735. Mr. John T. Roberts, ex Arbós

1735. Miss Kathleen Parlow, ex Dr. Luc

1735. M. Ján Kubelik, ex Petherick, ex Townley

1735. Mr. Rudolph Wurlitzer, ex Sennhauser

1735. M. Chardon of Paris possesses a charming quarter-size example (a child's violin)

The salient features of each of these specimens differ from those of its neighbour, not infrequently in a marked degree, and as long as the lover of the violin exists he will continue to pay ungrudging tribute to the master for that daring and diversified originality, of which his works furnish such eloquent proof.

Nothing would have been more simple than to reproduce that which had gone before—the many superb productions of Stradivari and the Amati, a large percentage of which were still finding a home in the Lombardy and Venetian provinces; instruments which must have been brought to Cremona from time to time for the purpose of repair and adjustment. We must remember that these instruments were then, so to speak, the 'chosen ones', and it speaks volumes for the robust faith of del Gesù to see him disregarding all others and keeping steadily to his ideals, apparently determined to work to the end in the path he had marked out for himself. Would that he could have been stimulated to greater industry! A matter of some significance in this connexion stands out conspicuously—a consideration which frequently in life leads men to better and nobler deeds. We refer to the presence of children in the household.

Now scan through with us the census returns and we shall find that they remain mute on this point. Both the master and his wife are regularly recorded there from the year 1731 to the time of his death; but there is never an addition to the family or to the household, not even an apprentice or a servant. And so matters remain until the very end.

We have already dwelt on the fact that there are extremely few of his violins which could be accepted as having been made prior to and including the year 1730, and we cannot find any sure ground for hoping that more than a solitary example here and there may be forthcoming in the future, for years pass without our becoming aware of the existence of any hitherto unrecorded instruments. Quite the contrary is it with Stradivari; rarely does a year pass without one or more fresh examples of his work being submitted to us.

E.

1731

Statur Animarum degentium sub hac Parochia
S.ti Prosperi Cremone hoc Anno Currenti 1731 de
Mense Martij

n.º 3   Casa d.l S.r Bernardo

Giuseppe Guarneri f.º Giuseppe   34   C C C

Catterina Roda mog.e f.a Gio   30   C C C

1737

n.º 8   Casino delli S.ri Benzoni

Giuseppe Guarneri f.º Giuseppe   40   C C C

Catterina Roda mog.e f.a Gio   36   C C C

1745

n.º 8   Casa delli Benzoni

Catterina Roda ved.a f.a Gio   44   C C C

1731
*Census of souls domiciled in this parish of S. Prospero, Cremona, in the present year, 1731
Month of March*[1]

No. 3.   House of Bernardo

*Giuseppe Guarneri (son) of the late Giuseppe, aged 34. Christened, confirmed, communicant
Catterina Roda,[2] wife, daughter of the late Giovanni, aged 30. Christened, confirmed, communicant.*

1737

No. 8.   Cottage of Count Benzoni

*Giuseppe Guarneri (son) of the late Giuseppe, aged 40. Christened, confirmed, communicant.
Catterina Roda, wife, daughter of the late Giovanni, aged 36. Christened, confirmed, communicant.*

1745

No. 8.   House of Count Benzoni

Catterina Roda, widow, daughter of the late Giovanni, aged 44. Christened, confirmed, communicant.

[1] It will be observed that the above extracts refer to the years 1731, 1737 and 1745; we have omitted the intervening years, i.e. 1732–6, 1738–44, because the returns are without exception simply a repetition of those given.
[2] Curiously enough, Catterina Guarneri has been cited, in some of the early books of the last century, as a violin-maker, but we are inclined to regard this attribution as purely legendary.

It may well be that del Gesù did not take his calling seriously during these years. He may have absented himself on and off from Cremona, and the statement that his wife came from the Tyrol lends colour to our previous suggestion that he married away from Cremona. But, let us hasten to place on record one all-important fact, viz. *no serious expert has ever claimed to have seen an example of his work made and dated elsewhere than in his native city.*

With the advent of the years 1731–5 the roll-call of production steadily augments, and, as we shall learn later, this year 1735 proves to be the most prolific in output of the maker's life, yet how relatively small when contrasted with 1709, the outstanding fruitful year of Stradivari.

No, the master's life was a comparatively brief and unproductive one. We have no definite reason for believing that he ever turned his attention to the making of either viola or violoncello. We have made minute inquiry during many years, and nothing has so far resulted to point to any efforts of his in that direction. On divers occasions both violoncellos and violas have been submitted to us, instruments put forward with definite pretensions, but in no case could they stand serious scrutiny.[1] We therefore conclude that only the making of violins appealed to him and that he was in this respect following in the footsteps of his godfather Pietro of Mantua. Also the actual labour involved in the construction of a violoncello is infinitely more strenuous than in the case of a violin; and we have a shrewd idea that the master throughout life generally took the line of least resistance!

The next five or six years, i.e. to 1740 or 1741, mark the zenith of Giuseppe del Gesù's achievements. We cannot subscribe to the correctness of the method of dividing the master's work into periods, for we find no dividing line that is at all perceptible, no decided changes of form or type which we are able to point to as the production of given years. The changes now are subtle ones; as we approach the forties the craftsmanship begins to betray here and there the less sure hand; but we are fully compensated by a more masculine treatment of the whole.

[1] Charles Reade (1814–84), the novelist, who as many of our readers may be aware, was at one period of his life interested in violin dealing as a business proposition, answered a correspondent who believed himself to be the fortunate possessor of a Guarneri del Gesù violoncello as follows: 'Thanks for your interesting letter. Nothing would give me more pleasure than to find a true bass by Joseph Guarnerius in your hands. But I must tell you I have ransacked Europe and never could find one; and the date you give me of ticket 1715 is against it. It is at least admitted on all hands at present that he began to work in 1724 or 5. However, the sum you mention is not excessive, if the bass is by Joseph Guarnerius filius Andrea, or by Carlo Bergonzi. Of course, if you choose to send it to me for inspection I will give you a faithful judgment, but alas, the chances are always against an odd instrument being the very thing it is represented to be.' (The violoncello on inspection turned out to be of old German work!—*Note by Authors.*)

Though form and general proportions remain as usual, we see a violin of heavier edges, less regular and deeper cut fluting, the inset of the purfling rough and ready, longer and at times protruding corners, broad open and lengthened sound-holes; no pair are alike, nor does the creation of one day resemble that of the morrow. The heads are bold and intensely original, carved with an ever-increasing freedom from all restraint. The model tends to be fuller, less correctly formed, at times somewhat angular at the centre and slightly scooped towards the flanks. In a word, the master lets himself go, and it is this very 'abandon', at times bordering on the audacious, which calls for our admiration. For, with it all, he never forgets the fundamentals of good construction. His strong characteristics are always there and, perhaps, it was for this very reason that he was indifferent as to whether his works went forth into the world signed or not, since he must have been conscious that his very distinctive touch was their true sign-manual.

Representative examples of these years are:

1736. Miss Amy Neill, ex Signora Teja Ferni
1736. Mr. J. F. Otwell, ex Soil
1737. Mr. Horace Havemeyer, ex Hawley
1737. Mr. Alfred San Malo, ex Lipinski
1737. Mr. Ralph H. Norton, ex Wanamaker, ex Marquise de Balâtre
1738. Mr. Rudolph Wurlitzer, ex Adam
1738. Mr. George Kemp, ex Posner
1738-9. Lyon and Healy, ex Consolo, ex Partello
1739. Mr. Rudolph Wurlitzer, ex Kortschak
1739. Mr. R. Cliff Durant, ex Papini
1740. M. Otto Senn, ex Lutti
Period 1740. Mme Alma Moodie, ex Kreisler
1740. M. Eugene Ysaÿe, ex Adam, ex Willemotte
1740. M. Adolf Rebner, ex Bonjour
1741. Mr. Robert A. Bower, ex Vieuxtemps
1741. M. Paul Kochanski, ex Davis, ex Enthoven
1741. M. Adolfo Betti, ex Sainton
1741. Miss Doubleday, ex Duvette
1741. Mr. Henry Ford, ex Doyen

Three more short years and the master's work on earth will have come to an end. He died in October 1744.

Now, according to most writers of the past this final period of del Gesù's life was a disturbed one, due in great measure to some serious offence committed by him, as a punishment for which he suffered several years of imprisonment. Count Cozio di Salabue states that the master received this punishment as the result of a brawl in which he killed one of his violin-making colleagues. Subsequent writers, amongst others, Fétis, have embroidered this story, adding a touch of romance by introducing the daughter of the jailer, who, moved by compassion, procured the necessary tools and materials for the master, so that it might be possible for him to continue giving shape to his beloved violins![1] A pretty legend, for legend we believe it to be, and the Italian adage, 'Si non e vero e ben trovato', very aptly applies.

We have been at some pains to unravel the origin of this story, and our conclusion is that Count Cozio was the first to give credence to that which up to then was probably no more than the outcome of vague gossip. The Count had formed, in the early part of the nineteenth century, a project for publishing some biographical notes concerning the celebrated Cremonese violin-makers (the project was never carried out), and obviously no writer could have had better opportunities for ascertaining the true facts regarding them. His interest was keen, his enthusiasm real; yet notwithstanding, we, who have studied his writings at the source and weighed their comments, find him superficial and frequently inaccurate, and his appreciation of the members of the Guarneri family forms no exception.

It is quite probable that some part of this information was gleaned from J. B. Guadagnini, with whom the Count was in close connexion at the period when he was working in Turin, i.e. 1770–85; and, mark you, Guadagnini, were he in reality a native of Cremona, might well have been personally acquainted with del Gesù. But was he a Cremonese? We doubt it. On the other hand we do know that he was

[1] It is instructive to note that the Abbé Sibire, when speaking of Guarneri, makes no mention of this legend, *La Chélonomie*, Paris, 1806. But the story became current some few years later, brought probably from Italy by Tarisio, the famous dealer, whose periodical visits to Paris commenced about 1825–7. In a rare pamphlet entitled *Archéologie du Violon*, by Cyprien Desmarais, published in 1836, we have the whole story recorded with all its picturesque details.

By a remarkable coincidence, Paganini, whose name is inseparable from del Gesù's in the story of the violin, was the victim of a similar calumny, the version most current being that 'he had suffered an imprisonment of eight years for assassinating a rival'. Paganini profited, by his durance, so the story ran, to attain his marvellous command of the violin. But del Gesù's imprisonment—note the inconsistency—caused the master to deteriorate and turn out his worst instruments. Why, we inquire, should the discipline and regularity of prison life bring about such opposite results? If, as tradition reports, del Gesù's habits were irregular and dissipated, prison control should have improved them, and restored some, at least, of his former skill.

working for a short time at Cremona in the year 1758, that is, within fourteen years of the master's death, a period when we should still be justified in believing that tradition was the outcome of some element of truth; and we should not be wise in lightly brushing aside tradition. But on the other hand there stand revealed the census returns of the Casa S. Bernardo together with that of the Count Benzoni; and regularly, without one omission, we see recorded from the year 1731 to 1744 both the names of Giuseppe Guarneri and Catterina Roda his wife. In the following year 1745 the *widow's* name only is given, and this entry is continued up to 1747, when she disappears. Her subsequent movements and the date of her death have eluded our search.

And what evidence can be adduced from the instruments supposed to have been made during this period of incarceration? A certain number of more or less commonplace crudities, some few the work of Italians, others made in the different countries of Europe, and mostly dating from the latter part of the eighteenth and beginning of the nineteenth centuries have, as a result of the general credence accorded to this story, been foisted with more or less success upon the reputation of poor Giuseppe del Gesù; instruments known here by the sorry appellation of 'Prison Joseph', and by our French neighbours as 'Guarnerius de la Servante'. Any ill-conceived production of flat orthodox model, always provided that the form could be manipulated to conform in a near or remote degree to the Guarneri type—eccentric f-holes, roguish-looking head, and a touch of the real Cremona varnish, red colour being a sine qua non—and it was forthwith provided with the true label and sent into the violin world to masquerade under the cloak of the unfortunate 'Joseph'! Readily as we admit the existence of authentic violins by the master the workmanship of which clearly points to decadence (and with which we will now deal), it is difficult to justify the acceptance of the above bogus specimens except by people of poor expert knowledge but rich imagination.[1]

We have already emphasized the fact that the master's initial works convey to our minds the impression of an expeditious worker—no second stroke of the tool where one would suffice—that his work was good and true at the start, revealing less care as the years passed by. And we can follow this course with considerable consistency up to the years 1741-2, really even to 1743, the year before his death. It is true that we see an increasing disregard of finish as we reach the forties; frequently weakness may

[1] The possession of this fertile imagination has frequently given material results!

be detected in the treatment or design of details, which gives rise to the suspicion that all is not well with del Gesù. The uneven finish of the edge, and the faulty inlay of the purfling, the irregularly shaped model, the truly amazing *f*-holes, not to speak of the palsied carving of the heads—all these are defects which betray an unsteadiness of mind and hand only too apparent. Yet in spite of this intermittent weakness we are indebted to these very years for some notably fine examples, in which we see the master's forcible character wonderfully sustained.

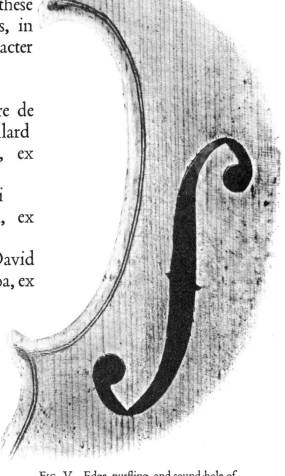

Amongst others, let us cite the following:

          1742. Musée du Conservatoire de Musique, Paris, ex Alard

          1742. Mr. Richard Bennett, ex Lord Wilton

          1742. Mme Soldat, ex Bazzini

          1742. Mr. Samuel Dushkin, ex Plowden

Period 1742. M. Jascha Heifetz, ex David

          1742. Municipal Palace, Genoa, ex Paganini

          1743. Dr. Felix Landau, ex Carrodus

          1743. Mr. J. S. Phipps, ex Leduc

How very comprehensible when we bear in mind that he would be in the plenitude of life in 1740, aged only forty-two years.

To what cause, then, are we to attri-bute this sapping of his vital forces? The

FIG. V. Edge, purfling, and sound-hole of an example of the year 1742.

answer can only be one of conjecture, for it is certain that the master came of healthy stock, judging by the longevity of both his grandparents and of his father and mother, all of whom reached the age of three score years and ten. His own brother too, Pietro of Venice, lived to the age of sixty-nine.

Now if we can accept the tradition handed down to us by the last of the Bergonzi[1] that del Gesù had led an irregular life, indulged in its pleasures, and was fond of wine, we have a sufficiently reasonable explanation to account for his state of health, and one which is supported by a survey of the actual work of these years. This road to ruin was and is still, alas, taken by many gifted men; and assuredly the Italian violin-makers were as human as all others. In order to live it was necessary to pro-duce; and when del Gesù was in chastened or degraded mood we see the result reflected both in the conception and finish of individual instruments. But we find no slackening in the pace of the master's productions during these last four years, for, besides those cited on the previous page, we are acquainted with more than twenty-five other violins belonging to this same period.

The example inseparably connected with the illustrious name of Paganini calls for more than a passing reference; and, as we have been privileged to examine it closely, we propose to describe the fiddle in a more intimate way than has been done before. The exact year of its birth is shrouded in doubt, the label it bears having been tampered with; the fourth figure may have been 3, but as there is a small hole at the lower part of the figure we cannot be sure. Originally it may equally well have been 2; but this figure of the inscription is not at all pure; so that we are reduced to conjecture. Now was this the label placed in the instrument by the master? We should say so, but certainly it is not *now* in the condition as left by him; and it passes one's wits to find any sane explanation of these petty acts of vandalism. All we dare say is that the label is an authentic one. A point of great importance is that the example does date from the 1739-44 period. On the balance of evidence we should prefer to assign it to the year 1742 rather than to 1743.

Of its superior merit there can be no two opinions; it ranks among the greatest. As we stood in the Council Room of the Municipal Palace of Genoa, we could not refrain from recalling the past, seeing a vision of that tall, weird figure with bow uplifted, the magic of whose playing resounded throughout the length and breadth of Europe, 'The glory, jest, and riddle of the World'! Then, taking up his violin, the silent witness of his many triumphs, destined like its owner to an everlasting silence, we contemplated its very virile construction, forcibly realizing why Paganini time and again rejected those new loves in the guise of fresh Stradivari[2] and Guarneri

[1] See footnote, p. 77.
[2] In 1817 Paganini purchased from Ct. Cozio di Salabue a violin of Stradivari of the year 1724, described on the receipt as a *chef-d'œuvre* of the master; the price paid was ninety-five Louis d'Or = £76.

which he acquired, all of which were set aside in favour of this instrument which, from the day of its possession remained throughout his career the one and faithful exponent of his art.[1] Its perfectly balanced form measures in length 14 inches less $\frac{1}{16}$; the widths are $8\frac{3}{16}$ and $6\frac{5}{8}$ respectively; the sides $1\frac{5}{16}$ and $1\frac{3}{16}$. The body stop is $7\frac{5}{8}$, an extreme measurement most exceptional with del Gesù. The neck—the original, and but slightly lengthened at the foot—measures $5\frac{1}{16}$ inches, nor are its general proportions at all small, either in thickness or width.

The fingerboard, which is of Italian work, and dates from about 1800–30, is throughout noticeably rounder in form than those used by the player of to-day; and this strongly arched board naturally carried a similarly curved bridge.[2] The construction from start to finish is beyond reproach, if judged from the Guarneri standpoint; the model is consistently worked with a gentle swell to both back and table—higher in the former than the latter; the sides are well and truly bent; and the head is of broad design in every respect, and carved with real power. No *f*-holes of del Gesù, either in their design, their pose upon the table, or in the cutting—even though that of the right is longer than the other—were ever more happily conceived. The edges, deeply fluted, are not too heavy in substance, and the purfling is inset with quite sufficient accuracy.

The varnish, of a rich red-brown colour, is of softish texture, and though laid on heavily is not in any sense overdone. As our illustration shows, the whole instrument is still fairly well covered. (See overleaf.)

The wood of the back, of foreign maple and of first-rate quality, is but moderately figured, similarly that of the head; but the sides, on the contrary, are cut from handsomely figured wood marked by a broader and well-defined curl. The pine of the table is admirable both as to quality and appearance; of an excellent width of grain, it readily conveys the impression of having been jealously chosen for this particular violin.

To sum up, we are here faced by an exceptionally happy work of the master, manly in every respect, rugged of finish, yet not exaggerated; a well-shaped model combined with an imposing height of sides, to which feature the handsome wood lends additional weight. Nor is the outline ordinary; the top curves are slightly

[1] 'His luggage caused no trouble as it consisted only of a small dilapidated trunk containing his precious Guarneri violin,' &c., &c. . . . 'He saw Paganini seated on a sofa, taking from its case the precious violin.' *Paganini in seinem Reise-*

wagen und Zimmer, George Harrys, 1830.

[2] Paganini's bridge is no longer on the fiddle; both it and the original strings are preserved in a sealed envelope.

more sloped than in many cases, and this counts for much to the player of great technical difficulties. The state of preservation points to loving ownership in the past,[1] for beyond a slight crack at the top left corner of the table it seems perfect, and the fiddle does not give signs of serious wear from the usage to which it had been subjected by Paganini. The edges of the back and table are nowhere worn down, and the corners of the latter, though somewhat rubbed off, are still intact. There is a rut running down from the top edge along the finger-board on the E string side, caused, we suggest, partly by the continued taking in and out of the bow which rubbed against the violin on every occasion when removed from the quaintly shaped case of the eighteenth century, which opened only at the end, and partly by the constant movement of the thumb when pizzicato passages were played.

We noted with interest that the spot on the back where the sound post stands is marked round with ink; Paganini had evidently found that the post so placed gave the best tonal results, and possibly modified a bad wolf-note!

'Lego il mio violino alla Citta di Genova onde sia perpetuamente conservato' wrote Paganini in his will; and though many of us doubtless deplore the fact that this great example of the master's work should be for ever silenced, yet we fear that but for Paganini's gift to his native city there would not be a single violin by Guarneri del Gesù remaining throughout the length and breadth of Italy. We are acquainted with none other in the hands of either dilettante or artist.[2]

Now the belief, as first recorded by Fétis, that Guarneri del Gesù died in the year 1745 has been generally accepted, and the only evidence in support of this assertion was that given by a label attached to a very fine violin, the work of the master, which

---

[1] Statements have been made that there are signs of worm ravage, and we are pleased to say that nothing of the kind exists.

[2] The published statement that Paganini was indebted for his (Guarneri) violin to the generosity of a French amateur, M. Livron of Leghorn, has been hitherto accepted without demur. But if we can believe the contents of a letter written by the violinist himself in April 1839 and addressed to his friend and lawyer Luigi Germi, an extract from which is contained in the procès-verbal drawn up at Genoa on the occasion of the reception of the violin by the City Authorities in the year 1861, it was given to him by the Italian General Pino. As a result of further inquiries we learn that the General, who was born and died in Milan (1760–1826), played a distinguished part during the Napoleonic régime in Italy, that he was an intimate friend of Paganini, and that the latter stayed with him at his villa on Lake Como. We can express no definite opinion in connexion with the above statement, but here again it should not be overlooked that Paganini owned various fine violins, and it is therefore quite conceivable that he may have been presented at some time with a second Guarneri del Gesù. M. Livron, a merchant, was in partnership with a compatriot M. Hamelin; both were living in Leghorn in 1800, and furnished the French army of occupation with supplies.

We are indebted to the late Sir Charles Lawes-Wittewronge for the following anecdote: When travelling on the Continent, his uncle, Andrew Fountaine of Narford Hall, the well-known amateur who possessed some very notable violins, called on Paganini, then, obviously, very ill, and was greeted by him with the words 'You come to buy my "Guarneri?" if only you had called three days ago, it should have been yours, now it is too late, for I have offered it to the City of Genoa.'

was owned for many years by a Parisian amateur by name 'Leduc'.[1] It had been purchased from Vuillaume—and this label apparently bore the date 1745.

This interesting instrument was brought to our country in 1880 by the late Mr. David Laurie, and it then passed into the Adam collection. Later, in 1894, it came into our hands; and at that time we saw no reason to doubt the correctness of the reading of its date; but owing to subsequent information we availed ourselves of an opportunity to re-examine both the violin and its label. Without hesitation we came to the following conclusion. The label is unquestionably original, and belongs to the violin, but the last figure of the date has been misread. It is a badly formed 3 and strongly resembles a French 5; but we have not a doubt that the correct date intended was 1743; and, we may add, we know but two violins bearing their original labels dated 1744, viz. that owned by M. Hoffmann of Prague, ex Earl of Harrington, and that owned by Mrs. Lyon, ex Ole Bull. Others exist, undoubtedly the work of the years 1740–4; but either their original labels have been removed, or still more probably they left the maker's hand unlabelled.

The following instruments are typical of these last four years:

Lord Coke, ex Gand
M. Gregorowitsch, ex Wolkoff
Miss Kneisel, ex Heath

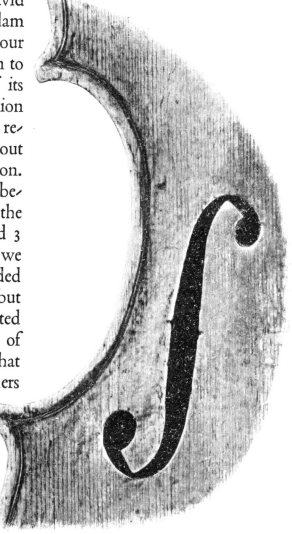

FIG. VI. Edge, purfling, and sound-hole of
an example of the period 1743-4.

[1] M. Leduc was, we believe, an architect. When writing to Mr. Plowden in 1855, Vuillaume says: 'I have been to see the "Guarneri" of M. Leduc; I find it superb, and it is useless for you to hope, for the owner is too much in love with it!'

Mr. Henry Ford, ex Doyen

Mr. Eric H. Rose, ex Hennell

The fact that the master died and was buried on the seventeenth day of October 1744—possibly he had died a day or two before—is placed beyond further controversy by the discovery of the burial certificate, a facsimile of which we reproduce, *F*.

F.

October 17th, 1744.

Dom. Giuseppe Guarneri, the husband of Cattarina Roda, about forty-seven years of age, having made his confession, received Holy Viaticum & Extreme Unction, passed away commending his soul to God. His body is interred in this church of S. Prospero.

It will be observed that he received the full Sacraments of the Church before expiring, and that he was buried in S. Prospero, and not in S. Domenico, in that Chapel of the Rosary devoted to Cremona's illustrious violin-making sons, where but seven years earlier the mortal remains of his greater contemporary, Antonio Stradivari, had been laid to rest.

In giving a resumé of the master's life-work we would again point out that it does not in our opinion permit of division into clearly definable periods as is permissible with that of Stradivari; from the very beginning the man shows himself to have been of erratic nature, and though we trace a considerable amount of consistency throughout the work and conception of his violins dating up to 1730-5, it becomes less apparent as we proceed onward to the year 1740, and still less so during the last four years terminating with his death.

We repeat that the instruments dating from 1730–35 represent his craftsmanship at its best; they embody much that is refreshingly original together with an added minimum of daring, and though they are with rare exception of small dimensions, this fact frequently passes unperceived owing to the broad treatment of their construction. In contrast we observe that the majority of the violins belonging to the years 1736–44 are still more broadly treated. The actual increase in size, when augmented at all, never goes beyond an eighth of an inch in length and the same in breadth; and we have never seen an authentic example measuring above the normal standard of fourteen inches. But the bold edges, heavier in wood and less regularly worked, the higher model in certain instances, at times again the abnormally high sides, and a varnish literally splashed on with lavish hand—all these features contribute in giving an ensemble which represents the acme of masculine construction.

That such productions, which, when new, were frequently of crude appearance and unresponsive in tone, could have really found favour at the hands of the cultured player is in the highest degree improbable. Think of the choice which was easily within his reach—the host of violins, the works of Stainer, the Amati, the Guarneri, and their pupils and followers, not to speak of Stradivari. No, del Gesù's productions were, unwittingly of course, for the use of futurity; and years were to elapse during which they were neither cared for nor seriously sought after.

At death the master left neither children nor known pupils; and we search in vain for any immediate sign that his work influenced that of contemporary violin-makers, either of Italy or other countries. With death and burial he passed into a long oblivion. Certainly the work of Michael Angelo Bergonzi shows some trace of his influence, but generally speaking no similarity worth noticing is to be detected; and it is only when we approach the end of the eighteenth century that we begin to perceive an awakening in favour of the late master.

Lorenzo Storioni, at this period, did undoubtedly here and there copy del Gesù, and one or two others contributed their feeble efforts;[1] but in the main, throughout Europe, there was a consensus of opinion in favour of Amati, Stainer, and Stradivari, a verdict given alike by players and makers.

The real awakening came with the new century—if slowly, yet surely. Several of the Italian violinists are found coming to the great centres, and performing upon del Gesù violins. They had recognized in them a 'something else' differing from the

---

[1] We have seen a copy by Valenzano, date 1794.

tonal qualities hitherto accepted; curiosity was thus aroused amongst the foremost makers and amateurs as to the merits of this particular member of the Guarneri family so far but little known and appreciated. And we see Nicolas Lupot, a most consistent admirer of Stradivari, making in 1806 a copy of one of the master's violins, inserting in it a reproduction of the Guarneri label, and then adding an inscription of his own, which stated that he had made it expressly for one of his patrons.[1]

But though the master's instruments were used thus by certain of the more discerning players, it still required the advent of Paganini to attract universal attention to the maker of his famed violin; and from that moment Guarneri del Gesù leaped into renown. The demand for 'Guarneris' became an ever more insistent one, and copies were produced by all the principal makers of Europe. But the more imaginative worker soon perceived that the real demand was for something that would more or less pass muster as an original work; in a word, the colourable imitation rather than the honest reproduction. He also realized that the master's eccentric irregularities gave rein to the would-be falsifier, and, as a result, not only were authentic 'Guarneri' made up of old parts called into being, but admirable imitative copies bearing all the appearance of age were made by Vuillaume, Georges Chanot, and other French and German contemporary makers, whilst here we had the Fendts and notably George and John Lott. To the latter we are especially indebted.

What is the actual number of violins which now exist and represent the master's life-work? We can, of course, only speak from the result of our own observations; but, always deeply interested in our subject, and with exceptional opportunities for judging, we believe that our deductions rest upon a sufficiently accurate basis.

We have seen that del Gesù's life was brief and probably an unsettled one, the exact contrary to that of his great compeer. Hence we neither expect nor do we find any such number of productions per annum; indeed our roll-call gives a sadly small return when compared with that of Stradivari. We are acquainted with a total of one hundred and forty-seven violins only, but we would add that we see reasons for admitting the possible existence of from thirty to forty other examples not hitherto verified by us; we say *possible* existence, because on a sober review of our facts we think this number exceeds rather than falls short of the actual total.

Undoubtedly the hand of time has dealt more harshly with Guarneri instruments

---

[1] This interesting inscription was, within the recollection of the writers, removed and destroyed in the process, by a former owner of the violin, now owned by the Curtis Institute of Music, Philadelphia, U.S.A.

than those of Stradivari; from their birth until the end of the eighteenth century and
even later they found themselves in less appreciative hands and were frequently subjected to careless usage. But, when generous allowance is made for these circumstances, we very much doubt whether Guarneri del Gesù's total production could
have exceeded two hundred and fifty violins; and, as stated before, we have no actual
knowledge that he made any stringed instruments of any other form.

The rarity of the master's early works, i.e. violins dated, or those conceivably
made prior to 1730, is extraordinary: we know of but seven examples.

From the year 1730, seven.

,,	,,	1731, four.
,,	,,	1732, thirteen—a notable increase.
,,	,,	1733, thirteen.
,,	,,	1734, thirteen.
,,	,,	1735, sixteen, the master's most fruitful year.
,,	,,	1736, ten.
,,	,,	1737, seven.
,,	,,	1738, eight.
,,	,,	1739, six.
,,	,,	1740, nine.
,,	,,	1741, eight.
,,	,,	1742, thirteen.
,,	,,	1743, seven.
,,	,,	1744, six.

We have previously commented on the fact that quite a number of these violins
do not bear the master's original label, and that in certain instances the labels which
they now bear are not of approximately correct date; therefore, in compiling the
above list, we have assigned such instruments to the year which we believe more
truly represents that of their production.

Of these existing violins, certain amongst them stand out pre-eminently, due
either to having been made in favourable circumstances, or falling into appreciative
hands during the greater part of the last two centuries, or perhaps more truly to a
combination of both these facts. Many now bear trace of hard and continuous wear;
they served indeed as 'Le cheval de bataille' to many a strenuous player of the past!
For in this connexion we must remember that a Guarneri could be purchased at the

beginning of last century for a sum representing approximately half that paid for a Stradivari. Once their outstanding tonal merits, however, became more widely recognized—between 1800 and 1830-40[1]—their value soon rose to a level approaching that attained by the violins of the great master, the value being to some extent enhanced by their rarity as compared with the far greater number of Stradivari. Our earliest records of price, though going back to the year 1800, are but meagre;[2] we find a Guarneri del Gesù brought here from Sicily, prior to the opening of that century, selling for fifty guineas, another example for fifteen guineas, and a third for thirty-seven guineas.

In the year 1830 we have an instance of £42 being paid, while in 1834 the violin presented by the late Gen. Kyd to Spagnoletti[3] (the player) was valued at £150.[4] No dates are given to these violins, an omission which makes the task of identification most difficult, nor did our ancestor Lockey Hill (1774–1835) nor John Betts (1755–1823), the foremost dealer of his day, attach the same interest to the recording of facts concerning Guarneri instruments that they did in the case of Stradivari. When we reach the fifties of last century we see the purchasing price of violins made by both makers fairly level: for instance, in the year 1857 at the 'Goding' Sale,[5] the Guarneri known as the 'King' was bought in at £260, and subsequently sold to the Vicomte de Janzé for £240, the fine Stradivari dated 1722 which formed part of the collection was sold, and purchased by Vuillaume for £200. In 1867, the year of the dispersal of the Plowden collection bought by George Hart, which consisted of four Guarneri and an equal number of Stradivari, two of the former were valued at £300 each, and two of the latter at the same figure. And henceforward as we trace the gradual rise in price taking place from year to year up to present times, we see it consistently applying to the violins of both masters.

In singling out the following examples which we feel may be cited as amongst

---

[1] 'In my youth' (Fétis was born in 1784) 'one of the best examples could be bought for 1,200 frs. = £48. Now (1866) as much as 6,000 frs. = £240 and even more is paid.' Fétis, art. 'Guarneri', *Dictionary of Music and Musicians.*

[2] Recu de Monsieur Potherat de Thon La somme de deux mille quatres cent Cinquant franc, pour un violon de joseph Guarneriuse que je lui evendu, et donc je lui garantie sans au cune fracture, est san au cune piece en dedont est avoir fourni une boite garni en cuivre.
A Paris ce 27 avril 1828.
                    Aldric
Luthier, Rue de Seibe No. 71.

[Aldric was a well-known luthier of his day, and the above receipt is an accurate transcription of one given by him. The sum referred to is the equivalent of £98.—*Note by the Authors.*]

[3] Paolo Spagnoletti (1761 (?)–1834) writes, in September 1823, to one of his musical friends as follows: 'Should you wish to have an "Amati", or a "Guarneri", or a "Stradivari", in really good condition, one would have to pay a high figure.'

[4] Paganini writing from Nice, in March 1840, to his friend, the advocate Luigi Germi of Genoa, states 'the Guarnerius in question is worth not less than 3,000 frs.' = £120.

[5] Sale held by Messrs. Christie.

the outstanding Guarneri we would justify our choice from the fact that the instruments mentioned possess in lesser or greater degree those all-round qualifications— tone, form, appearance, and state of preservation—and are throughout typical of the best features of a given period of the master's work. But we have to guard ourselves against pointing to any one of them as being superior to all the rest, although it is obvious that certain of the specimens would, for various reasons, command a far greater market value than the others. No supreme Guarneri exists, and all cited are possessed of individual charm—that mysterious something, so little, that counts for so much.

1730. Mrs. Francis G. Lee, ex Baron Vitta
1732. M. Blanco, ex Armingaud
1732. Baron Erlanger, ex Nothomb
1732. M. Zlatko Balokovic, ex Becker
1732. Mr. Sascha Colbertson, ex Carolina Ferni
1733. M. Fritz Kreisler, ex Junot, ex Mountford
1733. M. Jaroslav Siskovsky, ex Deichmann
1733. M. Duchamp, ex Alday
1734. M. Ferencz Hegedus, ex Lord Dunmore
1734. Mr. R. A. Bower, ex Soames
1734. Miss May Harrison, ex Lord Amherst of Hackney
1734. Mrs. Silcock, ex Capt. Frewin
1734. M. Bronsilaw Huberman, ex Alfred Gibson
1734. Mr. Richard Bennett, 'Violon du Diable', ex St. Léon
1735. Mr. Eric H. Rose, 'The King', ex Goding
1735. Prince Wilhelm of Prussia, ex D'Egville
1735. Mr. John T. Roberts, ex Plowden, ex Arbós
1735. Miss Kathleen Parlow, ex Dr. Luc
1735. M. Antonio Antoncich, ex Ward
1735. Mr. Rudolph H. Wurlitzer, ex Sennhauser
1735. Hon. Mary Portman, ex Murray
1735. M. Jan Kubelik, ex Townley
1735. A. C. Marshall, ex Muntz
1736. Miss Amy Neill, ex Signora Teja-Ferni
1736. Mr. J. F. Otwell, ex Soil

        1737. Mr. A. San Malo, ex Lipinski
        1737. Mr. H. O. Havemeyer, ex Hawley
        1737. Mr. Ralph H. Norton, ex Marquise de Belâtre, ex Wanamaker
        1738. Mr. George H. Kemp, ex Posner
        1738. Mr. Rudolph H. Wurlitzer, ex Adam
Period 1739. Mr. R. Cliff Durant, ex Consolo, ex Partello
        1739. Mr. Rudolph Wurlitzer, ex Hammig
        1740. M. Eugène Ysaÿe, ex Cte Baldeschi, ex Adam
Period 1740. Mr. Ralph H. Norton, ex Sauret
   „   1740. M. Camille Barrère, ex Rovelli
   „   1740. Miss Alma Moodie, ex Kreisler
        1741. Miss Doubleday, ex Duvette
        1741. Mr. Robert A. Bower, ex Vieuxtemps, ex Sons
        1741. M. Adolfo Betti, ex Sainton
        1741. M. Paul Kochanski, ex Davis, ex Enthoven
        1741. Mr. Henry Ford, ex Doyen
        1741. Mme Soldat, ex Bazzini
        1742. Mr. Samuel Dushkin, ex Plowden, ex Heath
        1742. Museum of the Paris Conservatoire, ex Alard
        1742. Municipal Palace of Genoa, ex Paganini
        1742. Mr. Richard Bennett, ex Lord Wilton
Period 1742. M. Jascha Heifetz, ex Ferdinand David
        1743. Dr. Felix Landau, ex Carrodus
        1743. Mr. John S. Phipps, ex Leduc
        1744. Mr. Eric H. Rose, ex Hennell
        1744. Mrs. Lyon, ex Ole Bull

If we were asked to make a final choice, we should name one or other of the following examples:

        1733. M. Fritz Kreisler
        1734. 'Le violon du Diable'
        1735. 'The King'
        1735. Mr. John T. Roberts
        1737. Mr. H. O. Havemeyer
        1742. ex Alard

1742. ex Paganini
1742. Mr. Richard Bennett
1743. Mr. John S. Phipps

We once more affirm that the above list embraces all that are known to us of fine and representative examples, instruments illustrating with but slight exception that which is typical of the life-work of the master from start to finish. It is true that we are not able to cite a violin quite of the first rank made prior to the year 1730, but we feel, and feel strongly, that no specimen can exemplify del Gesù in his mature youth more strikingly than that dated 1733 (Kreisler), which conceivably was made some years previous to that year. It stands on the threshold of the master's emancipation from the past; the f-holes still reveal his indebtedness to Stradivari, but model and form are his own, timid of conception, perhaps, when contrasted with the audacity of later years, yet admirably typifying those closely knit examples which, from a tonal point of view, stand up to the greatest. Both the Erlanger and Blanco violins of 1732 are, in character, slightly more advanced. The ex Gibson, the Hegedus, and the 'Violon du Diable' (1734) consistently follow on, the last named outstanding with its fuller model and fine appearance.

By 1735 we have the full development of that perfect combination of youthful finish and refined style—none exists surpassing those cited, notably, 'The King'. Then comes the ex D'Egville, more restricted as regards the flattened model and smallness of build, yet possessing withal great beauty. Again, the ex Plowden, in several respects the very brother of the last named, though somewhat bolder of conception and covered by a luscious red varnish which never can have been surpassed. A delightful pair indeed, and well might Vuillaume exclaim to Mr. Plowden, who then (1863) owned both instruments: 'Vous irez loin avant de voir de pareils Guarnerius!'

We see others dated from the following years upwards to 1740, here and there becoming more rugged of finish, even more forcible as to their character. The ex Soil (1736) and that of Mr. Kemp (1738) are equally notable examples; both are clothed with an attractive varnish of orange-brown colour, rather exceptional, both are of robust construction and finely preserved. The ex Hawley (1737) throws back several years as regards form and neatness of construction, its aspect enhanced by a back cut on the slab—most fascinating; that of Mr. Norton, ex Wanamaker, also of this same year, is again a choice example and, of 1740, we would make special mention of Ysaÿe's famed violin.

Lastly, we have some masterful specimens: here, the product of the maker when in eccentric mood, there, when in chastened mood, and both the one and the other thrill us by their intense originality.

Of 1741 none surpasses the ex Vieuxtemps, the ex Sainton, and that of M. Kochanski; 1742, the ex Heath and Plowden, the ex Alard, that of Mr. Bennett, and finally the ex Paganini; 1743, the ex Leduc and that of Dr. Landau, while of 1744 the ex Hennell is delightfully quaint in character and of picturesque aspect. Each and all these violins give of del Gesù in his varying moods; they stand among his highest achievements and for all time. The man possessed, beyond everything, an unquenchable vein of originality; it was born in him and his surroundings favoured its development. As he grew to manhood, he heeded neither father, uncle, nor elder brother, come what might, however badly he handled his tools—nor can it be gainsaid that he did here and there let himself go—his strokes give the impress of an indelible personality over which we love to linger. As long as the violin survives, so long will those who learn to understand del Gesù pay homage to him as one of Cremona's gifted sons.

With the master's death passed away, in reality, the greatness of the Cremonese School of violin-making. The last of the Amati and the two sons of Stradivari were dead; true, Carlo Bergonzi was still living, he was an old man and died in February 1747—but we see no signs of him at work, neither were his sons at all active.

Yes, Cremona's golden era of instrument making had indeed passed away, the founding of which was the direct outcome of that wonderful environment which we associate with the Renaissance period, a time of intense intellectual and artistic activity which spread throughout the land. The Church and the many noble families vied with each other in according their patronage to the host of skilled workers, and what more wonderful monument of this skill of man now exists than the famous Certosa of Pavia. Come, follow in our footsteps from Cremona to Pavia—no great distance—and there refresh your minds with the vision of this Monastery and its splendid contents. Surely none but inspired craftsmen could have thus wrought in stone, metal, wood, and other material! Time counted for naught, money value even less, and we assert once more and finally, that the paramount influence of the Church gave zest to the worker, whether high or low, exhorted him daily to pay tribute to the memory of the Saviour of mankind, and to this high ideal the violin-making sons of Cremona contributed their modest yet definite part.

With the exception of the improved adjustment more suited to the varying requirements of later generations of players, the violin stands where the last touch of
the master left it in the month of October of the year 1744—a year which marks the
centenary of the birth of Antonio Stradivari. What a host of remarkable instruments
had been produced within those hundred years, years during which the art of
violin-making reached the zenith of its fame, when the creative genius of Cremona's
sons, Amati, Guarneri, Rugeri, Stradivari, Bergonzi, and lesser luminaries shone
forth in all the glory of their respective attainment. Henceforth we shall find
instrument-making actively carried on for a further brief spell at Venice, Milan,
Florence, Rome, Naples, and other Italian cities, but we shall search in vain for the
fruits of that noble inspiration which had emanated from these several generations
of the Amati, Guarneri, and Stradivari.

> In the elder days of Art,
> Builders wrought with greatest care
> Each minute and unseen part;
> For the Gods see everywhere.

Joseph Guarnerius del Gesù fecit Cremonæ 1741

Joseph Guarnerius del Gesu fecit Cremonæ, 1741

CHAPTER V

GUARNERI DEL GESÙ VIOLINS
THE TONAL ASPECT

Ye, who to wed the sweetest wife would try,
Observe how men a sweet Cremona buy!
New violins, they seek not from the trade,
But one, on which some good musician play'd:
Strings never try'd some harshness will produce;
The fiddle's harmony improves by use.

(ANON.[1])

THE tone of the violins made by Giuseppe del Gesù had to be tested and approved by the skilled player and the cultivated listener, whose judgement would eventually determine whether or no it were of superlative merit. The test of time and use which had already confirmed the pre-eminence of the instruments made by del Gesù's predecessors—those famous makers of Brescia and Cremona—had to be applied also to his violins before their true tonal value could be ascertained.

The seasoning of the fabric to withstand the tension of the strings and the stress of playing, and the maturing of the tone by diligent and regular use, were processes which for their successful completion must be spread over a number of years. The knotty question of how long a period was required to bring the tone to an efficient degree of maturity calls for an attempt at unravelling, even though it may seem to lead us from the direct course of our subject.

To begin then with testimony drawn from seventeenth-century sources, from those who wrote of and used the instruments of that time.

In the second edition of Dr. Johnson's *Dictionary* we find the following appropriate extracts, quoted as 'authorities' for the employment of words bearing on music.

'*Sonorousness.* Enquiring of a maker of viols and lutes of what age he thought lutes ought to be to attain their full and best seasoning for "sonorousness", he replied that in some cases twenty years would be requisite and in others forty.'

[1] From *The Annual Register* of the year 1787.

'*Resonance.* An ancient musician informed me that there were some famous lutes that attained not their full seasoning and best "resonance", till they were about four-score years old.'[1]

On considering these extracts we observe that Boyle's questions concerned the lute only, still much in vogue; and that the answers to them were supplied by two experts, 'a viol and lute maker', and 'an ancient musician'.

The origin of the violin was but recent, and its use too restricted as yet to make it also an object of study or curiosity to Boyle, otherwise he might have elicited from the 'viol maker' some valuable or possibly piquant remarks conceived in the vein of Mace, such as: 'the scoulding Violins will out-Top them all.'[2]

However, the opinions of the two experts consulted by Boyle (to summarize them), that twenty or forty years in some cases were requisite for lutes to attain their full and best seasoning for sonorousness or resonance, are definite and precious evidence concerning a subject which exercises the mind of the violin lover in our twentieth century as much as it did that of the lute enthusiast in the seventeenth century.

Referring for testimony to the viol, that compeer of the lute and direct ancestor of the violin, the opinions expressed by Mace, an authority on both viol and lute, are quite emphatic as to the virtue of age for these instruments.

'At first, it is a New-made-Instrument; and therefore cannot yet Speak so Well, as It will do, when It comes to Age and Ripeness; yet it gives forth a very Free, Brisk, Trouling, Plump, and Sweet Sound: But 'tis Generally known, That Age adds Goodness, and Perfection to All Instruments made of Wood; Therefore Old Lutes, and Viols, are always of much more Value, than New Ones; So that if an Instrument be Good, when New, there is no doubt but It will be Excellent, when It is Old.[3] . . . The Reasons for which, I can no further Dive into, than to say: I Apprehend that by Extream Age, the Wood, (And Those Other Adjuncts) Glew, Parchment, Paper, Lynings of Cloath, (as some use) but above all the Vernish; These are All, so very much (by Time) Dryed, Lenefied, made Gentle, Rarified, or (to say Better, even) Ayrified; so that That Stiffness, Stubbornness, or Clunguiness, which is Natural to such Bodies, are so Debilitated, and made Play-

---

[1] These extracts, we assume, were taken from some piece of writing by the distinguished philosopher and scientist, Robert Boyle (1626–91), one of the founders of the Royal Society, which may have remained in MS., as we believe other of his papers have done.
[2] *Musick's Monument*, p. 233, T. Mace, 1676.
[3] Ibid., pp. 205–6.

able, that the Pores of the Wood, have a more, and Free Liberty to move, Stir, or
Secretly Vibrate; by which means the Air (which is the Life of All Things both
Animate and Inanimate) has a more Free, and Easy Recourse, and to Pass, and
Re-pass etc.—wether I have hit upon the Right Cause, I know not; but sure I am,
that Age Adds Goodness to Instruments; therefore They have the advantage of all our
Late Workmen.'[1]

We should bear in mind that the preceding statements represent the views and
experience of 'a viol and lute maker', 'an ancient musician', and an accomplished
player of both lute and viol like Mace—men whose profession it had been to make
instruments or play on them.

Now the Italian soloists of the seventeenth century, who advanced the art of violin
playing, were indebted beyond measure for their success to the instruments on which
they played—the violins which the skill and genius of the Brescian and Cremonese makers had already brought wellnigh to perfection. The pioneer violinists
of the century must have used the violins made by their contemporaries, Maggini
and the brothers Amati; for previous to 1600 the instrument was in its beginning;
and relatively few true violins had been made by Gasparo da Salò and Andrea
Amati, the two earliest makers concerning whom any trustworthy evidence exists.

Towards the close of the century, when the fine playing and remarkable composi-
tions of Corelli established the violin as one of the most important among instruments, we gather from several sources that one of his violins was made by Albani,[2]
and another by Andrea Amati.[3]

A comparison between the period which may be assumed to comprise the working years of Corelli's life (1670–1713 *circa*) and that of Albani (1674–98 *circa*),
taken from dates in authentic instruments, shows that Corelli played on an instrument which was the work of a contemporary maker, and could in no circumstances
have been more than a few years old. The Andrea Amati on the other hand would

---

[1] *Musick's Monument*, pp. 245–6.

[2] William Corbett (1668–1748), the English violinist, went
to Italy in 1710 and brought to this country a collection of fine
Italian instruments, which, enumerated in his will, includes an
Albani described as the violin of Corelli. Our study of Albani's
instruments and the researches instituted by us at Bolzani
(Botzen) have shown conclusively that there was only one
Matthias Albani, not two as usually stated, who made violins,
and he was of Italian origin. This statement is supported by our
finding in a viola of his making, which he subsequently had

repaired, an autograph inscription in *Italian* to that effect.

[3] Described as the violin of Corelli in a MS. note-book in our
possession, compiled at the beginning of the nineteenth century
by the well-known maker and dealer John Betts. 'Burney mentions Corelli's violin, then the property of Giardini, after whose
death we believe Mr. Salamon became its owner; it was made in
1578, and the case is said to have been painted by Annibal
Caracci.' Sandys and Forester, pp. 104–5. The date 1578 corro-
borates Betts's statement that it was an Andrea Amati.

have been close on one hundred years old, for we possess fairly conclusive data that by 1580 the master was no longer alive.

Corelli excelled as an orchestral leader as well as a soloist; and it is a reasonable assumption, one in accordance with the custom of many later violinists, that he used the Albani, the newer violin, to lead his orchestras, while reserving the Amati for the performance of his celebrated 'Twelve Solo Sonatas',[1] and other chamber music.

There is reason to believe that a specimen of the distinct form of Stradivari violin, known as the 'Long Stradivari' was introduced to London audiences soon after 1700; that is, within some fifteen years of its construction, for the master did not originate this pattern until 1690.

Our English maker, Daniel Parker, made from 1710 onwards some excellent violins, which embodied the special features of this particular type and other marked characteristics of Stradivari's style. The cause of Parker's departure from the orthodox Amati or Stainer models in vogue at the time can be traced, we believe, to the sojourn of Gasparo Visconti, the Cremonese violinist, in London, where he published in 1703 *Solos for a Violin with thorough Bass*,[2] dedicated to the Duke of Devonshire.

Fetis writes[3] that Visconti's 'counsels greatly aided Stradivari in the manufacture of his instruments'; and it is quite conceivable that he played on a 'Long Stradivari', and thus became the source of Parker's inspiration.

When Viotti in 1782 astonished the Parisians by his remarkable playing and demonstrated the transcendant qualities of the Stradivari violin, it is more than probable that he was using the choice example made in 1709, to which he himself refers[4] in his will, stating that 'it should realize a large sum'. Without allowing for any use of the instrument by Viotti prior to 1782, the Stradivari would be seventy-three years old at that date.[5]

The experience gained by the lute and viol players of the improvement wrought in their instruments by the 'seasoning' of age and use was to be repeated in the case of the violin players, as we believe will be shown by the preceding examples, and some others to follow in relation to the violins of del Gesù.

The earlier violinists, especially those of the eighteenth century, were gradually to

[1] *XII Suonate a violino e violone o cembalo*, Op. 5, Roma, 1700.
[2] *Opera Prima*. Printed for J. Walsh and J. Hare, London, 1703.
[3] *Nicolo Paganini*, Schott & Co., London, 1852, 2nd edition, p. 17.

[4] 'Viotti,' *Grove's Dictionary of Music and Musicians*, London, 1889.
[5] A generous Italian patron, the Prince de la Cisterna, is stated to have spent 20,000 frs. on Viotti's education, and probably started him on his career with the Stradivari.

acquire the knowledge of their forerunners: 'that twenty to forty years, and even fourscore years in some cases, were requisite' to play violins into a state of tonal efficiency. According to the nature of its construction and the quality of the materials employed, so would the number of years bestowed on the 'playing up' of an instrument necessarily vary.

By way of illustrating our argument we venture to tabulate the periods of time which we conjecture had been found necessary to season the tone of the most famous makers' instruments.

Stainer	from 10 to 15 years.
Amati, the average example	„ 20 „ 25 „
„ larger and more robust types . . .	„ 30 „ 35 „
Stradivari, the Amati types	„ 30 „ 35 „
„ „ Long and non-Amati . . .	„ 40 „ 50 „
„ „ years 1710–36	„ 50 „ 60 „
Guarneri del Gesù, small form 1726–36 . .	„ 40 „ —
„ „ most representative . .	„ 50 „ 60 „
„ „ massive, 1737–43 . . .	„ 60 „ 80 „
Carlo Bergonzi, average	„ 40 „ 60 „
„ „ most massive	„ 60 „ 80 „

In estimating the respective durations of time comprised in the foregoing table we have taken into account that as a general rule the 'old violin' was not subjected during its maturing stage to continuous and vigorous use for a definite series of years. The tone-seasoning process has in most cases been carried out in intermittent fashion owing to the limitations inherent to the pursuit of violin-playing and the vicissitudes common to human life, which would cause an instrument to be laid aside at times, changed for another, used but little or only feebly, and seldom allowing ten years to be devoted without a break to playing it up. Use, which implies age as well, is the real factor in maturing the tone: for age without use, though it does season the fabric, cannot to the same extent improve its sound,[1] or promote the necessary fusion between player and instrument. The negative result obtained by making violins of exceptionally old wood, an experiment tried by several French makers, is, so we believe, sufficient confirmation that our opinion is correct.

[1] 'Giardini, the Prince of Fiddlers, is expected in London in the course of this year with a cargo of "Cremonas", for the sole manufacture of which, it is said, he intends to apply for a patent. The art of making old fiddles of new wood will be a great acquisition to the musical world, particularly to the curious in "Cremonas".' (St. James Chronicle, 1786.)

We have recently come across a pronouncement by Spohr that supports the views here put forward, and which is entitled to the highest respect on account of its author's right to speak with authority on the subject. Describing the violins by great makers which he saw at Milan during his Italian tour in 1816–17, Spohr mentions the collection belonging to Count Cozio di Salabue, and draws special attention to four violins made by Stradivari, which formed part of it.

Noticing their new and unused condition 'as if just finished', Spohr proceeds to tell us that two of the four violins were made by Stradivari when he was an old man of ninety-three, as indeed the trembling of his hands betrays in the workmanship; whilst the other two are of great beauty, and date from the 'Artist's' best time. He concludes his account of them with the following criticism: 'Their tone is full and powerful, but still new and woody, and they must be played on for ten years at least to become first-rate.' Spohr's qualifications for 'playing up' a violin, his Herculean build and splendid health, which enabled him when studying under Eck often to spend ten hours a day at his violin, were altogether exceptional. Ten years of such usage would mature a 'new and woody tone' as effectively as forty or more years in a case where the violin could only be used in the intermittent fashion we have previously described.[1]

Now the earliest player of importance whom we can associate with the use of a del Gesù violin is Pugnani[2] (1727–1803), one of the most eminent among the many fine violinists who sprang from the prolific soil of Italy during the eighteenth century. Trained by Somis[3] according to the classical principles of Corelli, and later placing himself under the tuition of Tartini, Pugnani became a gifted exponent, both as performer and teacher, of all that was pure and fine in the art of violin-

[1] 'Violins and Violoncellos.

'Mr. Merlin begs leave to inform the Lovers of these instruments, that he has invented a contrivance to prevent their pegs getting loose, which also makes them turn with more ease and exactness than the common pegs do. *He likewise continues to alter the tone of the most common fiddle to that of the finest "Cremona", for one guinea each improvement.*

'N.B. Good allowance is made to the professors who honour him with their commands for his new invented violins and violoncellos etc.

'No. 66, Queen Anne St. East.
'Portland Chapel.'
(The Public Advertiser.) 1778.

[2] The earliest record of a violin by Guarneri in the hands of a player which we have succeeded in tracing occurs in the biographical notice of a little-known Italian violinist, Michel-

Angelo Bezegui, 1670–1744, who came to Paris when young and entered the service of M. Fagon, Intendant des Finances. Whilst on a visit to the latter's country estate he met with an accident, breaking his left arm, which prevented him from playing again, and he then presented his violin, 'un Guarnerius admirable', to M. de Saint-Saire, one of the best amateurs of the day. *Essai sur la Musique Ancienne et Moderne,* par Laborde, Paris, 1780.

[3] G. B. Somis (1676–1763). F. Giardini (1716–91), another pupil of Somis, was equally renowned for his tone. 'Shield (1748–1829), opera composer and violinist, went to Italy in 1792. He spoke of Giardini, who, He said, had the finest tone He had ever heard, when the strength of it was considered. In general those who produce fine tones have not much strength.' Farington, *Diary*, vol. i, p. 235.

playing. He founded a school of playing, that of Turin, whence issued many talented violinists, including his celebrated pupil Viotti.

Now a del Gesù of the year 1734—also the date of Saint Leon's 'Violon du Diable'—possessed the virility and latent force which would respond to the demands of a player in the 'grand style', such as Pugnani, who produced a large tone and played in a noble and animated manner, well exemplified by the *Prélude* and *Allegro* of his composition often heard to-day. If, as seems likely, he played on this del Gesù when he was in his prime and during the foreign tours which he made between 1754 and 1770, the date 1734 shows that it would be comparatively a new violin, perhaps twenty years old when first used by him.

We owe to Pugnani, though he was but ten years old at the time of Stradivari's death in 1737, the only account[1] which is extant of the famous maker's personal appearance and circumstances during the later years of his life. Pugnani's fondness for recalling his memories of Stradivari implies an interest in the Cremonese makers which may have led to some intercourse with del Gesù, and caused him subsequently to play on one of his violins.

Jarnowick[2] comes next in chronological order, among the eminent violinists traced by us as having played on violins by del Gesù. Endowed with the brilliant and elegant[3] qualities that make the popular virtuoso, he was notorious for his caprices, wilful temper, and irregular life. Congenial to Jarnowick's characteristics —a kindred spirit, in fact—must have been a violin made by del Gesù in 1741 (one year earlier than the famed one of Paganini), that period when the maker's life, judged by his work, seems to have been as erratic as that of the violinist! Without doubt brought from Italy by Jarnowick, and played on when he made a successful début at Paris in 1770, the del Gesù would be twenty-nine years old that year.

Spagnoletti,[4] much of whose musical life was passed in our country, where he led the best orchestra for some thirty years—Paganini insisted on his employment as leader at the concerts given by him—also used a del Gesù, made in the same year,

---

[1] Tradition handed down by his pupil Polledro (1781–1853).

[2] Giovanni Maria Giornvichj (1745–1804).

[3] Dragonetti is said to have declared that his playing was the most elegant he had ever heard before that of Paganini, but that it lacked power. *Grove's Dictionary*.

[4] P. Spagnoletti (1761–1834) was born at Cremona, earlier surely than the year usually assigned, 1761; for the young Mozart writes to his sister from Milan, 26th January 1770, of an

opera he had heard: 'At Cremona the orchestra is good, and the 1st violin is named Spagnoletta.' *W. A. Mozart*, by T. de Wyzewa et G. de Saint-Foix, vol. i, p. 267. At nine years of age it is improbable he would have been made the leader of an orchestra! Dittersdorf states in his autobiography that he accompanied Glück to Bologna in 1763, where he heard Spagnoletti, a famous violinist of Cremona! There probably existed two violinists, father and son.

1734, as that of Pugnani. This was Spagnoletti's favourite instrument according to tradition, though an N. Amati of the large form, dated 1682, which he also used, evidently bore a good share in the work of his active and long life. The fact of his being a Cremonese may have had some connexion with his ownership of a del Gesù at a later date; but we rather suspect that in his case, as also in that of Pugnani, an important compulsory reason for his choice of instrument was that a del Gesù violin could be bought for a sum which was within the means of the struggling artist, whereas the instruments of the earlier and more renowned makers, those of Stradivari and of the Amati,[1] had already appreciated in value.

Rode,[2] one of the outstanding names in the history of violin-playing, follows next on our list. An interesting document in our possession dated 1849 establishes beyond question that Rode habitually played at his concerts on a particular del Gesù violin; and this fact is vouched for by three men of such distinction as Vuillaume the violin-maker, Alard the violinist, and Clapisson,[3] the opera composer, violinist, and ardent collector of ancient musical instruments. Sandys and Forster support the truth of this in a reference to a fine specimen by the master, dated 1734, which had belonged to Mr. Mawkes,[4] and we quote it fully to show how highly Spohr esteemed del Gesù. 'He (Mawkes) bought it in 1831 at Spohr's recommendation from Professor Hoffmann[5] of Frankfurt, when he was studying under that celebrated musician at Hesse Cassel. Hoffmann bought it at the time Rode was at Frankfurt,[6] it having been a facsimile of an instrument of the same maker played on by him (Rode). Spohr told Mr. Mawkes, if he could purchase it, he would have one of the finest instruments in the world; and he would have given his famous Stradivari[7] in exchange for it.'

To revert to Rode's own del Gesù,[8] which, let us add, must have been nearly

---

[1] 'To be sold, a first rate Amati Violin, the property of a gentleman. To prevent trouble, the price is sixty guineas.
'Enquire at Mr. Bremner's Music Shop, opposite Somerset House, in the Strand.' *The Public Advertiser*, 1789.

[2] J. P. J. Rode, 1774-1830.

[3] *Les Trois Nicolas*, an opera produced by Clapisson in 1858, contains a short gavotte written as a solo for a Stradivari pochette, then his property, and now in the Paris Conservatoire Museum.

[4] Thos. Mawkes, violinist, 1810-80. His violin was purchased in London, from Mr. George Withers, by an American lady, on the advice of Wilhelmj, the violinist, about 1876. We have so far not succeeded in tracing its present ownership.

[5] H. A. Hoffmann (1770-1842) most probably, who was appointed 'premier violon' at Frankfurt in 1799, and later one of the 'chefs d'orchestre'. Fétis. Leading a series of quartette concerts at Frankfurt in 1818, Spohr mentions a 'Concert-Meister Hoffmann' as his second violin.

[6] Most likely in 1803, while Rode, on his way to St. Petersburg, was giving concerts in Germany.

[7] Spohr bought his 'famous Stradivari' at Gotha in 1822 from Madame Schlick, née Strinasacchi (1762-1839), the distinguished Italian violinist praised by Mozart for her 'expression, beauty, and power of tone', and with whom he played at her concert, Vienna 1784.

[8] Thibout, the French Luthier (1777-1856), made several copies of it, as stated on the label inserted.

sixty years old when he began to use it. Dating from the year 1734, one of the most prolific years of the maker, its tone must have contributed when Rode's powers were at their best—from 1794 to 1803—to the admiration which his playing won from all who heard him, including Spohr, the severest of critics. A very fine 'ornamented Stradivari'[1] of the year 1722 also belonged to Rode; but its exceptional state of preservation leads one to conclude that he owned it only during the later and less strenuous part of his career, and had used it but little as compared with the Guarneri.

Spohr, in spite of his admiration of del Gesù, was using, as already stated, a Stradivari violin in 1831, at the time of the incident just referred to in connexion with Rode. But as we learn from his autobiography[2] Spohr had played formerly on a del Gesù violin, one presented to him by M. Remi, a young French violinist and a member of the Tsar's Court-orchestra, whilst he and his master Eck[3] were staying at St. Petersburg in the winter of 1802–3.

His possession and enjoyment of the violin were of brief duration, for it was stolen from him in the following aggravating circumstances. He was taking a journey to Paris in 1804, and he narrates:

'I had a case made worthy of the splendid violin I had brought from Russia, viz. a very elegant one; and in order to protect this from injury I had packed it up in my trunk, between my linen and clothes.'

The trunk was fastened on behind the carriage in which he travelled, and it was cut away by thieves just outside Göttingen.

He adds: 'I passed a sleepless night in a state of mind such as in my hitherto fortunate career had been wholly unknown to me. Had I not lost my splendid Guarnerius, the exponent of all the artistic excellence I had till then attained, I could have lightly borne the loss of the rest.'

Although next morning the empty trunk, violin case, and the genuine Tourte bow, which in the lid of the case had escaped the thieves' notice, were found in the fields, Spohr's 'splendid Guarnerius' had vanished, and from that day up to now no trace of it has ever come to light.

It is worthy of comment that Paganini[4] and Spohr, each born in 1784, one to become the most extraordinary of virtuoso-violinists, the other the greatest of composer-violinists, should both have been presented with fine Guarneri violins at the

---

[1] Illustrated in our *Life of Stradivari*.   [2] L. Spohr, 1784–1859.   [3] F. Eck, 1774–1809?
[4] N. Paganini, 1784–1840.

outset of their careers, by enthusiastic admirers. Paganini was fifteen when he received his from M. Livron in 1799, Spohr nineteen when given his by M. Remi in 1803; and we have only to consider the circumstances attending the bestowal of these gifts to realize that the violins of del Gesù were already in favour and held in high repute.[1]

The reflection is possibly a saddening one to the violin-lover that the violins of both these great artists have long been silent; Paganini's mute in its glass case at Genoa, Spohr's voiceless in the 'place of lost things'.

It was a fortunate chance that placed in the hands of Paganini early in life the violin which enabled him to display so perfectly his wondrous gifts and skill. Made in 1742, this masterly production of del Gesù's genius in one of its happiest mani-festations was fifty-six years old when Paganini entered on the forty-one years collaboration which immortalized him and his instrument. The player of audacity and originality became indissolubly wedded to a violin, the work of a craftsman who in his own sphere was quite as astonishing and individual.

A feature of its tone to harmonize effectively with Paganini's style and composi-tions would be the 'incisive brilliancy', because, as Fétis has told us in a reasoned judgement, 'the poetry of the great violinist's playing consisted principally in the brilliancy of it'.[2] On the other hand, the extra force required to cope with the stiffish articulation of del Gesù tone, and to draw forth all its power, may seem in the light of to-day's knowledge to have been a drawback for a player, of whose tone a con-sensus of opinion has recorded that it lacked 'richness and sonority'. A violin similar to the 'Rode' would seem to have been better suited to the youth's gifts and attainments, rather than one of del Gesù's most massive productions of the type which more than any other has taxed the resources and time of the player 'to get the tone to go'.

However, at the exuberant age of fifteen, any such difficulty to be overcome would not weigh against the lucky fact that he, Paganini, was the recipient of a really fine violin, far superior in tone, we can safely assume, to any other previously used by him. His parentage and upbringing do not lead us to gather that the precocious boy had as yet had the advantage of playing on a violin of the highest quality. The del Gesù arriving as it did at a critical moment, when his gambling losses had left him

[1] When M. Remi proposed an exchange of violins in remem-brance of one another, Spohr exclaimed, 'A genuine Guarneri worth at least twice as much as mine!' and refused, but gave way when Remi insisted on making it a birthday present, it being Spohr's birthday. *Selbstbiographie*, vol. i, p. 55.

[2] N. Paganini, *Biographie Universelle*.

without any violin, served as a real godsend, stimulating him no doubt to conquer its secrets and resources, and by its magic aid urging him to excel all other violinists.

Finally, to illustrate the effect made by Paganini's playing, and the nature of the tone which he drew from his Guarneri, we shall cite some pertinent extracts from a little-known description by Moscheles,[1] the accomplished pianist and musician. Written in 1831, the year of Paganini's first visit to London, when Moscheles 'heard him frequently in order to study his manner and style more accurately', it presents the views of a competent and impartial critic, who was himself a remarkable soloist.

Moscheles in his diary complains of his utter inability to find language capable of conveying a description of Paganini's wonderful performance.

'Had that long-drawn, soul-searching tone lost for a single second its balance, it would have lapsed into a discordant cat's-mew; but it never did so, and Paganini's tone was always his own and unique of its kind. The thin strings of his instrument, on which alone it was possible to conjure forth those myriads of notes and trills and cadenzas, would have been fatal in the hands of any other violin player, but with him they were indispensable adjuncts, and lastly his compositions were so ultra original, so completely in harmony with the weird and strange figure of the man, that, if wanting in depth and earnestness, the deficiency never betrayed itself during the author's dazzling display of power. . . . I never wearied of the intense expression, soft and melting like that of an Italian singer, which he could draw from his violin . . . completely as he may annihilate his less showy colleagues, I long for a little of Spohr's earnestness, Baillot's[2] power, and even Mayseder's piquancy.'[3]

From *La Chélonomie ou Le Parfait Luthier*, by M. l'Abbé Sibire, published at Paris in 1806, we learn that the 'del Gesù' violin already enjoyed a high reputation, and that there were even then some enthusiasts who ranked it in tone as superior to the Stradivari.

L'Abbé Antoine Sibire was personally known, apparently, to Fétis,[4] then work-

---

[1] *Life of Moscheles, with selections from his Diaries and Correspondence*, by his wife, Hurst & Blackett, London, 1873.

[2] Mayseder's violin was a del Gesù, but Baillot played on a Francesco Stradivari, and evidently his power of tone compared favourably with that of Paganini and Mayseder.

[3] Ludwig Strauss, the violinist (1835–99), writing in 1893 of his boyhood says: 'I was allowed to play 2nd violin to Mayseder on every Tuesday night for 2–3 years at the house of Baron Heintl in Vienna; his playing of Hadyn was unique. I once plucked up courage of asking him what he thought of Paganini! We never heard anything like it before, nor shall we ever hear anything like it again—All of us wanted to smash our fiddles.'

[4] Fétis's father was a sound musician and talented violinist, and he himself had played the violin, a fact which accounts for the special interest displayed by him in the violin and its makers.

ing in Paris, and it is from his account of the author and book that we extract the following:

'An Amateur, passionately fond of the violin, which he played very badly, he frequented assiduously the workshop of Lupot, and thereby became smitten with a fanatical admiration for the instruments of the Cremonese makers. Lupot confided to him the manuscript notes and observations which he had made about the workmanship of these masters, and the qualities of their instruments.' Undoubtedly the book, the earliest to attempt a detailed criticism of the qualities distinguishing the famous Cremonese makers one from the other, owes its value and existence to the knowledge and enthusiasm of Lupot, as the Abbé affirms categorically in his preface and elsewhere.

By the dawn of the nineteenth century Paris had become paramount in fine violin-playing and all that related to its study, a result chiefly due to Viotti and the remarkable triumvirate of French violinists, Rode, Kreutzer, and Baillot, who were inspired by the great Italian's example.

The city contained at the same time the two finest craftsmen that France has produced in connexion with our subject, Lupot, the best violin-maker of his epoch, and Tourte, the greatest of all bow-makers. Evidently a discriminating and an enthusiastic public existed there ready to approve all that was progressive and sound.

Let us now consider what the Abbé Sibire has to say about the tone of the 'del Gesù' violin: 'One would suppose that he (del Gesù) had done his best to secure a tone of great volume, brilliancy more than fullness being his aim. If such were his purpose, it is certain that he was successful; not that his violins want power exactly, but an extraordinary brilliancy is their chief feature; the E string is sparkling, the A is its equal in brilliancy, and the D, likewise brilliant, possesses a certain roundness; but the G is dry 'as an almond', and stiff throughout its length, all the notes being stubborn, especially the B and C; it is completely sacrificed to the other three. For some time past his violins have been in favour. One perceives there are some musicians who place them above the Stradivari itself, so much does the extraordinary brilliancy of the first three strings (the E, A, and D) impose upon their ears. It is a great pity that this unhappy and overkind G string exhausts itself for the ungrateful others, which absorb it.'

When we unravel the meaning of these sentences from the fanciful and high-flown language in which it is cloaked, we find that the analysis of del Gesù's tone is substantially correct, except the part concerning the 'G' string, and in agreement with the experience of it by the whole century which has elapsed since the Abbé wrote. His error of judgement in this one detail should not cause us to underrate the criticism as a whole. In fairness to his knowledge we must point out that the Abbé had come in contact for the first time with a class of tone to which the violins of the older Italian masters had provided no exact parallel. The pungent brilliancy and concise power of del Gesù's tone introduced a new combination.

One must refer back to a contemporary of del Gesù, Carlo Bergonzi, or a successor, J. B. Guadagnini—to name two of the best known—to find violins which present a somewhat similar class of tone. But at the time when the Abbé wrote, these makers' violins were not widely known, and those of Carlo Bergonzi passed frequently as the work of del Gesù. The violinist who subsequently made the name of del Gesù universally famous, Paganini, did not play outside Italy until he appeared at Vienna in 1828. In 1806 he held an appointment at Lucca, the Court of Napoleon's sister, the Princess Eliza, and was then studying how to attain that special use and mastery of the 'G' string which added so much in later years to the fame of his playing and his violin. Paganini did not appear in Paris until 1831; and as the Abbé Sibire died about 1826 he escaped the humiliation of learning that he was totally wrong in describing so confidently the del Gesù tone on the G string as 'dry as an almond'.

Del Gesù, belonging to the third generation of a Cremonese family which had gained distinction in violin-making, inherited and acquired in the course of his training knowledge of the masterly and varied productions left by his famous forerunners in the art. He would be conversant with the distinct kinds of tone which were a consequence of the different types of violin, created by Gasparo-Maggini, the Amati, and Stradivari; for, as we have shown elsewhere, skill in playing as well as in making existed in the family. As he worked for years in close proximity to the workshop of Stradivari, he had every opportunity of acquainting himself with the great master's achievements. Stradivari features of design and construction accordingly present themselves; though it is soon apparent that in striving to express individual views and attain his own tone ideal, del Gesù was reverting for principles to Brescian sources. Perhaps he was prompted by the example of Stradivari, who in his 'long pattern' and later forms, leavened them with Brescian structural strength, in order to gain a fuller and bigger tone.

To the general trend of music, the advance of skill in playing, and in solo music written for the violin, we must look, then, for the causes that impelled del Gesù to bow to the influences and needs of his time, and introduce yet another category of tone. The eighteenth century in the course of its progress saw a continuous and growing appreciation of the violin by the musical world, and an employment of it in the chief forms of composition. In the Scores of Operas, Masses, and Oratorios, in purely instrumental works, Concerti Grossi, Overtures, Symphonies, Suites, &c. a most important role was allotted to the 'Strings', which became the backbone of the instrumentation.

With the passing of the Amati-Stradivari era, the monarch or the nobleman ceased to order from Cremona choice sets of instruments for his own use, or that of his Court band. All our evidence points to the conclusion that del Gesù, his fellow workers, and the post-Stradivari makers depended for their livelihood in a much greater degree than their predecessors had done on the demand for an instrument of sterling quality, which came from the professor and middle-class lover of the violin.

As the compass of the violin was extended upwards, and rapidity of execution in the high positions became an object, the soloists—especially virtuosi like Vivaldi, Locatelli, and Lolli—would desire incisive brilliancy in the tone, in order that feats of dexterity might be effective and easily heard in public performance; while to the violinists of average capacity, who greatly outnumbered the soloists and much of whose time would be spent in orchestral playing, a tone with 'bite' and 'driving force' was equally essential.

The tone of the del Gesù violin impresses us as being one of intense brilliancy, allied to concentrated power. Verging towards the metallic in quality on the E and G strings, the A and D possess that 'full body' which supplies so desirable an adjunct to the tone of the middle strings.

Some deviation from our estimate happens in occasional examples, as, for instance, a replacement of some of the brilliancy by increased mellowness in one violin; easier articulation and less sonority in another; while a third gains in penetration at the expense of richness of sound. Still, as might be anticipated from a craftsman whose divergences from his original design and set of principles relate to detail and not to substance, the maker adheres to his tone-standard quite as closely as to his method of construction. The Guarneri tone was said by Fetis[1] to be stronger

---

[1] *N. Paganini*, Schott & Co., London, 1852, p. 6, 2nd edition.

than the Stradivari, a belief held by others also; but the wider experience gained during the seventy years that have passed since he wrote, through the extended use of both makers' instruments, has not confirmed his statement. We can instance in disproof of it that the biggest and grandest tone heard in our time was that which Wilhelmj produced from his Stradivari.

Dogmatism is out of place in discussing this problem, because the solution of it depends on the contingency that while one soloist will get more sonority out of a Guarneri than a Stradivari, another will reverse the result, and obtain a larger tone from the Stradivari. The performer's physical endowment and method of playing are deciding factors—for the del Gesù violin needs to be attacked by a 'biting bow', and gripped by a 'strong left hand', if the whole extent of its tone reserve is to be brought out.

Our list of famous violinists, beginning from soon after the maker's death, who found in their violins a sympathetic medium for the display of their talents—the classicists Pugnani, Rode, and Spohr, the virtuosi Lafont, Jarnowick and Paganini, and the orchestral leader Spagnoletti—supplies convincing evidence that del Gesù tone could meet any demands which might be made on it, however distinct or varied their nature. Though the fascination of Paganini's playing added greatly to the reputation of del Gesù, in that it centred public attention on the maker's violins, a stronger proof of their intrinsic merits is afforded, we consider, by the many other soloists of eminence who have made them the instruments of their choice.

Simultaneously with the great virtuoso, Mayseder, Pixis, Lipinski, and Rovelli were performing on them; and subsequently Mori, David, Saint-Léon, Alard, Sainton, Carrodus, Vieuxtemps, Wieniawski, and Bazzini all became exponents of Guarneri tone.

The classical masterpieces among solo or concerted music, which form part of the present-day violinists' repertoire—a sonata, quartet, concerto, or whatever work it may happen to be—will lose nothing in the interpretation, and give none the less delight and joy to the music lover, whether the artist has chosen a del Gesù or a Stradivari as his means of expression.

'The tests of time and use' have established del Gesù beside Stradivari as one of the two greatest makers. His instruments are used by the foremost artists unceasingly to interpret musical works of the past and present, of the noblest inspiration and the most varied nature.

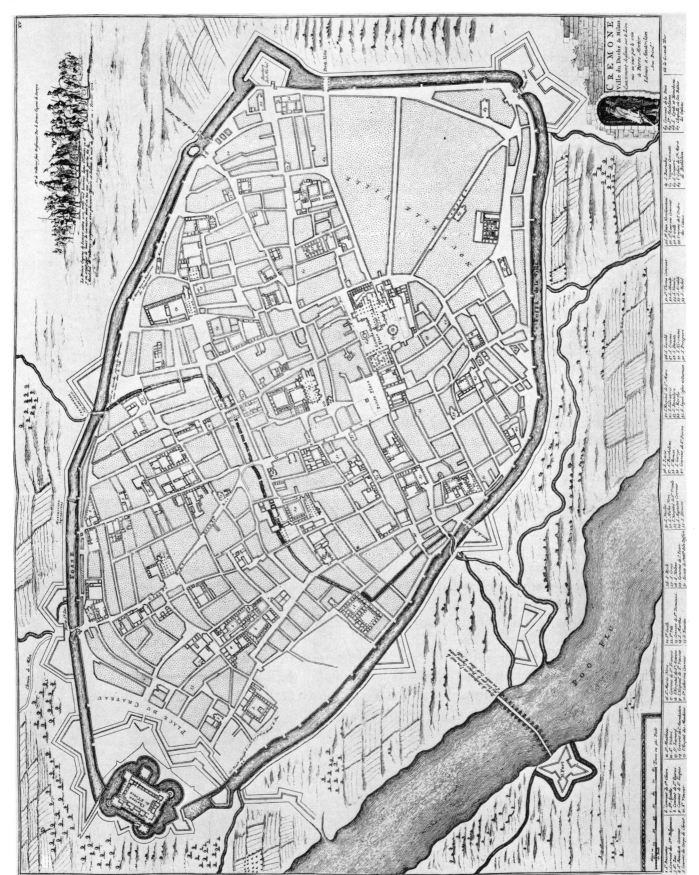

MAP OF THE CITY OF CREMONA, 1700

CHAPTER VI
THE CASA GUARNERI, 1654-1740

WE are fortunately in a position to give an illustration of the house known from about 1660 as the Casa Guarneri, previously the Casa Orcelli, the house which passed to Andrea through his marriage with Anna Maria Orcelli; and therein were born all the later generations of Guarneri violin-makers, including Giuseppe del Gesù.

It will be recalled that Andrea proceeded there with his bride of a few months on quitting the Amati household in 1654; and from that year onward until 1739-40 the house remained the home of the Guarneri family. In May 1740, after the death of Giuseppe filius, it was, as mentioned in Chapter IV, sold, being purchased by Giacomo Antonio Arrighi, who lived there until his death in 1746. We are also able to add a description of the interior as existing in the year 1728. Situated in the Piazza S. Domenico No. 5—now known as the Piazza Roma—within a few doors of the house of Stradivari, it formed one of a block of about twelve houses; and opposite, as shown in the illustration, is to be seen the projecting corner of the old Dominican Convent, a building which at the period of the French Revolution was utilized as barracks, and remained so until its demolition.

The house was of modest dimensions, narrow of frontage, yet having a fair depth, and opening at the back into the Strettino del Guasto (now Vicolo del Vasto), a small impasse, running for a short distance parallel to the Piazza. We learn from a contract drawn up by the Cremonese notary, Giuseppe Picenardi, dated 31st August 1728, that Giuseppe filius Andrea and his wife Barbara Franchi, being desirous of contracting a loan of 1,500 lire, had entered into the following agreement with Sig. Giovanni Ottina, a fellow Cremonese who carried on the business of merciaio (mercer). The loan was to be repaid within six years: interest on 900 lire to be paid regularly, whereas that due on the remaining 600 lire would be met if the borrowers agreed to allow Sig. Ottina to occupy part of their house (as a lodger). The following details and stipulations of the arrangements are given: 'a room on the second floor over the kitchen; a room and cabinet (or dressing-room) on the third floor over the shop, a loft for wood over the first-mentioned room, running through from one street to the other with its "stadiolo" (rack for wood); moreover the right to make use of the well, the "sedile" (seat), and the cellar in common with the master and his wife (*li detti Signori Jugali*), likewise the door opening on to the Guasto and the way through the shop when it is open.' Later the shop was occupied by a chemist, and within comparatively recent times it was the humble dwelling of a charcoal merchant and his family. Except that the front had been whitewashed from time to time, the house had remained unaltered from the period when the Guarneri dwelt therein. In the year 1869 the demolition of the Church and Convent of S. Domenico took place, and the result was the formation of a fairly large and open space, which was subsequently laid out as an attractive public garden. The surrounding property, in consequence, rose in value, and all the houses, including both that of the Guarneri and Stradivari, have been either rebuilt or in some measure reconstructed. One of the present writers revisited Cremona in 1925 in order to verify these facts.

We also adjoin a portion of the ground plan of Cremona, wherein were situated not only the Casa Guarneri but other houses of the celebrated violin-makers, this portion being an enlargement of the central part of the map¹ facing p. 123.

As in most of the mediæval cities, the active life of the community centred round the Duomo and Grande Place. Cremona formed no exception; and it is pleasant to picture to oneself the violin-makers in their modest dwellings working at their benches and planting the life of music in that large number of stringed instruments which were continually being constructed. Musicians or other emissaries came from far and wide, commissioned to give orders for or to purchase those works for which the city was so justly famed; and we cannot doubt but that much intimate inter-course took place between these men who made and those who played, as also between the various craftsmen thus living and working for generations in close proximity—all, too, at times intermingled for some common purpose, such as the annual celebration of the Fête of S. Cecilia, the Patron Saint of Music, and there-fore also of the instrument maker.

It will be seen on referring to the map that the principal places, parishes, and edifices are indicated and numbered, thus greatly facilitating the task of pointing out the spots in which our readers will be the more particularly interested. The Grande Place, the Cathedral dating from the twelfth century, and the site of the fine tower (marked *68*) will be observed on the plan; within a few hundred yards, marked *23*, we see the Church and Convent of S. Domenico, in the shadow of which centred

¹ Map dating from the period with which we are concerned.

the life of Stradivari. The Amati lived in the parish of S. Faustino (marked *25*) and
Andrea Guarneri and his son Giuseppe in that of S. Matteo (marked *24*) though
here we note that the church indicated on the plan is named in error S. Marta;
it should be S. Matteo.

The parish of S. Prospero, where Giuseppe del Gesù lived, but a short distance
away from the home of his ancestors, is marked *50*; and we would mention that
neither of the Churches of S. Matteo and S. Prospero now exists. We are able to
point out the approximately correct position of the Casa Guarneri and that of
Stradivari, both being situated where indicated by the figures *1* and *2* in the
Piazza S. Domenico; but we have failed to obtain similar information concerning
the houses of the Amati and Giuseppe del Gesù.

A.
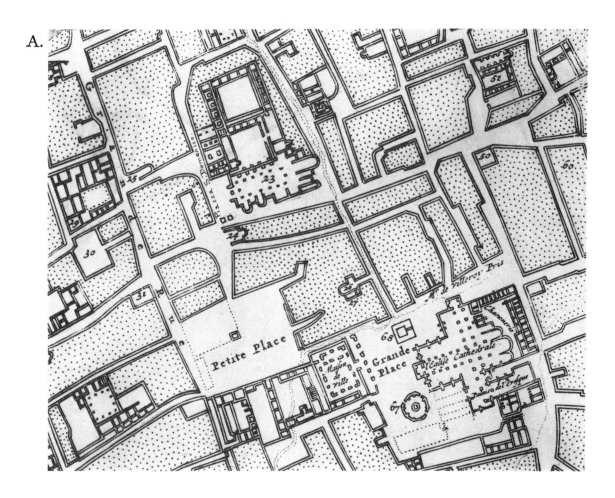

Casa Guarneri

CHAPTER VII
THE GUARNERI LABELS

ACLOSE study of the labels of the Guarneri as found inserted in their instruments is not without interest. Following the usual practice, their labels were printed from wood blocks and on hand-made paper, the text being invariably in Latin—with the exception of the Christian name 'Joseph'—and the orthography not always correct!

Not one of the Guarneri placed his label in a defined position as was the custom of Stradivari; in most instruments it will be found more towards the centre of the back, at times placed in a straight line when viewed through the sound-holes, at other times at varying angles. Andrea and both the Pietros appear always to have labelled their productions, though it is possible that the former may have occasion-ally inserted the name of Nicolò Amati in certain copies of that master's work made by him; but we ourselves have never been able to identify a violin giving definite evidence that such a practice had been resorted to by Andrea. The Rugeri certainly did so, and we have found the label of Francesco placed in one of his violins under-neath that of Nicolò Amati, who was his teacher;[1] nor did the Italian makers of later generations hesitate to ticket their productions—in certain cases copies—with the labels of their more famous predecessors.

We are decidedly of opinion, as stated and commented on in Chapter III, that the violins which issued from the workshop of Giuseppe filius Andreæ towards the latter part of his career, i.e. after 1715–20, and with which both Carlo Bergonzi and Giuseppe del Gesù were at times concerned, were generally sold without any in-scription whatsoever.

Labels of Andrea Guarneri.

If we now critically examine Andrea's labels, we find that the earliest hitherto seen by us is that of the year 1638—we have some evidence pointing to a violin label of still earlier date, namely 1635—and it is interesting to notice, in the first specimen, the master's statement, 'Alumnus Nicolai Amati', in the second, the in-accurate spelling of 'Allumnus', and, in the third, the 'ex Alumnis'. It is unfor-tunate that this last inscription records no date, but we believe that the violin which

---

[1] See *Life of Stradivari*, Chapter IX.

bears it is an early work of the master; it is reproduced from a tracing, whereas the others are direct photographs from originals. The label of 1668, all figures written, and that of 1682, all figures printed, are both exceptional; and if we had not our-selves found them in authentic instruments, and proved them on examination to be printed on old paper, we should have doubted their originality. The fifth ticket is a facsimile of the one most frequently met with, and which we see used from about 1660 to 1680–90. Note the bold figures and that they are invariably all written in. The tickets of the years 1690 and 1694 are specimens of those usually found at this period and to the end of the master's career inserted in instruments which we generally recognize to be the work of the son, Giuseppe. The inscription—'Sub disciplina', &c.—dated 1693 or 1695 comes from a violoncello, but we have seen a similarly worded label of smaller size in a violin; and our impression is that the instruments so labelled were productions in which the Guarneri had taken but a small part.

Labels of Pietro Guarneri of Mantua.

The son Pietro of Mantua apparently made use of but two types of label[1] during his career; and we have never learnt of the existence of an instrument signed by him when working at Cremona and prior to establishing himself at Mantua. It is definitely proved that he made violins whilst under the parental roof, and it is possible that we shall yet meet with an example bearing a Cremonese inscription. Both the tickets of small type were used up to about the end of the century; the earlier dated had three figures printed, and in the nineties the third figure was written over. Then in 1700 we see the adoption of a label of bolder type, which the master continued to use until his death in the year 1720. We give that of 1710 to illustrate his treatment of the figures; he simply did not trouble to efface the printed *o*, but penned *1* over it.

Labels of Giuseppe Guarneri, filius Andreæ.

The earliest label of the master, so far found by us, is one of the year 1690, which is identical with that of 1696—a type used by him whilst working in his father's workshop, i.e. prior to Andrea's death, and very rarely met with.

We have never seen a label dating from 1699; and when we recall that the father died in December 1698, also that Giuseppe had for some time been inserting the

---

[1] An inscription in Pietro's handwriting is reproduced in Vidal.

Andreas Guarnerius alumnus Nicolai Amati fecit
Cremonæ sub titulo Sanctæ Teresiæ 167

Andreas Guarnerius allumnus Nic a niti fecit
Cremonæ sub titulo Sanctæ Teresiæ 1655

Andreas Guarnerius ex alumnis Nicolai Amati
fecit Cremonæ sub titulo Sanctæ Teresiæ

Andreas Guarnerius Alumnus Nicolai
Amati fecit Cremonæ. 1668

Andreas Guarnerius fecit Cremonę sub titulo
Sanctæ Teresiæ 1676

Andreas Guarnerius alumnus
Nicola Amati fecit Cremonæ
sub titulo Sanctæ Teresiæ 1682

Andreas Guarnerius fecit Cremonæ sub
titulo Sanctæ Teresiæ 1690

Andreas Guarnerius fecit Cremonæ sub
titulo Sanctæ Teresiæ 16 4

Sub disciplina Andreę Guarnerij in eius
Officina sub titulo S. Teresię, Cremonę 16

LABELS INSERTED BY ANDREA GUARNERI

Petrus Guarnerius Cremonensis filius Andreæ
fecit Mantuæ sub. tit. Sanctæ Teresiæ 1686

Petrus Guarnerius Cremonensis filius Andreæ
fecit Mantuæ sub. tit. Sanctæ Teresiæ 1698

Petrus Guarnerius Cremonensis fecit
Mantuæ sub tit. Sanctæ Teresiæ 1703

Petrus Guarnerius Cremonensis fecit
Mantuæ sub tit. Sanctæ Teresiæ 1700

Ioseph Guarnerius Filius Andreæ
sub titulo S. Teresiæ Cremonæ 1696

Ioseph Guarnerius filius Andreæ fecit
Cremonæ sub titulo S. Teresiæ 1702

Ioseph Guarnerius filius Andreæ fecit
Cremonæ sub titulo S. Teresiæ 1710

Ioseph Guarnerius filius Andreæ fecit
Cremonæ sub titulo S. Teresiæ 1710

Ioseph Guarnerius filius Andreæ fecit
Cremonæ sub titulo S. Teresie 1712

Ioseph Guarnerius Filius Andreæ Fecit
Cremonæ, sub Titulo S. Theresie 1714

Ioseph Guarnerius Filius Andreæ Fecit
Cremonæ, sub Titulo S. Theresie 1731

LABELS INSERTED BY
PIETRO GUARNERI OF MANTUA
AND GIUSEPPE GUARNERI FIGLIO D'ANDREA

name of Andrea in his own productions, we think it quite probable that he only finally discarded this practice in the year 1700.

The second type is that dated 1702; note the change of wording, the small *f* of Filius, the different spelling of 'Teresię' and 'Cremonę'; the figures '17' only are printed, whereas in the previous label the last figure only is added with a pen.

The next two specimens of the plate are both dated 1710, and vary only in small detail; for instance, 'Andrea' is printed in the one case without the diphthong, and 'Teresię' has the long *s* of Gothic type, in the other the Latin *s*. Note also that the letter *i* and the figure 1 are at times dotted, but not invariably so; furthermore the date of the one label has 17 and the other 171 printed.

The exceptional feature of the fifth label is the group of figures entirely printed. The sixth and seventh, of altogether bolder type, are found in both violin and violoncello; see the curious addition of *h* to 'Teresia', and the three printed figures; in the last the printed 1 has been added to by pen in order to form a 3. Cremona is once more spelt with a diphthong; and it is of interest to observe that the actual type of block from which these labels were being printed are practically identical with those used by Andrea during the later years of his life.

Labels of Giuseppe Guarneri del Gesù.

Giuseppe del Gesù, contradictory though it seems, was most consistent as regards the form, figures, and composition of his label; he began by ignoring his parentage and Patron Saint, and he did not once vary the wording, or make any alteration whatsoever throughout his career. The type used for the printing is similar to that seen in certain of the labels of his father and grandfather, those of the years 1690–94 and 1714–31. Note the spelling of 'Cremone' with a cedilla under the *e*, and his adoption of the cipher I.H.S., an explanation concerning which is given in Chapter IV, page 71. His figures were well formed, the 17 always printed, the others added by hand; and in this connexion we note a slight yet curious addition from time to time; he added two strokes (we have seen three) with his pen when putting in the figures, and these strokes are found under the last figure of the date and the first letter of the monogram. Other than this curious feature we have observed no change; nor have we, as previously stated, ever come across a marginal note, or a line of his handwriting.

In a quite appreciable number of reproductions of the master's label it will be found that 'Cremonae' is spelt with a diphthong (see the father's labels of 1714 and 1731), but we have never in our experience come across an authentic label so spelt. Vidal[1] reproduces a ticket so worded, taken from the fine Guarneri violin ex Alard, now reposing in the Museum of the Paris Conservatoire of Music. We have been privileged to scrutinize this superb example on several occasions, and we do not believe its label to be an original. We would add, however, that a doubt as to the correctness of our judgement might be legitimately raised, for the inscription is obviously old, and printed in characters of the period; yet the fact remains that we have never in a single instance met with another authentic violin of the master bearing an original and a similar label, nor do the figures of the ex Alard satisfy our scrutiny. The last reproduction of those given is a replica of that frequently found in Guarneri copies, the work of Vuillaume, and which were so labelled by him; the spelling of Cremona will be noted as also the fact that the whole inscription is not a close imitation of an original.

Labels of Pietro Guarneri of Venice.

The first label that we know of inserted by Pietro was dated 1721, and used by him for his Cremonese work; note that he proclaims his parentage, and pays homage to the ancestral Patron Saint.

The next in chronological order, that of 1725, shows the master to be at Venice, and comes from a violoncello: hence its larger proportions. Observe the omission of the Patron Saint, and the different form of wording, also the spelling of the Christian name of his father, 'Josef', which is correct, and of 'Venetis' with one *i* only, which is incorrect. All the figures are printed.

The three following violin labels have each an elaborate border; in the one case it has been somewhat trimmed away, and note here the smaller type of printing. The others are decidedly decorative, and incidentally this points to the master's determination not to be outbid by his contemporary Santo Serafin. Perhaps that with the smaller border may have been inspired by the earliest label of Serafin!

The next ticket, dated 1739, is again taken from a violoncello; bold in character, it accords with its instrument (that belonging to Beatrice Harrison). Yet we see a return to the meagre border somewhat similar to the specimen shown above. Note that all the figures are written.

[1] Antoine Vidal, *La Lutherie et Les Luthiers*, 1889.

Joseph Guarnerius fecit ✠
Cremonę anno 172? IHS

Joseph Guarnerius fecit ✠
Cremonę anno 1732 IHS

Joseph Guarnerius fecit ✠
Cremonę anno 173? IHS

Joseph Guarnerius fecit ✠
Cremonę anno 1734 IHS

Joseph Guarnerius fecit ✠
Cremonę anno 1734 IHS

Joseph Guarnerius fecit ✠
Cremonę anno 1735 IHS

Joseph Guarnerius fecit ✠
Cremonę anno 1738 IHS

Joseph Guarnerius fecit ✠
Cremonę anno 174? IHS

Joseph Guarnerius fecit ✠
Cremonę anno 174? IHS

1735 IHS

1740 IHS

1741 IHS

* Joseph Guarnerius fecit ✠
Cremonæ anno 1735 IHS

LABELS INSERTED BY GIUSEPPE GUARNERI DEL GESÙ

* This label is fictitious: see text

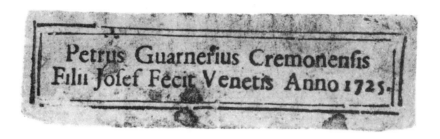

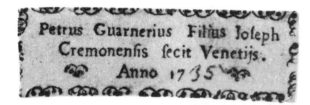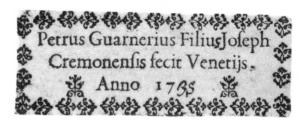

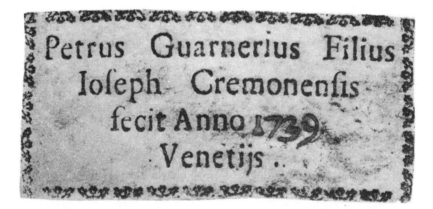

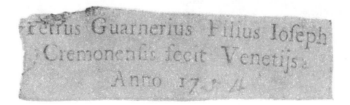

LABELS INSERTED BY PIETRO GUARNERI OF VENICE

The last two labels of this interesting series are in reality one and the same, with the exception of the irregularly formed border-line round that of the year 1750; the second and obscured date is 1754, and it records the latest work known to us of the master, who, so it will be recalled, died in 1760.

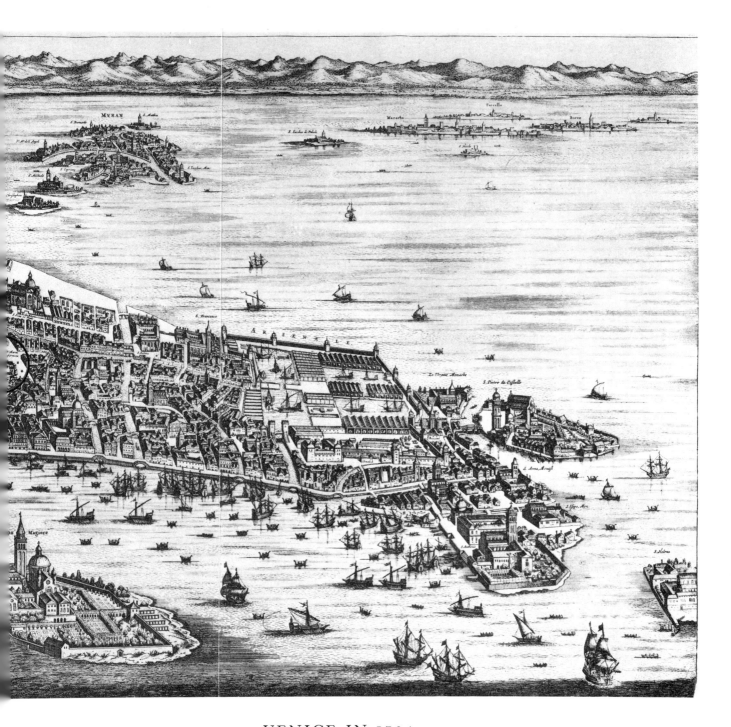

VENICE IN 1704

THE CHURCH OF S. LEONE, (NOW UNITED WITH THE PARISH OF S. MARIA FORMOSA)
WAS THE CHURCH WHERE PIETRO GUARNERI WAS MARRIED AND PROBABLY BURIED

THE CIRCLE INDICATES THE POSITION OF THE CHURCH

CHAPTER VIII
PIETRO GUARNERI OF VENICE
The last of all the Romans, fare thee well!

PIETRO GUARNERI, usually spoken of as Peter Guarnerius of Venice, was the second son of Giuseppe Guarneri figlio d'Andrea, and was born on the 14th of April of the year 1695. He died 7th of April 1762, and was destined to be the last of the Guarneri violin-makers.

In times gone by, when the present writers were young, considerable confusion existed concerning the two 'Peters'—uncle and nephew. The more general belief then held by the leading experts was that the elder Peter had worked respectively at Cremona, Mantua, and Venice, and he was frequently cited as the 'Venetian Peter' notwithstanding the different labels which clearly designated two distinct men.[1]

The early life of Pietro of Venice was, as far as we have been able to learn, quite uneventful. He was baptized on the 17th of April, *A*, and the census returns of his

A.

April 17th, 1695.

On the 14th day of the above month, was born Pietro, son of Dom. Joseph Guarneri & Barbara Franchi, his wife, and baptized by me, Francesco de Arquatis, Rector of S. Matteo, on the 17th day of the above month and year; Dom. Andrea, one of the clergy of the Parish of S. Nicolò, being the godfather.

---

[1] Piccolellis states that 'Pietro Guarnieri figlio di Giuseppe', cited in the works of Fétis and Vidal, represents a name unknown in Italy! *Liutai Antichi e Moderni*, 1885.

father's household make mention of him as an inmate up to and including the year 1718. He would then be aged twenty-three, and in all probability he had during the previous eight to ten years been trained by his father with a view to becoming a master craftsman of his art.

In 1719 Pietro no longer figures in the father's census returns; he had left for good. But we know that he did not immediately leave Cremona, for we are acquainted with several of his Cremonese-made violins, notably the example of which we give illustrations, bearing his authentic label, dated from the year 1721. This instrument came into our hands from the north of Italy in years gone by, and it was then practically in its original state.

It is not without interest to note that he worked under the auspices of S. Teresia,[1] thus upholding the tradition of his three ancestors; but once arrived at Venice he seems to have dropped this observance for good.

Seeing that the master remained at Cremona after leaving his parents, where was he living? Mystery indeed which the most sustained researches have been of no avail to unravel. If he had been exercising his calling with a modest show of dili-gence, we should now be able to point to some tangible proofs of his industry; but scan as we will the Cremonese work of this period, work in which there exists the possibility of identification with the name of Pietro, we have to confess to a result relatively speaking nil. With the exception of quite a few violins nothing whatever is forthcoming.

The probable explanation, as already offered,[2] is that the Guarneri—father and both sons—were at this time (1720-25) completely dominated by the masterful and numerous productions still coming from their neighbour in the Piazza S. Domeni-co; and perhaps this fact was partly the cause of Pietro's final decision to migrate to Venice. In the meantime he may have continued to co-operate in any work which was being done in his father's workshop. But apparently the orders received at the Casa Guarneri were few and far between!

There is just one other point worth considering, and that is whether Pietro may not have spent some time in Mantua shortly before or following on the death of his uncle in 1720.[3] We have seen that the uncle left unfinished instruments amongst the contents of his workshop, and we do recognize violins, which, though clearly related to those of Pietro of Mantua, are not quite the orthodox thing. It would not

---

[1] See ticket reproduced in Chap. VII.   [2] See Chap. III.   [3] See Chap. II.

Petrus Guarnerius filius Joseph fecit Cremonæ 1721

Petrus Guarnerius filius Joseph fecit Venetiis period 1730

Emery Walker Ltd. ph.sc.

be an unreasonable suggestion that the nephew spent a year or so in Mantua clearing up the contents of the workshop and finishing off these partly made instruments,

and that only after this task was terminated did he finally decide to establish himself in Venice. We would add, however, that we have so far never seen either ticket or inscription connecting the master with Mantua.

Pietro's Cremonese violins[1] are decidedly original, betraying less of the Guarneri character than is the case later as the master matured in his work. We see an outline distinctly reminiscent of an early work of Stradivari: dimensions some׳ what similar—i.e. length 14 inches, widths $8\frac{1}{16}$ and $6\frac{5}{8}$ respectively: sides left low, $1\frac{3}{16}$ and $1\frac{1}{8}$, for which a somewhat full and swelling model makes compensation. The substance of the edges, the purfling, and the corners are of Amati neatness, the corners being short, the purfling fine in substance and set close to the outer edges. The sound׳holes—somewhat inelegant—are noticeable on account of their extra length and the upright manner, close to the outer edge, in which they are set on the table: the broad bridge platform which this setting gives being quite out of the ordinary.

The head is first׳rate, bold in form and well cut (gouge marks visible), the treat׳ ment of the throat and back part of the fluting alone betraying the Guarneri

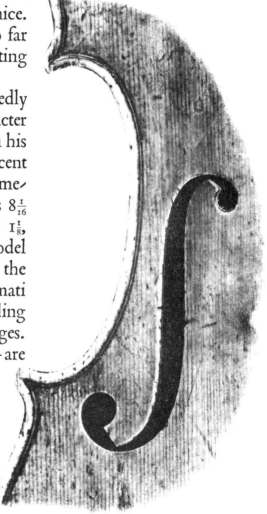

FIG. I. Edge, purfling, and sound׳hole of an example of the year 1721.

touch; on the other hand the carving and curves of the volute might at times be mistaken for the work of J. B. Rogeri of Brescia. The material from which this instrument was made calls for no special comment; the varnish is of fine quality and of an attractive red׳brown colour.

[1] See illustration facing p. 134.

Looked at as a whole we miss entirely the marked character of either the father or grandfather, and we find ourselves faced with a work which is refreshingly original; also it proclaims the maker as a thoroughly sound craftsman, one quite capable of upholding any fame which had been won by his forbears.

We do not know the exact year of Pietro's arrival in Venice, but would be in-clined to say that it was about 1722–24. Whether or not this surmise be correct, we are at least on sure ground in vouching for his presence there in the year 1725.[1] Three years later his marriage, the record of which we have succeeded in finding, took place on the 5th day of April 1728. He was married in the Parish Church of S. Leone to Angiola Maria, daughter of the late Signor Ferrari of Venice. Note that the certificate says: 'Pietro, son of Signor Giuseppe Guarneri of Cremona', B.

Now the claims of Venice to be ranked among the foremost centres of musical activity and progress in Italy—sharing that honour with Florence, Naples, and Rome—have been fully substantiated by many historians of the art. We propose here to try and indicate the causes that led, at the close of the seventeenth century, to the formation of the Venetian School of violin-makers, which became in order of merit second only to that of Cremona.

To some extent this happening may be ascribed to the residence in Venice of the remarkable composer Monteverdi, who from 1613 until his death in 1643 held the appointment of 'Maestro di Capella' at the famous Church of S. Marco, and by his virile and inspiring example stimulated the Venetians' innate taste for music. An accomplished violist, he had acquired through his Cremonese birth and upbringing a superior understanding of string instruments. The correspondence[2] which passed between the astronomer Galileo and his friend at Venice, the monk Micanzio, in 1637–38 concerning the purchase of a violin for the former's nephew, attests that Monteverdi's expert knowledge on the subject was recognized and sought; and shows moreover that he had kept in touch with Cremona and knew of its growing pre-eminence in violin-making. Monteverdi's special genius for writing dramatic music, his innovations in Opera, and in the treatment of instruments in his scores, contributed to the development of that passion for Opera which for a century or more markedly distinguished all classes among the citizens of Venice.

The first Opera House in Europe to admit the public by payment was opened at Venice in 1637; and between that date and the year 1700 no less than eleven

---

[1] See reproduction of label bearing that date, Chap. VII.   [2] See end of chapter.

B.

Adì 5 Aprile 1728.

Premesse tutte tre le Publicationi nella mia Chiesa li 28. 29. e 30. del mese decorso dopo hauer hauuto dalla Cancellaria di Monsig.mo Ill.mo et Rev.mo Patriarca mandato di Libertà soleñ.te di tutti due li contrahenti miei Parrochiani, Io Pievan infra.to questo giorno nella d.a mia Chiesa nella Capella della B.ma Verg.e de Sette Dolori, premesse anche le solite interrogationi, et obtenute le conuenienti risposte hò congiunto in Matrimonio solennem.te e Verba de presenti D. Pietro, figliolo di S. Giuseppe Guarnieri, da Cremona, e M. Angiola Maria, figliola del q. Simon Ferari, Veneta, et l'asseguentem.te li hò Benedetti nella solenità della Santa Messa. Testimonij: il Sig. Matteo Seles q. Giouanni stà à S. Saluador, et Girolamo Colutti del Sig. Antonio Chierico di Chiesa.

Simon Piazzola Pievano m.p.r.

April 5th, 1728.

Having published the Banns in my Church on the 28th, 29th, and 30th of the last month, and obtained from the Chancery of the Illustrious and Reverend Patriarch the permission sought by the contracting parties, my parishioners, I, the parish priest, have to-day joined them in Holy Matrimony, in the chapel of the Blessed Virgin of the Seven Dolours, in my church, after having put the usual questions and received the customary answers: the parties being Dom. Pietro, son of Signor Giuseppe Guarneri of Cremona and M. Angiola Maria, daughter of the late Simon Ferari of Venice, subsequently imparting to them the Nuptial Blessing during the solemnity of the Holy Mass. Witnesses: Signor Matteo Seles (son) of the late Giovanni of S. Salvador, & Girolamo Colutti (son) of Signor Antonio, Clerk of the Church.

Simon Piazzola, Parish Priest

theatres in the city were given over to the representation of Opera. The significance of this, from our point of view, is that it betokens the presence in Venice of a considerable number of skilled performers on string instruments, whether violin, viol, or lute.

At this early stage in the life of Opera the strings greatly outnumbered the few wind and other instruments which combined to form the orchestra for which the opera composer wrote. The requirements of the music performed in the many churches and palaces of Venice made a further call on the services of proficient violists and violinists. To illustrate what these were, we can cite the constitution of the orchestra attached to the Church of S. Marco after its reorganization by the able composer Legrenzi,[1] during his term of office from 1685-90 as Maestro di Capella. Consisting of thirty-four instrumentalists, twenty-eight of them 'strings', the combination was as follows: 'eight violons, eleven violes ou violettes pour les deuxième et troisième parties, two violes *da braccia* (tenors); three grandes violes *da gamba* et *violone* (contrebasse de viole), four theorbes, two cornets, one basson and three trombones.'

Legrenzi was a man of advanced ideas, skilful in instrumental composition, and had already published 'Suonate a due violini e *violoncello,* Venice, 1677', and it is noteworthy that he did not include any violoncellos in the orchestra of S. Marco, although he allotted the leading role to the eight violins, and relegated the treble viols to the playing of inner parts.

No precise details are forthcoming in connexion with the orchestras attached to the principal Opera Houses, but of those belonging to the four celebrated Conservatorios an enthusiastic and cultivated French dilettante, the Président de Brosses, who visited Venice in 1739, has left the following account. They consisted of talented girl students, chiefly orphans and foundlings, and de Brosses described their performance in glowing terms. 'The girls sing like angels, play the violin, the flute, the organ, the oboe, the violoncello, the bassoon; in short, there is no instrument so large as to frighten them. . . . They alone form the executants, and at each concert the orchestra is composed of about forty young ladies. I assure you that there is nothing more delightful than to see a young and pretty novice, dressed in white with a bunch of pomegranate flowers behind her ear, conduct the orchestra and beat the time with the utmost grace and precision. . . . Of the four Conservatorios that

[1] Legrenzi, G., 1625-90. Fétis, *Biographie Universelle des Musiciens.*

which I frequent the most and obtain the greatest enjoyment from, is the Pietà; it is also the foremost for the perfection of instrumental music.'[1]

The distinguished violinist and composer Vivaldi held the directorship of the Pietà, a fact which would account for its superiority in instrumental music, and we may add the comment that an orchestra thus composed wholly of ladies is not the novelty we might be tempted in these days to imagine!

The widespread study and use of the violin described in the course of these chapters show that there was nothing fortuitous about the growth of a fine school of violin-making at Venice. The numerous students, professors, and amateurs created an imperative demand for skilled makers and repairers, to continue the supply of new instruments of a good class as well as to carry out the adjustment and repairs which all string instruments periodically need.

It thus becomes evident that, in leaving Cremona to settle in Venice, Pietro Guarneri was entering into the life of a far more populous and wealthy city, where the taste for music and the patronage of it and the sister arts offered fuller scope for the exercise of his talents, and promised possibly a better pecuniary result and a higher social position.

Did Pietro immediately establish himself as a master liutaio? One cannot be sure about this, though we do know he was working in that capacity in the year 1725. To whom could he have addressed himself if he did give prior service to one or other of the Venetian makers? Previous to about 1680, strangely enough, we have no proof of the existence of a purely violin-maker in Venice; we say purely as contrasted with the lute, guitar, and viol-makers, who worked there in earlier times, and may possibly have made an occasional violin, though we have no personal knowledge of any such instrument now existing. Mattio Gofriller[2]—a German by birth—was about the first true violin-maker; and he shows himself to have been a master both distinguished and industrious. His violoncellos are especially fine. Then we have the Tononi, father and son. Joannes[3] the father may have migrated from Bologna in his later years—not a long way from Venice, but the son Carlo appears to have worked but little elsewhere. He was already in Venice in 1703, and he has left us some fine works amongst his fairly numerous productions.

Francesco Gobetti was working as late as 1720 onwards. Here again was a maker of

---

[1] *Lettres écrites d'Italie publiées pour la première fois en l'an XIII.* (1805.)　　　[2] Spelt at times Goffriller.
[3] We have never seen an instrument dated from Venice. He died in 1713.

real distinction who made some admirable violins; and we should say unhesitatingly that he and Carlo Tononi were connected.

FIG. II. Edge, purfling, and sound-hole of an example of the period 1725.

Then came Domenico Montagnana and Santo Serafin,[1] certainly the two most reputed of the Venetians; neither of these men was of Cremonese origin; nor, which is of equal importance, did they in our opinion receive their teaching in Cremona. But it is beyond discussion that they and all others were directly or indirectly indebted to the Cremonese. Besides the above mentioned there were several other makers working in close proximity to Venice; and the combined efforts of all these men meant an annual production of a goodly number of instruments. Those makers whose names we give were certainly the most representative, and if Pietro did give service to one of them prior to 1725, we should point to either Tononi or Serafin as being the men of our selection. We do recognize features in the work of Pietro—the modelling, f-holes, and especially the head—where we can trace similarity of conception; but though we may search for signs of the master's own early formed individuality in the productions of Tononi, Serafin, Montagnana, or any of their contemporaries, we find nothing to support any theory of co-operation.

Here then was the new environment of Pietro Guarneri. As already recorded, there was much musical activity in Venice; and the superb works of the Amati, Stainer, and their various pupils and followers—not forgetting Stradivari—were in

[1] Santo Serafin was born in 1699 and came to Venice from Udine, his birthplace, in 1717. He followed first the art of painting, and only later took up violin-making. We note that the name is spelt at times Seraphin, Serafino, Serafini, and Serafin.

the hands of the players, and were continually resounding through the many churches, theatres, and palaces of the nobles. What finer inspiration could her contemporary craftsmen ask for? Indeed, the more we ponder, the more clearly do we visualize that the possession of these instruments did serve as their guiding light. Strange though it be, Stainer influence was first and foremost, then came the vogue of the Amati, and lastly the finality of Stradivari.

Who in the main were Pietro's principal competitors? We unhesitatingly name Santo Serafin and Domenico Montagnana; yet if the reputation of the last named had depended entirely on his violins we venture to suggest that he would be less considered. For his strength revealed itself in the remarkable violoncellos which he constructed and left to posterity, and to which we continue to pay a real tribute of admiration.

With Serafin matters are somewhat reversed; his violin production was considerable, and in the majority of instances the violins were made of choice material and of finely finished workmanship. Clearly it was he who occupied the predominant position amongst the Venetian makers, and we are not surprised to learn from our researches that he was patronized by various noble Venetian families.

We have spent some time in trying to give an impression of the environment of Venice at the period when Pietro came to spend the remainder of his life there; and whatever reputation the master has achieved is due to the instruments which we shall from now onwards see him making in the city.

The earliest of Pietro's Venetian works hitherto met with is represented by a violoncello of the year 1725, an example in which the master clearly betrays his Cremonese ancestry and teaching—infinitely more so than is revealed in the violin made at Cremona in 1721. Both form and proportions are obviously inspired by those of Stradivari at his best, though modified in the total length, which measures 29½ inches (Stradivari 29⅞ inches). Edge, corners, the fuller model and the fluting of the edges are strongly reminiscent of the father, Giuseppe filius; and in his 1690–1700 period the *f*-holes again are of Stradivari character whilst the head is less so, and we perceive once more the family touch with a something added which reveals his fresh Venetian entourage. The varnish, thickly laid on, was originally of a rich red colour, but it has shrivelled up, as frequently found in Montagnana's instruments, and furthermore has suffered from exposure in an Eastern climate, and the condition of the whole instrument does not point to careful ownership in the past—quite the contrary. To sum up, we realize in contemplating this example that the master had profited by the past; he was here trying his hand at the construction of an instrument on Stradivari lines, modified in accordance with his own ideas. And well had he succeeded. We learn from the present owner that it was found in the early part of last century in Cephalonia, one of the Ionian Islands. Who knows but that it was taken there direct from Venice?

Following on in chronological order we have a violin (see plate facing p. 140) and a second violoncello, instruments possessing much charm and distinction; and here we clearly trace relationship with contemporary Venetian work. There is something reminiscent of Tononi and equally so of Serafin; but unfortunately neither of these instruments bears its original label, and we are consequently unable to state the exact years of their production. We would suggest the early thirties.

We see a violin of attractive Amati-like form, the same small and neatly worked edge, purfling, and corners, as found in the Cremona-made fiddle; the modelling is full and more gracefully shaped, the f-holes of long form and cut open at the wings, set less close to the outer edge, and placed slightly less upright—note that the wide platform for the bridge is still retained—a head inspired by Serafin, and the Guarneri touch in the forming of the volute and fluting of the back. The whole work is lightly knit together, revealing Amati tradition.

The violoncello[1] is an equally choice work; it stands in fact amongst the foremost of the Venetian creations. All the salient features of the violin are reproduced—model, edge, corners, f-holes and finish of work—in reality an aggrandisement of the violin. Finely proportioned in form, and of well-balanced contours (see Appendix) it reveals a creative side in Pietro which we had not so far suspected. Founded in form on Amati, it reminds us more of the violoncello of Andrea Guarneri the grandfather than of anything else, though Montagnana must not be entirely ignored; and in the finished workmanship, and lastly in a peach-red varnish of soft texture it rivals Santo Serafin at his best.

Instruments of this period of the master's life are extremely rare, as much so as those made in Cremona.

Henceforward from 1730–5 we begin to meet more frequently with violins; the master was steadily producing, for quite a number exist, and indeed these are the instruments which with a few exceptions stand for his life's work.

[1] See illustration, facing p. 142.

Four more violoncellos only and the original head of a fifth specimen have been identified by us, and we cannot point to the existence of a single viola. All these signed Venetian productions range in date from 1725 to about 1760, a full period of thirty-five years.

From 1740 onwards Pietro's violins assume a heavier character throughout the details of their work. They are generally of broader form, and we see him favouring the work of his uncle of Mantua distinctly more than that of his father. This fact possibly supplies the reason why these instruments were assumed in the past to have been made by one and the same man.

The outline is founded upon Amati tradition rather than that of any one else, but both top and bottom curves are left squarer, and the corners somewhat protrude. The length is frequently a little less than 14 inches and at times $14\frac{1}{16}$ and even $14\frac{1}{8}$; the respective widths are $8\frac{3}{16}$ and $6\frac{5}{8}$, occasionally narrower; the sides instead of the standard $1\frac{1}{4}$ inches are more often $1\frac{1}{8}$ and even as low as $1\frac{1}{16}$.

The model is generally of a full Amati-like swell, closely resembling certain examples of Serafin in this feature; but we do here and there see a specimen the model of which is relatively flat. The fluting around the edge is in most cases left fairly deep, dug in at the corners, but it is less accentuated than in the work of the uncle, and the edges are not quite so rounded.

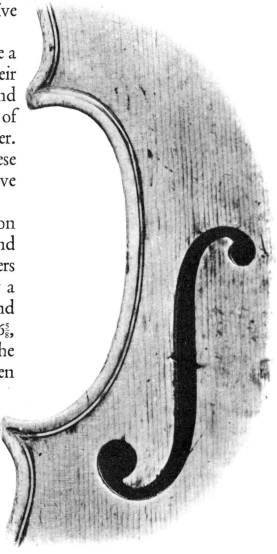

FIG. III. Edge, purfling, and sound-hole of an example of the period 1745-55.

The purfling of his early years was light in substance, and the mitres pointed up the centre of the corners, but with the advance of time we meet with purfling of a heavier kind, indeed so heavy that we should assume it had been intended for a violoncello. We see this same change with regard to the thickness of wood left in the edges—at first on the light side, later of sufficient substance to serve for those of a viola—and we also note a generous margin of edge left around the sides.

Pietro's bold and open-cut f-holes are strongly characterized, and here we are reminded of those of Serafin—a certain blending of the Amati and Stainer conception. They are set, and not unrarely, somewhat low down upon the table, and although so placed, the stop is not invariably lengthened, seeing that the nicks of the f-holes are higher up than usual. But occasionally we do meet with an abnormal stop of $7\frac{13}{16}$ (normal stop $7\frac{10}{16}$).

In scrutinizing the heads[1] carved by the master, one is struck by their relationship with those of the uncle; true, we miss the latter's more finished and symmetrical curves, that precision and grace which pervades the whole. In place of it we see a more rugged work, the gouge marks left around the deeply cut volute, a fairly heavy chamfer, a broad back part with fluting dug in similar to that of Montagnana; yet, after all, there is felt that quite unmistakable family touch which can be sensed in the great majority of the Guarneri heads.

The interior work is heavy, the blocks and linings are of willow wood, the latter left broad. The corner blocks are massive, those of the top and bottom shaped after Stradivari; and either three or four nails are inserted in the former to fix the foot of the neck. The thicknesses are good, approximating to those of Stradivari, though at times we find the centre of the back stouter and more in accord with the practice of del Gesù.

The wood used by Pietro was seldom handsomely figured, nor do we recall, except on rare occasions, a violin made from such choice material as that which so frequently came from the workshop of Santo Serafin; it was he, we repeat, who enjoyed the highest patronage of the Venetians, and the master together with others supplied the wants of the more humble fiddlers, who then as now worked hard but earned little.

The maple thus utilized by Pietro was generally of foreign growth; the backs moderately figured, sometimes quite plain; and he favoured those of one piece. The sides and head as a rule were on the plain side.

The varnish used by the master was of an oil basis and at times of considerable beauty—the colour yellow, golden brown, and on rarer occasions brown-red. He

---

[1] See plate of heads, facing p. 146.

Petrus Guarnerius filius Joseph fecit Cremonæ 1734

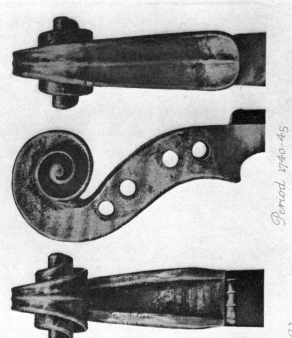

Period 1725-30

Period 1740-45

Period 1721

Period 1730-35

Heads of Pietro Guarneri of Venice

applied it with skill, though we have seen examples where it was laid on with a heavy hand, or again where we should suggest insufficient oil to render the varnish elastic; so much so that it tends to chip away unduly from the wood. Here and there we note the use of dryers, though less often than in the case of his contemporary, Domenico Montagnana.

The following violins may be cited as representative examples:

1721	made in Cremona	M. Wolfman
1721		Miss Helen Egerton
1721		Miss Beatrice Lutyens, ex Cte de Sasserno
1725 period, Venice .	.	Mr. Alfred J. Clements, ex Pickering
1725–30 . . .	.	Mrs. Hodgson, ex Dr. G. Birch
1734–5 . . .	.	Miss Wilkinson
1735	. .	Mr. John Pennington
1735–40 period .	. .	Dr. Otto Krebs, ex Wieniawski
1740	. .	M. Th. Haemmerle, ex Baron Knoop
1747	. .	M. Carl Flesch, ex Duc de Camposelice
1750	. .	Mr. Joseph Haft, ex Waddell
1750	. .	M. Louis Bailly
1754	. .	Miss M. Miles, ex Baron Rothschild

We have already praised the violoncello made by Pietro in earlier years: there also exists another example dating from 1739 which, practically speaking, is of the same proportions; and in considering it we can rightly re-echo the words of M. Vidal,[1] who, commenting upon this very instrument, says: 'It entitles Pietro Guarneri to be placed amongst the greatest of the Italians.'

Made from choice material and covered by a soft varnish of red-brown colour, it stands out as an exceptional work, and could we but learn the history of the past we should find that it was specially commanded by one of the great noblemen of Venice, purchased at Trieste towards the middle of last century, taken to Vienna and thence found its way to Moscow, where the late M. Déprets, its former owner, lived. It is now in the possession of that accomplished violoncellist, Beatrice Harrison.

This example differs from the first one in a broader treatment of the edge and corners and in slightly heavier construction. The f-holes are more curved at both

---

[1] *La Lutherie et des Luthiers*, Antoine Vidal, 1889.

wings and placed lower down on the table and the finish of the work, especially that of the head, is less refined. Otherwise they are brothers, and indeed a noble pair.

Pietro's other efforts in violoncello making followed closely upon the lines of one of the two forms initiated by Serafin, viz. an excellently proportioned instrument though of small dimensions. Two specimens only are known to us, the earlier dating from the year 1735.[1] Here we again see that the players and makers of the day were undecided as to what form and proportions would give the best all-round results; and accordingly the Venetians varied the size of their violoncellos as their earlier and contemporary Cremonese colleagues had done and as their Milanese followers were to do later.

The six violoncellos hitherto identified by us are the following:

                1725. Mr. Carl Hamburger
    Period 1730. M. Waddington, ex Van Gelder
                1735. Mr. J. H. Newcomb, ex Hoare
          1735–39. Miss Wilson, ex Muntz
                1739. Miss Beatrice Harrison, ex Déprets
          1740–50. Museum of the Conservatoire of Paris

The remarkably high standard reached by the Venetians in their violoncellos, whether they made, as in the case of Serafin and Pietro, only a few, or, as in that of Gofriller and Montagnana, a number, points to the existence of a considerable and lucrative clientèle.

The numerous churches and theatres of Venice required for their orchestras a fair number of violoncellists; and in addition there would be the girl players belonging to the orchestras of the three Conservatorios, and the wealthy dilettanti, who supported orchestras, or who themselves were players.

Whether the demand for so many fine violoncellos was created by the fact that the composers of Venice gave the instrument a prominent part in their scores, or whether it sprang from the existence in the city of distinguished violoncellists, or of a fine school of playing, are questions which naturally present themselves.

Marcello, the Venetian nobleman, statesman, and gifted composer, wrote six solo Sonatas for the violoncello, and also gave it an obbligato part in some of his celebrated Fifty Psalms, published between 1724 and 1727; and he alone among the famous Venetian composers has shown a predilection for the violoncello.

[1] Maybe that these smaller instruments were made specially for the lady players at the Pietà (see p. 139).

Of the city's association with any fine violoncellists or any special school for training players no information has yet come to light.

As regards the variation in the dimensions of the violoncellos produced by the Venetian makers, orchestral violoncello parts were at this period of an easy nature; and the player on the larger-sized Gofriller or Montagnana found no difficulty in executing his part whether the music was sacred or secular. The sonorous and massive tone flowing from the lower strings of these majestic instruments was in perfect keeping with the character of Church music, and at the same time provided a supporting bass to the voices, the effect of which was truly admirable.

Obviously the physical limitations of the girl students at the three Conservatorios called for a smaller and an easier speaking violoncello; but the impelling motive for one of more convenient dimensions being introduced was the advent of the virtuoso-cellist, who in rivalry with celebrated soloists on the viol-da-gamba demanded, in order to obtain greater brilliancy and facility in execution, an instrument designed more after viol-da-gamba proportions.

To return to Pietro's life, we see no real signs of any co-operation with his brother del Gesù; nothing but a vague and distant intimacy is to be found in certain of the details of their work. Yet both of them drew their early inspiration from a common source—that of their father.

How marked is the contrast when we consider the brothers Amati, whose individual works we find great difficulty in distinguishing!

Pietro and del Gesù must have met occasionally, the cities of Venice and Cremona being situated at no great distance from each other. They would certainly have spoken together concerning their work, and looked at the instruments which each was shaping. Yet neither brother was in any real sense influenced by the production of the other. Each went his own way and so continued till the end of the chapter!

On one occasion, and once only, we came across a violin which furnished a direct proof of working intimacy having existed between the two masters. This instance was revealed through our examining closely the original head of a violin, the work of del Gesù, dating from the year 1734. We were struck by the clearly recognizable impress of Pietro's touch. He had obviously carved it or taken part in its carving; and it was this small incident which first turned our thoughts to the possibility that a more intimate relationship existed than that hitherto supposed by the expert writers of the past.

Thanks to the untiring efforts of Signor Livi we are in a position to impart a few facts concerning Pietro's home life. Married as we have seen in 1728, the master was blessed with ten children, five sons and five daughters, several of whom died young. The first child, a son, was born in February 1729, and baptized in the names of both grandparents Giuseppe Simone. Other children followed as the years passed on, the last being a son, Bortolo Mattio, born in February 1743. We note with interest that the god-father was the Venetian noble, Signor Girolamo Ascanio Giustiniani,[1] C.

There is no word or sign that any of the sons embraced the family career, now carried on for upwards of a century. It had ceased at Mantua with the death of the uncle Pietro. Del Gesù had left no successor at Cremona; and the passing of Pietro of Venice closes the last chapter connecting this singularly interesting family with the art of violin-making.

The master died on the 19th of April of the year 1762;[2] and the certificate of death which we reproduce, taken from the Register of the Parish of S. Leone, now united with the Parish of S. Maria Formosa, reads as given, D.

His wife survived him until 1777, dying on the 22nd of February of that year, aged about seventy-two. We also note the death of the son Giuseppe in January 1790, aged about sixty years. We have no knowledge as to the calling he pursued.

With the death of Pietro the knell of instrument-making sounded at Venice as at Cremona with the death of Giuseppe del Gesù; for the art was steadily decaying. What more significant fact could be brought forward in evidence of this decline than that all the Venetian makers previously mentioned, with the sole exception of Serafin, who was timidly followed by his nephew Georgio,[3] had left neither direct nor serious successor to carry on their craft. Georgio Serafin and Anselmo Belosio, both pupils of Santo Serafin, alone gave some distinction to their work; but neither of them furnish proof of any real industry.

Violin-making in Italy had, in fact, seen its zenith; it was no longer being patronized by the wealthy. Large numbers of fine Italian instruments were in

[1] This noble stood sponsor to one of the daughters in 1735. He is then described as son of the late Most Illustrious Girolamo, Procurator di S. Marco.

[2] The latest work of Pietro hitherto identified by us is a violin of the year 1757.

[3] We learn from the Venetian Archives that Georgio was the son of Giovanni Battista Serafino, and that he married, on 21st November 1751, Signora Antonia Anna, fourth daughter of the *late* Signor Domenico Montagnana.

C.

Feb. 25th, 1743.

Bortolo Mattio, son of Pietro Guarnieri (son) of the late Giuseppe, and Angiola (daughter) of the late Simon Ferrari his wife, was born yesterday. Held at the Sacred Font by the above-mentioned Illustrious Sig. Girolamo Ascanio Giustinian (son) of the Most Illustrious Girolamo, Procurator of S. Marco, of the parish of S. Salvador, (&) Sig. Giuseppe Senche (son) of the late Giambattista, his Agent. Midwife, Antonia Costa of the parish of S. Giacomo d'allorio. Baptized by me, Simon Piazzola, Parish Priest.

D.

The 19th of the same month, 1762

Pietro Guarneri (son) of the late Giuseppe, aged 66, died, after seven days (illness) at one o'clock this morning, of pneumonia. Assisted by the Rev. Giuseppe Favina & buried by P. e. C.

E. E.

circulation, times were less prosperous, and in consequence the demand for the high standard of excellence had now lapsed. Also we must take into consideration that the Italians had found many apt imitators in France, the Low Countries, Germany, the Tyrol, England, Spain, and elsewhere. From about 1700 onwards all these countries were producing instruments that sufficed amply for the average musician, with the result that over-production (rather than under-production) was becoming the order of the day. Italian violins of a cheaper kind were however still in request; for the majority of players could as yet have gained no deep understanding of the lasting merits of instruments made by the great Cremonese of the past.

Revert for one moment to that past, to the beginning of the Guarneri and the decade of 1630 which heralded the start of their career as violin-makers. Let us contrast the then prevailing situation with that of 1760 by giving our attention to the correspondence between Galileo and Fra. Fulgentius Micanzio, who was a former pupil of the famous astronomer.

From Galileo to Father Fulgentius Micanzio in Venice:

Arcetri, Nov. 20th, 1637.

. . . When you receive the amount of my small pension, please keep it until my nephew Alberto, who is in the service of His Serene Highness the Prince of Bavaria and is now staying with me here, passes through Venice on his return journey to Munich and pays his respects to your Most Reverend Paternity. He wishes to purchase a violin there, either of Cremonese or Brescian make, being a very good performer on that instrument; and the said small pension will help to pay for it. I suppose that these instruments, though made elsewhere, can be found in Venice; but should that not be so, and it becomes necessary to obtain one from somewhere else, you will greatly oblige me by making arrangements so that some competent musician shall select one from Brescia, an instrument of the highest order. . . .

From Father Micanzio to Galileo:

Venice, December 5th, 1637.

I have received your most kind letter of the 20th of last month, and I have already obtained the amount of your small pension by inducing the Most Illustrious Baitello to give an assurance to that scamp Arisio that you are still alive. Concerning the violin which your nephew on passing through here wishes to buy, I have spoken to the Musical Director of the Concerts of St. Mark's (Maestro di Concerti di S. Marco), who tells me that I can easily find Brescian violins, but that those of Cremona are incomparably the better—in fact they represent the non plus ultra; and by the medium of the Cremonese Signor Monteverdi, Chapel-Master of St. Mark's, who has a nephew living in Cremona, I have given the order for a violin to be sent here. The difference in the price will show you the superiority, for those of Cremona cost at the lowest twelve ducats each, whilst the others (Brescian) can be had for less than four ducats. As your nephew is in the service of His Highness of Bavaria, I think he will prefer by far the one ordered to be sent to Venice as soon as possible. . . .

From Father Micanzio to Galileo:

Venice, Jan. 16th, 1638.

If I have delayed writing to you it is only because I am still awaiting that blessed violin from Cremona, for which Signor Monteverdi assures me he has made so many repeated applications, yet, notwithstanding, it does not appear. . . .

From Father Micanzio to Galileo:

Venice, March 20th, 1638.

I am still pining for that blessed violin. Every day I am shown letters which explain that in order to construct a perfect instrument it has been found necessary to wait until the cold weather has passed away, and that in a couple of days, it will be ready; still, there is no end to the delay. You may rest assured that I do not cease from pressing them. . . .

From Father Micanzio to Galileo:

Venice, April 24th, 1638.

Concerning the Violin, Signor Monteverdi has recently shown me a letter in which his nephew writes him that the new one is in progress, but as he wishes to send an instrument of exquisite work, it cannot be brought to perfection without the strong heat of the sun; he can, however, offer an old one of superlative merit, but the price asked is two ducats more—that is, fourteen. I have requested him to have this one sent at once, irrespective of the price; he has promised to do so, and I am expecting it from day to day.

Having been obliged to negotiate this matter through other hands, you must excuse me (for the delay). I give you my word of honour that I have not neglected it; on the contrary, I have left no stone unturned. And now, kissing your hands, believe me, &c.

From Father Micanzio to Galileo.

May 28th, 1638.

As regards the violin, Signor Monteverdi read me a letter which he had received from his nephew, in which he wrote that he had the violin, and that it proved on trial to be a singularly successful instrument; that he had consigned it to a boatman who lay at anchor, and was on the point of starting for Venice; that he had not been able to get it for less than fifteen ducats, besides the expenses of the carriage and the case. I replied that I would settle everything, and begged the gentleman not to delay any longer, as too much time had already been wasted over such a trifle. As soon as it arrives, I will at once consign it to the illustrious Signor Residente Rinuzzini. . . .[1]

---

[1] These letters are taken from our *Life of Stradivari* (pp. 241–2).

Surely we obtain from these letters much food for reflection; we learn authorita-
tively that the fine instruments were only produced slowly—the sun played an important part (the drying of the varnish and the fabric) and it is obviously due to this
slowness of production that we find the cost enhanced. Again, we learn that the
fame of the Cremonese violin was such—and in this connexion we would recall
to our readers the date 1637-8, i.e. before the birth of Stradivari—that it became
necessary to pay a figure represented by three times as much as that which would
buy the violin of Brescia.

So, with all things mortal, the passing of time brought different ideas into vogue.
These slow and old-fashioned methods of working were to be modified. The violin
could and should be produced more cheaply, and, since the spirit of the age demanded it, it was done. Northern and Central Italy were still fairly active, Naples
even more so; but all vied in making the four-ducat rather than the twelve-ducat
instruments and the mass of less discriminating players were quite satisfied.

But, even though time brings changes in ideas and demands, the fundamental
truth persists that one must drink fully of the past if one would build well for the
future. The present writers express the hope that these pages will help to enforce
that lesson on those who to-day are interested in the craft of violin-making.

A little learning is a dangerous thing;
Drink deep, or taste not the Pierian Spring.

Petrus Guarnerius filius Joseph fecit Venetiis (period 1725)

Petrus Guarnerius filius Joseph fecit Venetiis 1750

Emery Walker Ltd ph.sc.

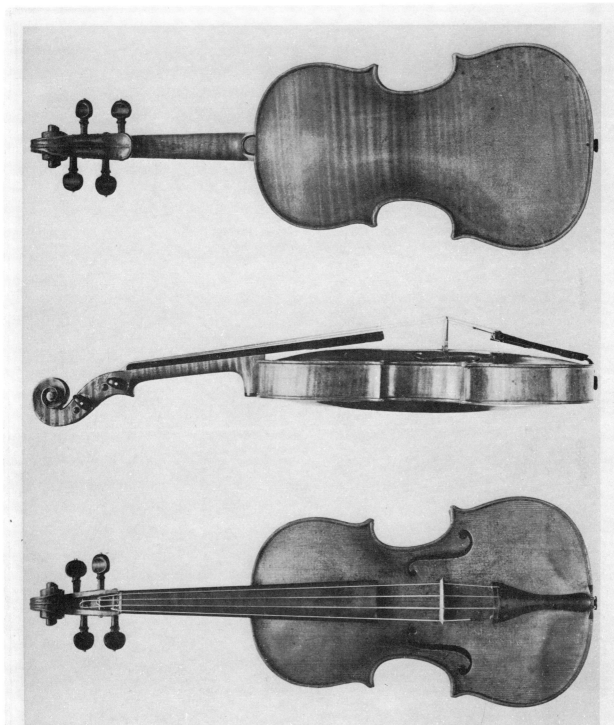

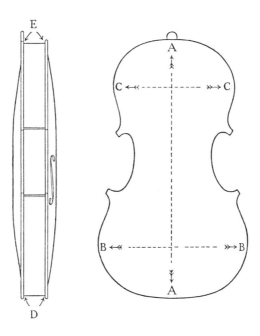

APPENDIX I TO CHAPTER I

Table of Measurements of Instruments made by Andrea Guarneri

Violin dated 1638.

Length A to A .	.	14 inches
Width B „ B .	.	$8\frac{3}{16}$
„ C „ C .	.	$6\frac{5}{8}$
Sides D „ D .	.	$1\frac{3}{16}$
„ E „ E .	.	$1\frac{1}{8}$

Violin dated 1655.

Length	.	.	$13\frac{15}{16}$ inches
Width	.	.	8
„	.	.	$6\frac{1}{2}$
Sides	.	.	$1\frac{3}{16}$
„	.	.	$1\frac{1}{8}$

Violin dated 1660.

Length	.	.	$13\frac{3}{4}$
Width .	.	.	$7\frac{7}{8}$
„ .	.	.	$6\frac{5}{16}$
Sides .	.	.	$1\frac{1}{8}$
„ .	.	.	$1\frac{1}{16}$

Violin period 1660-70.

Length	.	.	$13\frac{13}{16}$
Width .	.	.	8 bare
„ .	.	.	$6\frac{3}{8}$
Sides .	.	.	$1\frac{3}{16}$
„ .	.	.	$1\frac{1}{8}$

Violin dated 1676.

Length	.	.	14
Width	.	.	$8\frac{1}{8}$
„	.	.	$6\frac{9}{16}$
Sides .	.	.	$1\frac{3}{16}$
„ .	.	.	$1\frac{1}{8}$

Violin dated 1678.

Length	.	.	$13\frac{11}{16}$
Width	.	.	$8\frac{3}{16}$
„	.	.	$6\frac{1}{4}$
Sides .	.	.	$1\frac{1}{8}$
„ .	.	.	$1\frac{1}{16}$

Violin 1680-90.

Length	.	.	.	$13\frac{15}{16}$ inches
Width	.	.	.	8
,,	.	.	.	$6\frac{1}{2}$ full
Sides	.	.	.	$1\frac{3}{16}$
,,	.	.	.	$1\frac{1}{8}$

Viola dated 1676.

Length	.	.	.	$16\frac{5}{16}$ inches
Width	.	.	.	$9\frac{3}{4}$
,,	.	.	.	$7\frac{3}{4}$ full
Sides	.	.	.	$1\frac{3}{8}$
,,	.	.	.	$1\frac{1}{4}$

Violoncello dated 1669.

Length	.	.	.	$31\frac{3}{4}$
Width	.	.	.	$18\frac{1}{2}$
,,	.	.	.	$15\frac{1}{16}$
Sides	.	.	.	6 bare
,,	.	.	.	$5\frac{3}{4}$
Stop	.	.	.	$17\frac{5}{16}$

Violoncello period 1690-95.

Length	.	.	.	$29\frac{5}{16}$
Width	.	.	.	$17\frac{5}{8}$
,,	.	.	.	$14\frac{3}{8}$
Sides	.	.	.	$4\frac{1}{2}$
,,	.	.	.	$4\frac{5}{16}$
Stop	.	.	.	$15\frac{1}{2}$

Violoncello dated 1692.

Length	.	.	.	$29\frac{1}{8}$ inches
Width	.	.	.	$17\frac{5}{8}$
,,	.	.	.	$14\frac{1}{2}$
Sides	.	.	.	$4\frac{1}{2}$
,,	.	.	.	$4\frac{1}{4}$
Stop	.	.	.	$15\frac{1}{2}$

APPENDIX II TO CHAPTER II

Table of Measurements of Violins made by Pietro Guarneri of Mantua

Violin dated 1676
(bearing a label of Andrea).

Length A to A	.	.	$13\frac{15}{16}$ inches
Width B „ B	.	.	$8\frac{1}{16}$
„ C „ C	.	.	$6\frac{9}{16}$
Sides D „ D	.	.	$1\frac{3}{16}$
„ E „ E	.	.	$1\frac{1}{16}$ full

Violin dated 1685.

Length	.	.	. $13\frac{15}{16}$ inches
Width	.	.	. 8
„	.	.	. $6\frac{9}{16}$
Sides .	.	.	. $1\frac{3}{16}$
„ .	.	.	. $1\frac{1}{16}$

Violin dated 1698.

Length	.	.	. $13\frac{7}{8}$
Width	.	.	. $8\frac{1}{8}$
„	.	.	. $6\frac{5}{8}$
Sides .	.	.	. $1\frac{3}{16}$
„ .	.	.	. $1\frac{1}{16}$

Violin dated 1703.

Length	.	.	. $13\frac{15}{16}$
Width	.	.	. $8\frac{1}{8}$ bare
„	.	.	. $6\frac{9}{16}$
Sides .	.	.	. $1\frac{3}{16}$
„ .	.	.	. $1\frac{1}{8}$

Violin dated 1709.

Length	.	.	. 14 inches
Width	.	.	. $8\frac{1}{8}$
„	.	.	. $6\frac{5}{8}$
Sides .	.	.	. $1\frac{3}{16}$
„ .	.	.	. $1\frac{1}{16}$

APPENDIX III TO CHAPTER III

Table of Measurements of Violins made by Giuseppe Guarneri, figlio d'Andrea

Violin dated 1696.

Length A to A . . $13\frac{7}{8}$ inches
Width B „ B . . $7\frac{5}{16}$
„ C „ C . . $6\frac{5}{16}$
Sides D „ D . . $1\frac{1}{8}$ full
„ E „ E . . $1\frac{1}{8}$

Violin period 1700.

Length . . . $13\frac{7}{8}$ inches bare
Width . . . $7\frac{7}{8}$
„ . . . $6\frac{3}{8}$
Sides . . . $1\frac{1}{8}$
„ . . . $1\frac{1}{16}$

Violin dated 1702.

Length . . . 14 bare
Width . . . 8
„ . . . $6\frac{9}{16}$
Sides . . . $1\frac{1}{4}$
„ . . . $1\frac{3}{16}$

Violin dated 1709.

Length . . . 14 bare
Width . . . 8
„ . . . $6\frac{1}{2}$
Sides . . . $1\frac{3}{16}$
„ . . . $1\frac{1}{8}$

Violin dated 1710.

Length . . . $14\frac{1}{8}$ bare
Width . . . 8 full
„ . . . $6\frac{9}{16}$
Sides . . . $1\frac{3}{16}$
„ . . . $1\frac{1}{8}$

Violin period 1710.

Length . . . $13\frac{7}{8}$
Width . . . $7\frac{7}{8}$
„ . . . $6\frac{3}{8}$
Sides . . . $1\frac{1}{4}$ bare
„ . . . $1\frac{3}{16}$

Violin dated 1712.

Length . . . $14\frac{1}{16}$
Width . . . $8\frac{1}{8}$
„ . . . $6\frac{5}{8}$
Sides . . . $1\frac{3}{16}$
„ . . . $1\frac{1}{8}$

Violin dated 1716.

Length . . . $14\frac{1}{8}$
Width . . . $8\frac{1}{4}$
„ . . . $6\frac{11}{16}$
Sides . . . $1\frac{1}{8}$
„ . . . $1\frac{1}{8}$

Violin period 1715-20.

Length . . . 14
Width . . . 8
„ . . . $6\frac{9}{16}$
Sides . . . $1\frac{1}{4}$
„ . . . $1\frac{3}{16}$

Violin period 1720.

Length . . . $14\frac{1}{8}$
Width . . . $8\frac{1}{4}$
„ . . . $6\frac{5}{8}$
Sides . . . $1\frac{3}{16}$
„ . . . $1\frac{3}{16}$

Table of Measurements of Violoncellos made by Giuseppe Guarneri, figlio d'Andrea

V'cello period 1700.

Length A to A	.	.	$29\frac{1}{4}$ inches
Width B „ B	.	.	$17\frac{1}{2}$
„ C „ C	.	.	$14\frac{1}{8}$
Sides D „ D	.	.	5
„ E „ E	.	.	5
Stop .	.	.	$15\frac{3}{4}$

V'cello dated 1708.

Length	.	.	$29\frac{1}{4}$ inches
Width	.	.	$17\frac{3}{16}$
„	.	.	$14\frac{1}{8}$
Sides .	.	.	$4\frac{7}{8}$
„	.	.	$4\frac{1}{2}$ bare
Stop .	.	.	$15\frac{3}{4}$

V'cello dated 1709.

Length	.	.	$29\frac{1}{2}$
Width	.	.	18
„	.	.	$14\frac{1}{2}$
Sides .	.	.	$4\frac{7}{8}$
„	.	.	$4\frac{3}{4}$
Stop .	.	.	$15\frac{3}{4}$

V'cello dated 1712.

Length	.	.	$28\frac{5}{8}$
Width	.	.	$16\frac{7}{8}$
„	.	.	$13\frac{11}{16}$
Sides .	.	.	$4\frac{5}{16}$
„	.	.	$4\frac{1}{4}$
Stop .	.	.	$15\frac{1}{4}$

V'cello dated 1721.

Length	.	.	29
Width	.	.	$17\frac{3}{8}$
„	.	.	$13\frac{7}{8}$
Sides .	.	.	$4\frac{1}{2}$
„	.	.	$4\frac{1}{4}$
Stop .	.	.	$15\frac{3}{4}$

V'cello dated 1731.

Length	.	.	29
Width	.	.	$17\frac{3}{8}$
„	.	.	$14\frac{1}{8}$
Sides .	.	.	$4\frac{7}{8}$
„	.	.	$4\frac{5}{8}$
Stop .	.	.	$15\frac{3}{4}$

APPENDIX IV TO CHAPTER IV

Table of Measurements of Violins by Giuseppe Guarneri del Gesù

Violin dated 1726.

Length A to A	.	.	14 inches bare
Width B „ B	.	.	$8\frac{1}{16}$
„ C „ C	.	.	$6\frac{9}{16}$
Sides D „ D	.	.	$1\frac{1}{4}$
„ E „ E	.	.	$1\frac{3}{16}$

Violin dated 1730.

Length	.	.	$13\frac{7}{8}$ inches
Width	.	.	$8\frac{1}{16}$
„	.	.	$6\frac{9}{16}$
Sides	.	.	$1\frac{1}{4}$ full
„	.	.	$1\frac{3}{16}$

Violin dated 1731.

Length	.	.	$13\frac{7}{8}$ bare
Width	.	.	8
„	.	.	$6\frac{1}{2}$
Sides	.	.	$1\frac{1}{4}$
„	.	.	$1\frac{3}{16}$

Violin dated 1732.

Length	.	.	$13\frac{7}{8}$
Width	.	.	8 bare
„	.	.	$6\frac{1}{2}$
Sides	.	.	$1\frac{3}{16}$ full
„	.	.	$1\frac{1}{8}$

Violin dated 1733.

Length	.	.	$13\frac{15}{16}$
Width	.	.	$8\frac{1}{8}$
„	.	.	$6\frac{5}{8}$
Sides	.	.	$1\frac{3}{16}$ full
„	.	.	$1\frac{3}{16}$ bare

Violin dated 1734.

Length	.	.	$13\frac{7}{8}$ bare
Width	.	.	$8\frac{1}{8}$
„	.	.	$6\frac{1}{2}$
Sides	.	.	$1\frac{3}{16}$
„	.	.	$1\frac{1}{8}$

Violin dated 1735.

Length	.	.	$13\frac{13}{16}$
Width	.	.	$8\frac{1}{8}$
„	.	.	$6\frac{9}{16}$
Sides	.	.	$1\frac{3}{16}$
„	.	.	$1\frac{1}{16}$

Violin dated 1736.

Length	.	.	$13\frac{13}{16}$ full
Width	.	.	8
„	.	.	$6\frac{7}{16}$
Sides	.	.	$1\frac{3}{16}$
„	.	.	$1\frac{1}{8}$

Violin dated 1737.

Length	.	.	14
Width	.	.	$8\frac{3}{16}$
„	.	.	$6\frac{5}{8}$
Sides	.	.	$1\frac{5}{16}$
„	.	.	$1\frac{1}{4}$

Violin dated 1740.

Length	.	.	$13\frac{15}{16}$
Width	.	.	$8\frac{1}{8}$
„	.	.	$6\frac{1}{2}$
Sides	.	.	$1\frac{3}{16}$ full
„	.	.	$1\frac{3}{16}$ bare

Violin dated 1742.

Length	.	.	. $13\frac{11}{16}$ inches
Width	.	.	. $8\frac{3}{16}$
,,	.	.	. $6\frac{5}{8}$
Sides .	.	.	. $1\frac{1}{8}$
,, .	.	.	. $1\frac{1}{8}$

Violin dated 1742.

Length	.	.	. $13\frac{15}{16}$ inches
Width	.	.	. $8\frac{3}{16}$
,,	.	.	. $6\frac{5}{8}$
Sides .	.	.	. $1\frac{5}{16}$
,, .	.	.	. $1\frac{3}{16}$

Violin dated 1743.

Length	.	.	. 14 bare
Width	.	.	. $8\frac{1}{8}$ full
,,	.	.	. $6\frac{11}{16}$
Sides .	.	.	. $1\frac{5}{16}$
,, .	.	.	. $1\frac{3}{16}$

Violin dated 1744.

Length	.	.	. $13\frac{7}{8}$
Width	.	.	. $8\frac{3}{16}$
,,	.	.	. $6\frac{9}{16}$
Sides .	.	.	. $1\frac{1}{8}$ full
,, .	.	.	. $1\frac{1}{8}$ bare

Table of thicknesses of Violins by Giuseppe Guarneri del Gesù

Pre-1730 period.

Back, centre	.	.	$\frac{12}{64}$ inches
,, post .	.	.	$\frac{11}{64}$
,, flanks	.	.	$\frac{7}{64}$ to $\frac{5}{64}$
Table, all over	.	.	$\frac{8}{64}$ full

Violin dated 1733.

Back, centre	.	.	$\frac{11}{64}$ inches
,, post .	.	.	$\frac{11}{64}$
,, flanks	.	.	$\frac{10}{64}$ to $\frac{6}{64}$
Table, centre	.	.	$\frac{7}{64}$,, $\frac{6}{64}$
,, flanks	.	.	$\frac{8}{64}$,, $\frac{6}{64}$

Violin dated 1735.

Back, centre	.	.	$\frac{12}{64}$
,, post .	.	.	$\frac{11}{64}$
,, flanks	.	.	$\frac{7}{64}$
Table, all over	.	.	$\frac{8}{64}$

Violin dated 1736.

Back, centre	.	.	$\frac{12}{64}$
,, post .	.	.	$\frac{12}{64}$
,, flanks	.	.	$\frac{10}{64}$ to $\frac{7}{64}$
Table, all over	.	.	$\frac{8}{64}$

Violin dated 1741.

Back, centre	.	.	$\frac{12}{64}$
,, post .	.	.	$\frac{12}{64}$
,, flanks	.	.	$\frac{8}{64}$ to $\frac{6}{64}$
Table, centre	.	.	$\frac{8}{64}$
,, flanks	.	.	$\frac{8}{64}$ to $\frac{6}{64}$

Violin dated 1742.

Back, centre	.	.	$\frac{10}{64}$
,, post .	.	.	$\frac{13}{64}$
,, flanks	.	.	$\frac{7}{64}$ to $\frac{8}{64}$
Table, all over	.	.	$\frac{8}{64}$,, $\frac{7}{64}$

Violin dated 1742.

Back, centre	.	.	$\frac{12}{64}$
,, post .	.	.	$\frac{12}{64}$
,, flanks	.	.	$\frac{7}{64}$ to $\frac{8}{64}$
Table, all over	.	.	$\frac{6}{64}$,, $\frac{7}{64}$

Violin dated 1742.

Back, centre	.	.	$\frac{10}{64}$
,, post .	.	.	$\frac{13}{64}$
,, flanks	.	.	$\frac{7}{64}$ to $\frac{8}{64}$
Table, all over	.	.	$\frac{7}{64}$,, $\frac{8}{64}$

APPENDIX V TO CHAPTER VIII

Table of Measurements of Violins made by Pietro Guarneri of Venice

Violin dated 1721.

Length A to A	.	.	$14\frac{1}{16}$ inches
Width B „ B	.	.	$8\frac{1}{16}$
„ C „ C	.	.	$6\frac{5}{8}$
Sides D „ D	.	.	$1\frac{3}{16}$
„ E „ E	.	.	$1\frac{1}{8}$ full

Violin period 1730.

Length	.	.	$13\frac{15}{16}$ inches
Width	.	.	8
„	.	.	$6\frac{1}{2}$
Sides	.	.	$1\frac{1}{4}$
„	.	.	$1\frac{3}{16}$

Violin dated 1734.

Length	.	.	14
Width	.	.	$8\frac{3}{16}$
„	.	.	$6\frac{5}{8}$
Sides	.	.	$1\frac{1}{4}$
„	.	.	$1\frac{3}{16}$

Violin dated 1735.

Length	.	.	$14\frac{1}{8}$ bare
Width	.	.	$8\frac{3}{16}$
„	.	.	$6\frac{11}{16}$
Sides	.	.	$1\frac{1}{8}$ full
„	.	.	$1\frac{1}{16}$

Violin dated 1740.

Length	.	.	$14\frac{1}{16}$
Width	.	.	$8\frac{3}{16}$
„	.	.	$6\frac{5}{8}$
Sides	.	.	$1\frac{1}{4}$ full
„	.	.	$1\frac{1}{8}$

Violin dated 1745.

Length	.	.	$14\frac{1}{8}$
Width	.	.	$8\frac{1}{4}$
„	.	.	$6\frac{11}{16}$
Sides	.	.	$1\frac{1}{4}$
„	.	.	$1\frac{1}{8}$

Violin dated 1754.

Length	.	.	14 inches
Width	.	.	$8\frac{3}{16}$
„	.	.	$6\frac{9}{16}$
Sides	.	.	$1\frac{3}{16}$
„	.	.	$1\frac{1}{8}$

Violoncellos

V'cello dated 1725.

Length A to A	.	.	$29\frac{1}{2}$ inches
Width B „ B	.	.	$17\frac{1}{2}$
„ C „ C	.	.	$13\frac{1}{2}$
Sides D „ D	.	.	$4\frac{7}{8}$
„ E „ E	.	.	$4\frac{1}{2}$
Stop	.	.	$15\frac{7}{8}$

V'cello period 1730.

Length	.	.	$29\frac{7}{16}$ inches
Width	.	.	$17\frac{3}{8}$
„	.	.	$14\frac{1}{4}$
Sides	.	.	$4\frac{3}{4}$
„	.	.	$4\frac{5}{8}$
Stop	.	.	$15\frac{7}{8}$

V'cello dated 1735.

Length	.	.	.	$27\frac{3}{4}$	inches
Width	.	.	.	$16\frac{1}{2}$	bare
,,	.	.	.	$13\frac{3}{8}$	
Sides	.	.	.	$4\frac{7}{8}$	
,,	.	.	.	$4\frac{1}{2}$	
Stop	.	.	.	$14\frac{5}{8}$	

V'cello period 1735-39.

Length	.	.	.	$27\frac{7}{8}$	inches
Width	.	.	.	$16\frac{1}{2}$	bare
,,	.	.	.	13	
Sides	.	.	.	$4\frac{3}{4}$	
,,	.	.	.	$4\frac{7}{16}$	
Stop	.	.	.	15	

V'cello dated 1739.

Length	.	.	.	$29\frac{3}{4}$	
Width	.	.	.	$17\frac{3}{4}$	
,,	.	.	.	$14\frac{5}{16}$	
Sides	.	.	.	$4\frac{3}{4}$	
,,	.	.	.	$4\frac{1}{2}$	
Stop	.	.	.	16	

V'cello period 1740.

Length	.	.	.	$29\frac{5}{8}$	
Width	.	.	.	$17\frac{5}{8}$	
,,	.	.	.	$13\frac{3}{4}$	
Sides	.	.	.	$4\frac{3}{4}$	
,,	.	.	.	$4\frac{3}{4}$	
Stop	.	.	.	$15\frac{3}{4}$	

INDEX

Personal names in *italics* are those of present owners of instruments made by members of the Guarneri family